Enthusiasm and Enlightenment in Europe, 1650–1850

Enthusiasm and Enlightenment in Europe, 1650–1850

edited by Lawrence E. Klein and Anthony J. La Vopa

Huntington Library —— San Marino, California

Cover illustration

"The Soul Exploring the Recesses of the Grave," design by William Blake, engraved by Louis Schiavonetti. Plate from Robert Blair's *The Grave* (London, 1808).

Acknowledgments

This volume is based on a workshop, "Enthusiasm and Modernity in Europe, 1650–1850," which was sponsored by the UCLA Center for 17th- and 18th-Century Studies and the William Andrews Clark Memorial Library, held 3–4 May 1996.

J. G. A. Pocock's essay appeared previously in *The Certainty of Doubt: Tributes to Peter Munz,* edited by Miles Fairburn and W. H. Oliver, published in 1996 by Victoria University Press, Wellington, New Zealand.

Simultaneously published as *Huntington Library Quarterly,* volume 60, numbers 1 & 2

CATALOGING-IN-PUBLICATION DATA

Enthusiasm and Enlightenment in Europe, 1650–1850 / edited by Lawrence E. Klein and Anthony J. La Vopa.
    p.   cm.
   "This volume is based on a workshop, 'Enthusiasm and Modernity in Europe, 1650–1850," which was sponsored by the UCLA Center for 17th- and 18th-Century Studies and the William Andrews Clark Memorial Library, held 3–4 May 1996"—Acknowledgements.
   Includes bibliographical references.
   ISBN 0-87328-200-0 (pbk. :alk. paper)
   1. Enthusiasm—History—Congresses. 2. Enlightenment—Congresses. 3. Europe—Intellectual life—Congresses. I. Klein, Lawrence Eliot. II. LaVopa, Anthony J., date.
BF575.E6E58 1998
128'.3--dc21
                                                      98-44003
                                                      CIP

ISBN 0-87328-200-0

1151 Oxford Road ✄ San Marino, California 91108
Editorial office: 626.405.2174/ e-mail: sgreen@huntington.org
Sales: 626.405.2172/ e-mail: booksales@huntington.org
Fax: 626.585.0794

Contents

This volume is based on the proceedings of a workshop sponsored by the UCLA Center for 17th- and 18th-Century Studies and the William Andrews Clark Memorial Library, held on 3–4 May 1996. The editors and the Huntington Library Press acknowledge with great appreciation the support for this project given by Peter Reill, director of the Center.

Introduction

Lawrence E. Klein and Anthony J. La Vopa

Although today a mild and innocuous word, "enthusiasm" was, from the Reformation through the nineteenth century, a term of great power with a wide range of referents. In religious controversies, as well as in debates about physiology, psychology, society, politics, and aesthetics, enthusiasm played an important but highly unpredictable role. The term's complex resonance makes it a promising point of entry for exploring diverse but often overlapping discourses. The essays collected here aim to extend the contextual study of this term's field of meanings in several directions. By complicating our understanding of the role of enthusiasm in early modern discourses, we come closer to appreciating its full significance for early modern history and culture.

Enthusiasm has a history going back to the ancient world. The term was explored by Plato and so entered early into Western discussions of inspiration in either a religious or an artistic sense. This pedigree authorized an idea of enthusiasm as a positive condition offering commendable opportunities for the expansion of human capacity and, indeed, opportunities for transcendence. Throughout the early modern era the reformulation of positive estimations of enthusiasm remained a standing option.

But there were also negative associations, evocations of impending dangers of individual and collective disorder, evident from the time of the Reformation in the European discourse of enthusiasm. Luther himself at once attacked the concept and tied it to a particular German tradition, using the term *Schwärmerei*. Certainly in all the lands where Protestantism made headway, enthusiasm came to be identified as a menace in many areas of life. (On the contrasting positions of enthusiasm in Protestant and in Catholic countries, see Jan Goldstein's contribution to this volume.) Though its early modern career as a term of abuse began in religious discourse as a way to asperse certain kinds of religious habit and affiliation, its use as a pejorative spread to such domains as politics, philosophy, and learning. The critique of enthusiasm was launched in the name of multiple and divergent projects. It was considered a threat to authority and order, not only in various forms of religious excess, but also in more secular guises of hyper-rationality, isolated introspection, mass conformity, and so on.

Much of the scholarly work on the subject of enthusiasm has been synthesized recently in Michael Heyd's important study, *"Be Sober and Reasonable": The Critique of Enthusiasm in the Seventeenth and Early Eighteenth Centuries* (Leiden: E. J. Brill, 1995). Heyd's main achievement is to trace the shifting intellectual bases of the critique of enthusiasm. He follows a series of projects in religion, science, philosophy, and social thought that were defended, at least in part, as attempts to define and contain a phenomenon called "enthusiasm." In the course of the seventeenth century, attacks on enthusiasm that originated in the languages of humanism, scholasticism, and Galenic medicine were recast in terms of new theological, medical, and scientific idioms. The Enlightenment discourse of reason—almost a cult of "Reason"—experimental method, and the mechanization of medical discourse all helped to displace (though not totally supplant) the older forms of argumentation. Thus, in Heyd's view, the reaction against enthusiasm in the early modern period had a formative role in the changes of outlook that, for better or worse, are often summed up in the term "secularization," a key aspect of the discourses of Enlightenment as well.

Since the new idioms were all allied with defenses of the social and political order, their introduction had implications for the way Europeans understood themselves. To bring the attacks on enthusiasm under historical scrutiny in this way is to advance our understanding of the changing ways in which established orders were legitimated in early modern Europe.

The essays in this volume share with Heyd's approach an interest in the conceptualization of enthusiasm by those who saw it as negative, or at least problematic. The agenda is primarily, though not exclusively, to recover the perceptions of, or rhetoric about, enthusiasm, rather than to penetrate behind stereotypes to the individuals or groups to which the term referred. The essays thus extend what Heyd has provided us in the way of a history of abuse and of the efforts to channel at least part of its meanings into a positive notion of creative spontaneity and inspiration.

In several ways, however, this collection marks a new departure, a commitment to directions not pursued by Heyd and the scholarly literature his work summarizes. The collection moves out beyond intellectual history, and especially the history of theology and philosophy central to Heyd's investigations, to new areas of cultural, and, in a loose sense, social history. It also extends the period of investigation. Although Peter Fenves begins his account with Plato and Anthony La Vopa begins his with Luther, the essays are largely concerned with the eighteenth century. The contribution by Jon Mee carries the story of enthusiasm into the early nineteenth century. And finally, by devoting to France and Germany the focused attention that has been brought to the study of enthusiasm in England, these essays (most explicitly, that of Jan Goldstein) seek to bring some comparative perspectives to bear on the subject.

It is perhaps a scholarly truism that in their attacks on enthusiasm, seventeenth- and eighteenth-century Europeans became self-conscious about modernity and about Enlightenment values, and sought to identify what they welcomed and feared about them. However, the words of seventeenth- and eighteenth-century writers have often been taken at face value by modern scholars. Oddly, this is true both of scholarship in the liberal vein (which tends to take for granted the value of reason and Enlightenment, and so forth, along with the progressive teleology folded into these terms) and of scholarship in the postmodern vein (which, while questioning Enlightenment values and claims, often reduces them to a simple, univocal, and successful program). The essays here share a commitment to complicating the story and thereby challenging these oversimplifications of the intellectual history of the seventeenth and eighteenth centuries. The discourse of enthusiasm proves an excellent vehicle for this sort of exercise.

For one thing, while enthusiasm might serve well as the foil for numerous projects of Enlightenment, it was a a foil that was difficult to control. Employed to erect intellectual and cultural boundaries and thereby to marginalize certain phenomena, the discourse proved quite volatile, and could in the end work to disparage those who launched the original attack. For another, while Enlightenment did seek, often, to found itself on the ruins of enthusiasm, the defense of Enlightenment could equally rely on enthusiasm. The cultures of modernity are as generously laced with attempts to preserve or reinvent enchantment as they are with attempts to abolish it. There is a fear that modernity—in the forms of rationalism, secularism, and so on—impoverishes, even among those intent on instituting it. The preservation of enthusiasm could thus be used to compensate for modernity's costs. It is a form of compensation, of course, that has its own dangers: the embrace of enthusiasm, however cautious, may pull one into a treacherous world of self-absorption and self-delusion. By looking at both the endorsements of enthusiasm and the attacks on it in a variety of Enlightenment contexts, we see better how modernity constituted in one way or another as the obverse of enthusiasm was neither stable nor unified.

There are several strands of modernity that the essays in this volume help to problematize through examinations of the discourse of enthusiasm:

Modernity and epistemology. In the first place, modernity in the seventeenth and eighteenth centuries was given a cognitive or epistemological identity. The attempts to define "reason," "philosophy," and "Enlightenment" were all attempts to discipline the human pursuit of and claim to knowledge. Certainly, in this process, enthusiasm was a frequent target. But the relation between enthusiasm and the categories of Enlightenment was not a simple one of dichotomy. Those who attempted to discipline cognition were worried by the impoverishment of cognition that might accompany these efforts. Thus, in the eighteenth century, attacks on enthusiasm called forth new forms of enthusiasm, legitimate and even indispensable, such as those defined by the third earl of Shaftesbury (see Lawrence Klein's essay), or in the *Encyclopédie* (see Mary Sheriff's) or by Coleridge (see Mee's). What those who would discipline cognition through an attack on enthusiasm repeatedly discovered was that their own efforts could be characterized as enthusiastic. This is the major theme in J. G. A. Pocock's contribution to the volume, but a similar dilemma confronts Kant and other *Aufklärer* in Germany (see the essays by La Vopa and Fenves) as well as Coleridge and others of the generation that spanned revolution and romanticism (see Mee's essay).

Modernity and religion. In the literature synthesized by Heyd, secularization is a defining trait of modernity, and this secularization is built, in part, on the critique of enthusiasm. The essays in this volume do not justify a total abandonment of the category of secularization, but they do remind us of the complexity of the process it describes. There was an obvious shift in the discourse of anti-enthusiasm from theological polemic to new languages of science and medicine. Perhaps more interesting, however, are the underlying continuities and structural affinities, revealed in these essays, between sacred and secular discourses. Most striking is the migration of the discourse of enthusiasm from the domain of religious polemic to the recognizably modern political contestation of the later eighteenth century, especially in the 1790s. As both Mee and La Vopa make clear, the discourse of enthusiasm was appropriated by both radicals and anti-radicals. Elements of this political dialectic were already evident in earlier periods. The attacks on "democrats" and other political radicals in the revolutionary era echoed two earlier rhetorical campaigns: the one against sectarian dissent and the one against philosophical system-builders.

Modernity and the public sphere. The issues about knowledge and power that pervade the discourse of enthusiasm point to the emergence of a public sphere as a distinctive phenomenon of European modernity and as a distinctive element of its self-perception. Claims about reason, philosophy, and Enlightenment were not used simply to define what constituted knowledge; they identified who could claim knowledge, who had cognitive authority, who could speak and write, and what kind of speech and writing were normative in the public world. When a public distinguished by its rationality was juxtaposed to a mob disfigured by the contagion of enthusiasm, the underlying point was to distinguish between legitimate and illegitimate ways of communicating and receiving ideas. The discourse marked a conflict about where the line should be drawn between public and merely private language, between the respectable and the wild, the coherent and the incomprehensible. Although the enlightened might project an enthusiasm as a foil against which to define what constituted rational behavior in the public sphere, we can think of the enthusiasts themselves as trying to assert counter-publics, in defiance of a would-be rationalist hegemony (see Mee's essay). Set within this discursive arena, the intellectual's ambivalence in the face of an expanding audience of readers, and indeed in the face of reading itself, becomes more understandable. The consensus generated by a public of autonomous and rational readers was constitutive of the public sphere. And yet reading itself could be figured as a symptom or cause of enthusiasms (see the essays by La Vopa, Sheriff, and Fenves).

Modernity and the social self. From the seventeenth century onward, European projections of modernity involved revaluations of selfhood and subjectivity. On the one hand, the modern self was supposed to be an autonomous self, a bounded subjectivity. Such a self could be contrasted with that of the enthusiast—unbounded, self-devouring, heteronomic. On the other hand, the modern self had to submit to the disciplines of sociability and civility: this self could also be juxtaposed to the subjectivism of the enthusiast, which sought to break through all social mediations. However, in either case, the normative boundary between the configurations of self was slippery. The essays in this volume (especially those by La Vopa, Klein and Goldstein) investigate those zones where the privacy of conscience slipped into isolated, self-absorbed, and self-delusional enthusiasm, where self-mastery slipped into artifices of social self-presentation, where the rational self became a self effaced by rationality, and where the commitment to community became self-abandonment in collective frenzy. All of these issues were complicated by the fact that the self as defined in the new discursive context was often given a gendered identity. Sheriff's essay explores how the best efforts of enlightened males to distinguish the creative enthusiasm of the male from the nymphomaniacal excess of the female obscured the very boundaries on which they insisted.

Sheriff's piece is emblematic of a central motif in the collection. The discourse of enthusiasm was repeatedly used to marginalize and thereby silence, according to class or gender or cognitive mode or religious affiliation. It was used to constitute authority against forms of power that were perceived as threatening. It was used to constitute disciplines (cognitive, political, social, psychological) against threatening forms of unchanneled energy (psychic, sexual, emotional). However, in most cases, the energies that were to be proscribed turned out to be, at the same time, necessary. While Enlightenment was often described as being founded on the prohibition of enthusiasm, it was, more accurately, reliant on the phenomenon that was supposed to be eliminated.

Enthusiasm:
The Antiself of Enlightenment

J. G. A. Pocock

W e are moving toward a reassessment of Enlightenment, in which there will no longer be "The Enlightenment,"a unitary and universal phenomenon with a single history to be either celebrated or condemned, but instead a family of discourses arising about the same time in a number of European cultures, Protestant as well as Catholic, insular as well as peninsular, and certainly not all occasioned by the Parisian intellectual hegemony that sought to establish itself among them. This view reasserts the diversity of cultures, some of them national and some of them built by states, in a Europe presenting itself at the end of the twentieth century as a cultural homogenization bent on the destruction of both states and nations; in resisting this aggression, the study of Enlightenment discourses seeks to maintain the open society by articulating the diversity of voices within it. Within a family of Enlightenments, furthermore, there is room for the recognition of family quarrels, some of them bitter and terrible in their conduct; and in escaping the false unity of "The Enlightenment," we escape the error of regarding "it" as culminating in "The Enlightenment Project," a construct invented by both left and right in order that they many denounce it (thus imposing on the open society the poverty of historicism). This enterprise, however malevolent, focuses on a problem others may wish to discuss: how it was that Enlightenment, very often at its beginnings a program of persuading the human mind to recognize its limitations, in certain cases became a program of revolutionary triumphalism. This did sometimes happen; the historicist error is that of supposing that all roads led to this conclusion. By first pluralizing the Enlightenments, and then by focusing upon the concept of enthusiasm—one of the key words in the Enlightened lexicon—this essay attempts to show that the Enlightenments from their outset recognized the possibility of an intellectual fanaticism arising within as well as without the enterprises in which they were engaged.

Some further generalizations are needed at the outset, to draw the stories to be recounted together and make a family of them. It will be proposed, therefore, that a narrative of Enlightenment may begin by supposing a family of intellectual and political programs, taking shape in several west European cultures between 1650 and 1700, with the shared but diversified intention of seeing that there should be no recurrence of the Wars of Religion. This is a hypothesis supported by a wide range of the apparent facts, but it is not being put forward as a covering law to be falsified so much as—since this is history— a means of bringing together a number of narratives that do seem to have occurred: to have been both constructed and experienced by various actors, and to have constituted aspects of what we term Enlightenment and what the actors themselves referred to by such terms as *lumière, Aufklärung,* and "this enlightened age."[1] There are other narratives that can be constructed and can usefully interact with the vocabulary of Enlightenment then and now; insofar as they set limits to the narrative to be recounted here, they may be said to falsify it but not to destroy it, merely indicating the limits within which it is useful.

It is further proposed that the liquidation of the Wars of Religion—a fear of whose recurrence long outlasted the Treaties of Westphalia in 1648—was perceived as entailing a reduction of the capacity of spiritual authority to challenge civil authority and incite a drawing of the sword in the name of Christ. Spiritual authority of this kind might be lodged in highly institutionalized churches, apparently part of the ruling social order, or in voluntary sects and "gathered congregations," in some cases very subversive of that order indeed. It will be found that it was particularly in connection with the latter that the term enthusiasm was conspicuously employed. Churches and sects were alike in being, or claiming to be, vehicles of the divine: gatherings of humans in or through whom the persons of the Christian Trinity—the Father who gave law, the Son who brought redemption, the Spirit who gave evangelical or charismatic energy—acted and gave humans authority to act, after the ascension of the Son and before his return and/or the reign of the Spirit. It was this which was meant by spiritual authority, whose capacity to disturb civil authority and even civil society had been so dreadfully displayed in the Wars of Religion as to give immediacy to Christ's saying that he brought not peace but a sword. It was therefore the capacity of church or sect to act, not merely in the divine name, but as representative or extension of one or more of the divine persons, that had to be challenged and reduced; and since the

---

1. The phrase in English was in use in the eighteenth century and is an indicator of the extent to which the people we call enlightened spoke of themselves in similar language. I am indebted to Dr. B. W. Young of the University of Sussex for information on this point.

divine persons actualized themselves through action in this world, it was hard to reduce spiritual authority without at the same time reducing the divine person itself. This is why the processes we are designating by using the term Enlightenment in this way were so often processes of disputatious theology— which reproduced the great debates of Nicaea and the other fourth- and fifth-century councils—seeking to diminish the full unity of divine and human nature in Christ, or the full equality of divine persons in the Trinity, reiterating many of the heresies of Arius, Sabellius, and others by the way. Even the full mockery of anti-Christian Enlightenment, which mobilized the new epistemology with the intent of reducing all theological dispute to absurdity, could not always escape this entanglement in renewed patristic theology; it was the greatness of Edward Gibbon to have perceived that you could not dismiss theology without at the same time learning to write its history.

We must further propose that the Wars of Religion did not, as conventionally supposed, end at the Peace of Westphalia in 1648, but were continued past that date in various forms. This enables us to treat the War of the Three Kingdoms, of which the English Civil War was part, as a war of religion of a peculiar and insular kind, occasioned not by the direct collision between Calvinist and Tridentine Catholic religion as were the wars in western peninsular Europe, but by tensions between the Catholic and Calvinist components of that unique body the Church of England. The War of the Three Kingdoms, brought about in part by attempts to extend the Church of England's authority in Scotland and Ireland, was not determined until 1660, 1688, or even 1745.[2] To say this permits us, further, to present the beginnings of Enlightenment in the British kingdoms as brought about in large measure by the endeavors of the Church to reestablish itself at the turning points of a series of crises; and at the same time allows us to draw near an understanding of the term enthusiasm.

✌ ✌

The Greek *enthousiasmos* carries the Latinate meanings of infusion and inspiration: the in-pouring or in-breathing of the divine, which comes to inhabit the person possessed, as it did the inspired pythoness at Delphi, bringing the power to prophesy, which in turn can come to mean both to foretell and to speak with tongues not one's own. In Christian religion, it is possible to be

2. For this reading, see particularly John Morrill, *The Nature of the English Revolution* (London, 1993); Brendan Bradshaw and John Morrill, eds., *The British Problem* (London, forthcoming); and Conrad Russell, *The Fall of the British Monarchies, 1637–1642* (Oxford, 1991).

possessed by the Spirit, as the Hebrew prophets spoke the word of the Lord and the apostles at Pentecost were moved to speak with many tongues; but there are also false prophets, and the term enthusiasm very often indicates the delusion or imposture of those who falsely believe or profess that they are or have been possessed by the Spirit. This negative secondary meaning of "enthusiasm" tends to take precedence over the original primary meaning of *enthousiasmos,* and the history of its usage is often that of a weakened and generalized term of abuse; but the original meaning was not lost, even at the heart of its negative employment.[3]

In Europe at the end of the Wars of Religion, it was very well known what "enthusiasm" meant and what context of theology it belonged in. Prominently, it denoted the fury of the millennial sects, expressed by those who had figured in the Peasants War in Germany and the Anabaptist rebellion at Münster, in whom the Spirit seemed to have come to overturn the Law and to have inspired an antinomian determination to destroy the ruling structures of church, state, and land, together with conventional morality; perhaps the saints were so fully justified that what was sin in others was testimony to the Spirit's immediacy in the sectaries. After Bernhard Knipperdolling and Jan Bockelszoon at Münster, belief that this had happened was more important than the question of how far it had. England at the end of the Interregnum had seen nothing on the level of the Münster antinomians; the Ranters were as much myth as reality;[4] but enthusiasm had taken a highly political form. Probably because the Church of England was an aspect, rather even than an arm, of the national sovereign government, the sects that arose within that church and separated from it were disposed to antinomian perceptions of that government, and some had developed radical programs for the reconstruction of the parliamentary franchise or the tenure of property in land; and, if the Levellers and Diggers were largely forgotten by 1660, the Quakers survived as the objects of a fear they found hard to shake off. There had been the phenomena of "the world turned upside down," as we have learned to call them from Christopher Hill; and, at a few moments in 1647, 1649, and 1653, it had seemed possible that the enthusiasts were in actual power. And this memory apart, there was the appalling and unforgettable fact of the regicide itself, which could not have been accomplished without those who were willing to wait upon the Lord and obey his voice when he told them that all covenants

3. I regret that Michael Heyd's *"Be Sober and Reasonable": The Critique of Enthusiasm in the Seventeenth and Early Eighteenth Centuries* (Leiden, 1995) did not reach me until this essay had already been completed.
4. See J. C. Davis, *Fear, Myth, and History: The Ranters and the Historians* (Cambridge, 1986).

were dissolved and all earthly power overturned. Oliver Cromwell, in one perspective the chief enemy of the sects, was in another the chief of enthusiasts; this duality accounts for his subsequent reputation as a hypocrite.

It is therefore not surprising that a sustained polemic against enthusiasm began in the later years of the Protectorate and formed part of the discourse of restored England through the years of the Napoleonic Wars: but this is the point at which it forms part of the discourse of English Enlightenment. After generations of historians who found it hard to see Enlightenment in England because there were no anti-Christian *philosophes* with projects for the liberation and reconstruction of society, we are learning to recognize that Enlightenment existed—paradoxically, to the earlier understanding—in clerical and conservative forms, the product of the Church of England's program to reconcile itself with the governing classes. Because that church was both apostolic and Erastian, it was threatened by its own Catholic components, which seemed to claim for it a spiritual authority independent of the king's; because the Stuart kings had nevertheless supported its hierarchy against their critics, it (and they) were threatened by its Calvinist and Puritan components, who in their reaction against the supposed popery of bishops paradoxically claimed for the ministers the same independence of the civil magistrate that they denounced in the bishops. Seeing the origins of this claim in the Calvinist decrees of absolute grace, a party among the English episcopacy had allied themselves with the Arminian movement disturbing the Calvinist churches of western Europe with its proposals for modifying those decrees.[5] It is here that we have good cause to find one of the origins of Enlightenment, since the Arminians tended to replace a religion of grace and justification with one of rational and sociable theology, out of which could emerge the Socinian conclusion that Christ had come with no other purpose than to reinforce the moral law, and was therefore a being divine in mission but not in nature. Such modifications of Incarnation and Trinity were much to the purposes of those desiring to diminish the claims of the churches to spiritual authority, and by the end of the century Pierre Bayle was writing of a prevalent belief that all the princes of Europe would establish Socinian religions of state if they dared.[6] But in England—perhaps only in England—it was the Episcopal and ritualist wing of a divided church that adopted Arminian theology, with the result that "Arminianism" became a hostile byword for alleged catholicizing and crypto-papist designs. To the left

5. See Nicholas Tyacke, *Anti-Calvinists: The Rise of English Arminianism, c. 1590–1640* (Oxford, 1987); and H. R. Trevor-Roper, *Catholics, Anglicans, and Puritans* (Chicago, 1988).
6. Pierre Bayle, *Dictionnaire Historique et Critique* (Rotterdam, 1696–97), 2:1065, 1070–74 (in the article "Socinus").

of the great debate within the state religion—the Episcopal and anti-Episcopal wings each accusing the other of rendering spiritual magistracy independent of civil—arose the enthusiasms of the sects, insisting that the Spirit might at any time be active in the congregation or even in the individual and stood in no need of the authority of hierarchy or magistrate. This is a schema only, but it shows how it was that the Church of England restored in 1660–62 was under threat from enemies within and without—Catholic, Calvinist, and enthusiast—and badly needed means of insisting that the Spirit ordinarily acted only through channels consistent with the authority, civil and ecclesiastical, of the Father who brought the law and the Son who brought the church and its priesthood. Whether this could be maintained without diminishing the person of the Spirit, the Son, and the whole Trinity was the next question.

The error to be avoided at this point is that of constructing a whiggish history of English Enlightenment, in which the first step away from orthodoxy is irrevocable and the outcome in secularization inevitable. That was in fact the Catholic position, and it has always been odd to see secularist historians adopting it. There was general recognition that a slippery slope yawned at the foot of the Arminian position, whose downward stages were clearly marked: Arian, Socinian, deist, skeptic, and—least clearly signposted—atheist. But the Church of England abounded with able theologians, resolved to retain the Trinitarian theology while maintaining the alliance between church and state and unintimidated by the complexities of doing so; it is for the historian of theology to tell their many stories.[7] This does not mean, in turn, that the possibility of a radical subversion did not exist or went unrecognized; it had been dramatically evident since 1651, when Thomas Hobbes, not ordinarily considered an Enlightened philosopher, announced what was to be a drastic, though not necessarily a drastically anti-Christian, Enlightened program in the history of philosophy. For about two thousand years, he said, philosophy had been on the wrong track, and it was time to make a new beginning; he was prepared to offer his own works as a *novum organon* to replace Aristotle's in the universities.[8] The original error had been that of the Greeks, who had held up before the intellect the inherent substance of things spiritual and material—Platonic ideas, Aristotelian essences—to be contemplated and comprehended.

7.　See, for example, John Spurr, *The Restoration Church of England, 1646–1689* (New Haven, Conn., 1993); J. A. I. Champion, *The Pillars of Priestcraft Shaken: The Church of England and Its Enemies, 1660–1730* (Cambridge, 1990); John Gascoigne, *Cambridge in the Age of the Enlightenment* (Cambridge, 1990); and B. W. Young, *Religion and Enlightenment in Eighteenth-Century England: Theological Debate from Locke to Burke* (Oxford, 1998).

8.　Thomas Hobbes, *Leviathan*, ed. Richard Tuck (Cambridge, 1991), 458–74 (chap. 46).

From this error had arisen many systems propounding an indwelling spirit capable of inhabiting and entering the universe: the God of the philosophers, made actual—Hobbes did not say—when the Logos became flesh, as the God of the Christians. In what manner of God Hobbes himself believed, if he believed in any, became from that point the subject of debate. He made it clear, however, that the doctrine of real essences was the source of the "kingdom of darkness" and the "kingdom of the fairies," denounced in *Leviathan* in language initially satisfying and afterward deeply subversive to the Protestant and Anglican mind.

His first and easiest target was the Catholic doctrine of transubstantiation as Protestants understood it: the doctrine that the divine nature in Christ was capable of transforming matter so that the bread and wine literally became the substance of his body and blood. But if that were abandoned, what was the status of the divine nature of Christ? This had been incessantly debated in the patristic age, and it was possible to reopen the debate. Hobbes showed, however, a way of doing so that condemned the entire discourse of Nicene theology as founded on the error of real substances; it had been wrong to suppose a Logos and then to suppose it made flesh. If that were accepted, however, the doctrine of Christ's nature must be reconsidered; or rather, it must be terminated, on the ground that the very concept of "nature" had made it a *question mal posée* from the outset. Here, said an acute Anglican observer, Hobbes's system became "a farrago of Christian atheism."[9] Superficially, however—though nobody is known to have read Hobbes superficially—he was following the strategy of Anglicanism, and attacking popery and enthusiasm by turns. If it was wrong to suppose that Christ could enter and transubstantiate—not merely transform—the elements, wrong to suppose that the Church could become his mystical body and the pope speak with the authority of that body, it was wrong to suppose that the Spirit proceeding from him could enter the body of the congregation or the intelligence of the individual, and there speak with a voice of its own. Hobbes was attacking the sects as well as the Catholic Church, though he spent far more time denouncing the latter, following the Anglican premise that the pope was always the greater danger. In replicating the Anglican strategy, however, he was subverting its foundation: the doctrine of Christ as God made man because spirit made flesh, on which all Christian belief and even Christian disputation rested. He might attack the enthusiasm of the sects that declared that the Spirit moved in the congregation, and all Anglican clergy would applaud; but had he not implicitly revealed that the

9.   Henry Hammond in 1651; see Richard Tuck, "The Civil Religion of Thomas Hobbes," in Nicholas Phillipson and Quentin Skinner, eds., *Political Discourse in Early Modern Britain* (Cambridge, 1993), 122.

greatest *enthousiasmos* was the doctrine of the Word made Flesh, the opening of the Fourth Gospel, the doctrine of the Incarnation itself? Proleptically and by anticipation, he had displayed to the Anglicans of the Restoration how easily their attack on transubstantiation to their right and enthusiasm to their left might become an attack on the presence of God in the world, and therefore in the Church.[10]

A direct polemic against enthusiasm may be seen beginning five years after *Leviathan,* with the publication in 1656 of Meric Casaubon's *Treatise Concerning Enthusiasm* and Henry More's *Enthusiasmus Triumphatus.* Both—but especially Casaubon—were concerned to show enthusiasm as a delusion rather than a heresy, a possibly diagnosable disease of body and mind, akin to hysteria in women (who were peculiarly liable to it), encouraging the fantasy that the personality was possessed by alien forces. Of the two, it is More who is problematic and raises questions important to our understanding of the concept of enthusiasm and the polemic against it, though some of these questions did not become salient until after the Restoration of 1660. In the first place, *Enthusiasmus Triumphatus* is not simply a polemic against the radical gathered congregations, with their unlearned preachers, women testifiers, and millennial and antinomian visions. It is also a debate with a Rosicrucian, a brother of the poet Thomas Traherne; and at this point we learn that the polemic against enthusiasm could become a debate among the learned as well as a defensive action by the learned against the vulgar, and that there were philosophies, or at least complex systems of written discourse, that could be condemned as "enthusiasm," thus modifying the meaning of the word. Rosicrucians were not prophetic or Pentecostal Christians; it could be questioned whether they were Christians at all: they upheld a system that presented the world as pervaded by occult spiritual forces, which the intellect might apprehend and of which it might make itself the mouthpiece. Here the Hebrew prophet is joined, or superseded, by the Greek oracle, and the term enthusiasm begins its journey toward applicability to any system that presents the mind as of the same substance, spiritual or material, as the universe that it interprets, so that the mind becomes the universe thinking and obtains an authority derived from its identity with its subject matter. There had been systems of this sort since at least the days of the Gnostics, and the learned of seventeenth-century Europe had a good deal of knowledge of them.

In the second place, Henry More was one of a number of divines whom we know as "the Cambridge Platonists," further known as "latitudinarians," as

---

10. See J. G. A. Pocock, "Within the Margins: The Definitions of Orthodoxy," in Roger D. Lund, ed., *The Margins of Orthodoxy: Heterodox Writing and Cultural Response, 1660–1750* (Cambridge, 1995), 33–53.

they were called at the time. Some of them had held ecclesiastical office and discharged its duties under the non-Episcopal church settlements of the Inter-regnum, and now saw no reason why they should not continue doing so under the restored episcopacy. Those who had upheld the Episcopal cause during its eclipse, however, were not always disposed to welcome them back. In arguing for good standing and the right to continue in office, they adopted positions that were "latitudinarian," in the sense that they held it possible for reasonable members of the same church to maintain conversation and diminish dogma on points of substance on which they might disagree. This approach did not always satisfy the orthodox, who saw in it the possibility of either heresy or indifference; for, if Christ were a being concerning whom one held opinions rather than a being with whom one was in communion, conversation con-cerning his nature might of itself modify or diminish that nature; and indeed a Socinian undercurrent within the Church of England is detectable from this point.[11] Latitudinarians thus viewed stood at the point where their church was tempted to de-emphasize dogma for the sake of peace, first reducing Christ to the subject of conversation and then reducing the intensity of the conversation to the level attained by that perhaps legendary divine whose tombstone declares that he served his Maker for fifty years without the smallest sign of enthusiasm. Such almost invisible spirituality is not unknown among the Anglican clergy and was sometimes accompanied by a refusal to debate the interpretation of Christ's nature to which they otherwise subscribed.

But a systematically antidogmatic religiosity might be accompanied by an epistemology that put the mysteries of dogma out of reach of the intellect, or capable only of a probabilist discourse. The Cambridge men who were both latitudinarians and Platonists present the problem that their philosophy was precisely that being blamed for creating the mysteries in the first place. More and the others professed reason to be "the candle of the Lord," a reasonable and eirenic spiritual illumination that rendered the mind proof against both angry dogmatism and ecstatic enthusiasm; the spirit of Socrates rather than of the prisoner in the cave who has escaped to view the sunlight. They seem hardly to have realized how easily their Platonism—which was in some measure Neo-platonism—could be represented as that doctrine of sensible Ideas that was the source of both transubstantiation and enthusiasm, or their "candle of the Lord" as that "Inner Light" that moved Cromwell and the Quakers to the con-viction that the Spirit was moving in them. Ten years after *Enthusiasmus Tri-umphatus,* these possibilities were brutally pointed out to More by Samuel

11. See H. J. MacLachlan, *Socinianism in Seventeenth-Century England* (Oxford, 1951).

Parker in his *Impartial Examination of the Platonick Philosophie* (1666). For Parker, the future bishop of Oxford,[12] Plato (rather than the Neoplatonists) was the source of both popery and enthusiasm, because he was the source of all false doctrine that the essences of things could be immediately perceived by the mind; and Parker expressed an open preference for the philosophy of Bacon and the Royal Society, according to which it was possible to perceive things only in their behavior. Nothing less, he said, could teach the vulgar to know their place and abstain from speculation about questions that they should leave to the experimentation of their betters. Parker's assault on the spell of Plato hardly expressed a preference for the open society.

In combination with his militant support of the civil magistrate's supremacy over the Church, Parker's anti-Hellenism sounded decidedly Hobbist, and this may have been one reason why he devoted many pages to attacking Hobbes in terms that interestingly equate that philosopher with the Hellenism he desired to destroy; the multiple body of *Leviathan*'s frontispiece is compared with the multiple emanations of the Gnostics. The target here is Hobbes's materialism, which appeals to the enthusiasm of the vulgar and helps create a phobia against spirit so extreme as to be itself akin to enthusiasm. It was beginning to emerge that there could be such a thing as a materialist enthusiasm, and this underlines the extent to which the diatribe against enthusiasm was moving away from its original concern with the excesses of the prophetic and the Pentecostal, to fasten upon heresy and error at the level of the philosophical. Plato had filled the universe with ideas, the Neoplatonists and Rosicrucians with occult qualities; the mind could intoxicate itself with the phantasmata of these unreal entities, and fancy itself possessed by them. But a Democritean or Hobbesian materialism reduced universe and mind—sometimes even God—to atomic particles, and thought to the movement of these particles; from which it followed that the mind was of the same substance as the universe it thought about, and might be considered as matter thinking about itself. To the orthodox critics of materialism, it was clear that here was a special case of the heresy, error, delusion, or mental sickness of supposing that ultimate reality poured itself into the intelligence and directed its thoughts; whether that reality were supposed to be spirit or matter, the term enthusiasm was equally applicable.

12. On Parker, see Gordon J. Schochet, "Between Lambeth and Leviathan: Samuel Parker on the Church of England and Political Order," in Phillipson and Skinner, *Political Discourse in Early Modern Britain*, 189–208; and "Samuel Parker, Religious Diversity, and the Ideology of Persecution," in Lund, *The Margins of Orthodoxy*, 119–148. See also J. G. A. Pocock, "Thomas Hobbes: Atheist or Enthusiast? His Place in a Restoration Debate," *History of Political Thought* 11 (1990): 737–49.

In a time when natural philosophers were interested in equating the energies of matter with spirit and speaking of "spiritual mechanics" as if the terms matter and spirit were interchangeable, this particular peril gained prominence. It has been shown how, in the controversy between Hobbes and Boyle over the vacuum, each side could rhetorically accuse the other of enthusiasm: the Hobbist declaring that the vacuum if it existed would become filled with spirit, the Boylean that the plenum if it existed must be already filled with a matter and spirit indistinguishable from each other.[13] Each was accusing his opponent of abolishing God in favor of a primary substance to which mind must necessarily submit and belong—a charge to which Hobbes might be more vulnerable than the pious Boyle. This was the point at which Christians and clerics went in search of a theistic natural philosophy in which the movements of matter were directed by an independently existing God, who made himself known by the wonders of his works, seldom by direct revelation, and never by his immanence or inherence, which he had made the human mind incapable of grasping.

It has been emphasized—though this emphasis is now criticized for supposed excess—how first Boyle and then Newton, as leaders of the Royal Society to which Hobbes was not admitted, supplied the Restoration Church's need for a God who stood apart from his creation, and a creation whose movements could be understood but neither their essence nor his ever apprehended.[14] Before the impact of Newton, the Cambridge Platonist Ralph Cudworth, writing against Hobbes in *The True Intellectual System of the Universe* (1679), had sought just such a rational theism in Plato himself, insisting that the preponderant philosophers of Greek antiquity had conceived of a God who was neither absent nor inseparable from his creation (also, less fortunately, that they had access through a pre-Christian cabala to foreknowledge of the Trinity). Cudworth aimed to attack atheism, of which he found two kinds in both antiquity and modernity; the commoner kind, represented by Democritus and Hobbes, insisted that nothing was to be found but matter, and that the free fall of atoms was undirected by any intelligence whatsoever. But he also detected a "Stratonical" or "hylozoistic" atheism, which invested the universe with a vegetable, animal, or even an intelligent soul, thus making it indistinguishable from God and removing God from all possibility of independent existence. Here Cudworth's text, a long invective against Hobbes, begins to display references to a recent work called the *Tractatus Theologico-Politicus*, a modern representative

13. Steven Shapin and Simon Schaffer, *Leviathan and the Air-Pump: Hobbes, Boyle, and the Experimental Life* (Princeton, N.J., 1985).
14. See Margaret C. Jacob, *The Newtonians and the English Revolution, 1689–1720* (Ithaca, N.Y., 1985).

of this ancient heresy. Spinoza had acquired his role as an atheist who was also a pantheist, one who abolished God by retaining him as identical in substance with his creation.[15] A hylozoistic materialism was far more conducive to enthusiasm than a strictly atheist atomism; it offered the mind opportunity to believe itself matter capable of consciousness and thought, and at the same time to believe itself the active operation of a God who became actual through the operations of the mind. A circle could be completed.

∾   ∾

We may now leave behind—though we may not forget—the English clerical enlightenment, with its memories of regicide, civil war, and the rule of the saints. In so doing we continue to follow the trajectory of the concept of enthusiasm from the prophetic to the philosophical and have arrived at a point where it might denote any intellectual system of the universe in which the mind was of the same substance as the universe it apprehended. How such systems originated is a problem for our understanding of European intellectual history; it was a problem also for the systems of intellectual history generated in eighteenth-century Europe. In Protestant Europe other than England there was one set of reasons for a concern with the phenomenon of enthusiasm; in Catholic Europe, whether Gallican or papal, there may have been others. For a philosophical history on the grand scale in which enthusiasm was made visible in a central role, we may turn to a Lutheran work. Jakob Brucker's *Historia Critica Philosophiae*,[16] a history whose power, sweep, and brilliance are concealed from the eyes of a degenerate modernity by its embodiment in six volumes of a thousand pages each and a prose of intense and erudite latinity; it is our misfortune if we consider this monumental achievement archaic or ludicrous. Brucker, an acquaintance of such major scholars as Isaac de Beausobre and Johann Lorenz von Mosheim,[17] knew that the history of philosophy must be written as both a history of the truth and a history of contingency, meaning

15. This may be a better account of how Spinoza was perceived than of how he wished to be understood. For accounts of "Spinozism" in the English Enlightenment, see Margaret C. Jacob, *The Radical Enlightenment: Pantheists, Freemasons, and Republicans* (London, 1981); Robert Sullivan, *John Toland and the Deist Controversy* (Cambridge, Mass., 1982); and Stephen Daniel, *John Toland: His Methods, Manners, and Mind* (Kingston and Montreal, 1985). More generally, see Yirmiyahu Yovel, *Spinoza and Other Heretics: The Marrano of Reason* (Princeton, N.J., 1990).
16. *Historia Critica Philosophiae a mundi incunabulis ad nostram usque aetatem deducta* (Leipzig, 1742–).
17. Isaac de Beausobre, pastor to the Huguenot congregation at Berlin, *Histoire Critique de Manichée et du Manicheisme* (Amsterdam, 1734); Johann Lorenz von Mosheim, chancellor of the University of Göttingen, *Institutiones Historiae Christianae* (Göttingen, 1775).

by the latter a history of what those whom we chose to call philosophers had found it possible to say, given the conditions of their times. With these ends in view he went back to a time before the appearance of what was strictly to be termed philosophy: to the "Axial Age" in our parlance, when a diversity of Eurasian sages from Zoroaster to Buddha[18] had generated systems, said Brucker, that were less philosophy than theogony. Of these the genesis of enthusiasm had been a central feature.

Our Axial Age was Brucker's history of the Gentiles. The true religion had been known only to the patriarchs Abraham, Isaac, and Jacob with their special revelations and covenants, which freed them from all need of philosophy; but among the Gentiles, who comprehended most of the human race, powerful minds had appeared who sought to grapple with the spiritual and intellectual darkness that followed the Confusion of Tongues. In that darkness had existed a proliferation of superstitions, polytheisms, and mythologies; and the Gentile sages had perceived that each and every one of the tales constituting these belief systems was a myth, in the sense of the poetic expression of an apprehended truth or reality. They had proceeded to syncretize these myths, supposing that each of them encapsulated some aspect of a reality too vast to be apprehended by any mind or captured in a single formula; and the most farseeing among them had supposed this to be a primal absolute reality undifferentiated into categories, an original Not Being that had preceded even the differentiation of being from its own negation. Satisfied that every myth represented this differentiation in a poetic form suited to the vulgar understanding, the sages and their disciples had gathered in esoteric brotherhoods to worship that which lay behind every popular cult or superstition, while encouraging the vulgar to continue cultic religion after their own fashion. In patronizing and manipulating the religions of the peoples, these primeval masonries had played the role of priests; at the same time, in their secret rituals they had worshipped that which they believed to be manifest in themselves and in all reality emanating from it, and in this capacity had exercised the role of enthusiasts. It was this duality of the ancient esotericisms, we may gloss, that explains the uneasy relationship between Sarastro and the Queen of Night; his austere veracity can never escape the sinister charlatanry that is its shadow.

Brucker, a sound Protestant if not necessarily an orthodox theologian, sought for the moment at which philosophy had escaped from its magian

---

18. Known to scholars of the age only as "Fo." See J. G. A. Pocock, "Gibbon and the Idol Fo: Chinese and Christian History in the Enlightenment," in David S. Katz and Jonathan I. Israel, eds., *Sceptics, Millenarians, and Jews* (Leiden, 1990), 15–34.

prehistory, and found it in the life, but not the death, of Socrates. He presented that philosopher as Enlightenment saw him: a moralist who had turned away from Ionian nature-philosophy to study the laws of human conduct and from them deduce the necessity of a rational and benevolent creator. But this had been too much for the poetic and political theologies of Athens, and, following Socrates' execution on a charge of blasphemy, his disciple Plato had been exposed to Pythagorean systems in Italy and magian systems in Egypt and had reinstated the undifferentiated first matter in the form of the Idea or essence of all things. Plato had been the great betrayer of ancient philosophy, restoring that kingdom of unreal or pseudo-real primal substance that underwrote superstition in the priests and enthusiasm in the philosophers. In Neoplatonic and Aristotelian forms, the kingdom of darkness had lasted nearly two thousand years, until Bacon, Grotius, and Locke had restored an empirical philosophy and ethics in which Christian belief was freed from its magian and Hellenic encumbrances. Here again we find the morality guaranteed by theism to which Christian Enlightenment reduced the revealed religion, bringing it close to the philosophical deism with which it could never quite join.

In Brucker's system, most philosophy and all enthusiasm were the products of Gentile history, lying outside the small Judaic world of antiquity and obtaining a mainly malignant authority over the Christian message when it was communicated to the Gentiles. This has been the world of the heathen legislators—Orpheus, Zoroaster, Pythagoras, Brahma, Manco Capac, and latterly Mani—geniuses benign in their intentions, who had given law to heathen mankind, but in order to do so had laid claim to divine guidance. Confucius alone in antiquity had avoided imposture, and in later times Mohammed's austere and simple monotheism had separated him from the esoteric worship of the absolute and patronage of popular superstition, which had made secret enthusiasts of the sages of ancient Gentilism. To the philosophers of French Enlightenment, the primary error of the legislators was the central tragedy of history: in feigning dreams and oracles they had opened the door to superstition, in adopting or inventing magian religion they had opened the door to philosophic enthusiasm, and in both they had prepared the way for the perversion of their own work by the rule of priests. Raynal and Diderot made this the recurrent theme of the *Histoire des Deux Indes*,[19] while for Anquetil-Duperron, Zoroaster had been the first of enthusiasts, whom he divided into impostors who had pretended to inspiration and then came to believe their

19. G. T. F. Raynal, *Histoire Philosophique et Politique des Etablissemens et du Commerce des Européens dans les Deux Indes* (Geneva, 1780), 1:39, 59, 61, 64. These passages are among those thought to have been inserted by Diderot.

own fictions, and legislators who had thought it necessary to reinforce moral truths by pseudo-spiritual falsehoods.[20] The concept of enthusiasm was broadening to include all claims to the presence of the divine in human affairs; God might still be the object of belief, but never of experience.

A sharply differentiated, though related, account of enthusiasm was put forward by the Scotto-British historian David Hume, in a series of essays and chapters that return us to the context of seventeenth-century British history. In an essay "Of Superstition and Enthusiasm,"[21] Hume was content to define the former as produced by the fears of the human mind and the latter by its excessive hopes, the two together making up most of what constituted religion; but in the far more comprehensive treatise *The Natural History of Religion*,[22] Hume blithely bypassed the five centuries of pre-Christian philosophy to announce that, until seventeen centuries before his time, the generality of mankind had been polytheists, the impure monotheism of a single people (the Jews) and the speculations of a few philosophers (the Pythagoreans and Platonists) forming no exception worth regarding. It was not easy to understand why Hume surrendered the opportunity to ground Christian theology in Hellenic philosophy and magian theogony, since he went on to explain that it was the combined effect of monotheism and philosophy that had brought the claim to truth-status to statements concerning the gods, replacing the purely mythopoetic discourse of polytheism, in which disputation, intolerance, and persecution had been unthinkable. Perhaps he was conducting an experiment in theoretical history; perhaps he wished to idealize the paganism of the Roman empire, in which the innumerable superstitions of the people had been supervised by magistrates who were Epicurean skeptics, not by brotherhoods of philosophic enthusiasts. For if philosophy brought in the twin possibilities of theology and persecution, it also brought in the possibility of enthusiasm; it converted beliefs into intellectual propositions, concerning which the intellect could become fanatical. It remains unclear why Hume did not ascribe this to "the spell of Plato," insisting on dating it to a moment no earlier than the advent of Christianity, since it was already a commonplace that the Platonic Logos was more ancient than its Johannine Incarnation.

Hume went on to make it clear that superstition was the worship of the godhead in material things and social practices, whereas enthusiasm was the

20. A. H. Anquetil-Duperron, *Zend-Avesta. Ouvrage de Zoroastre . . . Traduit de l'original Zend* (Paris, 1771), 2:65–66.
21. First published 1741. See David Hume, *Essays Moral, Political, and Literary*, ed. Eugene F. Miller (Indianapolis, 1985), 73–79.
22. First published 1757. See David Hume, *Four Dissertations*, ed. John Immerwater (Bristol, 1995), 1–117.

worship of the godhead in the ideas that the human mind formed concerning it, and then disastrously supposed to be the godhead itself, working within the mind, inspiring and possessing it. There is a hint that this is a strictly intellectual phenomenon, inseparable from the history of philosophy and theology; the trances and possessions of shamans and pythonesses are not mentioned. It is this self-deification of the auto-intoxicated mind that gives enthusiasm its terrible power; while enthusiasm lasts, says Hume, the normal operations of history are suspended, and things are done that would be impossible at any other time and are unpredictable even when they occur. Here the problem of liberty makes its appearance. Superstition is conducive to the rule of priests, fatal to all civil society and therefore to civil freedom; the explosive energies of enthusiasm sweep away all religions and their hierophants except the mind's worship of itself; its freedom is total and so also is its power. Without Puritan enthusiasm, expressed in the most absurd and abject language, the English would never have reconquered their constitutional and civic freedoms; but they could renew the constitution only by destroying it and living for a while under the despotism of Cromwell, the most dangerous of hypocrites because he was an enthusiast who believed every word by which he deceived himself.[23] But enthusiasm burns itself out. The mind that has destroyed everything except itself is left alone with itself, and in the absence of God must sooner or later turn to the only available source of reality, the opinions that it forms as a result of living in society. Hume led Voltaire, Raynal, and Diderot in observing the phenomenon of the wildest and most anarchic of sects mutating in a single generation into the most sociable, reasonable, and untheological of non-dogmatic believers: the Quakers (we would add Muggletonians) in England;[24] the Anabaptists who survived in Germany;[25] the Quakers, Moravians, and Mennonites in Pennsylvania.[26] Enlightenment idealized quietism as the only religion that could be trusted to secularize itself.

But it might not be necessary to pass through the fires of enthusiasm. Hume was the last man to welcome the experience of revolutionary dialectic; he understood very clearly the capacity of the human mind to oscillate between extremes, but thought it the aim of government to contain this tendency as far as possible. There was something to be said for superstition; imprisoning the godhead in things and practices, it directed the mind toward material and social reality, which perhaps need not be left to re-emerge after the deluge of revolu-

---

23. David Hume, *The History of England,* rev. ed. (1778; reprint, Indianapolis, 1985), 5:66–68, 131, 212–14, 450, 498–99, 6:5.
24. Hume, *Essays,* 78; *History,* 6:142–46.
25. Voltaire, *Essai sur les Moeurs,* ed. R. Pomeau (Paris, 1963), 240.
26. Raynal, *Histoire des Deux Indes,* bk. 18, chap. 75.

tion. In his *History of England,* where he stressed the necessity for enthusiasm to resist despotism, he showed a noteworthy sympathy for the Catholicizing ritualism associated with the name of Archbishop Laud.[27] A benignly supervised superstition freed the mind from the Lucretian fears and Protestant despairs that were the prelude to enthusiasm, and so long as the priests were the subjects of the civil magistrate and the practices of society, superstition might lead men into sociability, instead of out of it into the twin menaces of priestcraft and enthusiasm. The masses, wrote Hume in company with most of the *philosophes,* were incurably superstitious; but there is an element of wish-fulfillment about this statement. If they were superstitious, it was that they might not be enthusiastic. Together with that Enlightened utopia, so nearly realized, in which a philosophical pope should dissolve the Jesuits and rule inoffensively as an improving Italian prince, there was the vision of a cultic and tolerant Anglicanism, presided over by bishops—of whom some there were—who subscribed to the Athanasian Thirty-Nine Articles in public and maintained Socinian opinions in private conversation. Yet Hume knew that these utopias were out of reach. The demon of truth had entered the Eden of mythopoeia, the paganism of antiquity could never be recaptured, and the enthusiasm of crowds who experienced God in their beliefs concerning him might again invade the London streets. Four years after Hume's death, the Gordon Riots confronted Edward Gibbon with the sight of "forty thousand Puritans, such as they might be in the time of Cromwell . . . started out of their graves."[28]

❧ ❧

We are pursuing the history of enthusiasm as Enlightened thinking described it: the marriage of Athens and Jerusalem, philosophy and monotheism, for which the Enlightened desired to substitute an empirical philosophy, a morality of sociability, and a God who could be inferred rather than known. This analysis requires us to remain within the parameters of Enlightenment not completely secularized, not altogether detached from the religious matrix within which it had first taken shape. There was plenty of Enlightenment of this sort in eighteenth-century experience, both European and American, and its exponents knew very well how to diagnose enthusiasm as they understood it. Hume's skepticism did not divorce him from his Moderate friends in the

27. Hume, *History,* 5:459–60.
28. J. E. Norton, ed., *The Letters of Edward Gibbon* (London, 1956), 2:243.

Edinburgh clergy, and Gibbon was able to remain on terms of courteous dis-agreement with at least the Socinian strain within the Church of England. The unbelief of these philosopher-historians was not condemned until 1789, and Gibbon was able even then to make the point that the atheists of Hol-bach's circle in Paris had "laughed at the skepticism of Hume" and con-demned all forms of religion with the "bigotry of dogmatists."[29] Even Voltaire, Gibbon thought, was in the last analysis a bigot;[30] his irony had not been ironic enough. It is important not to let the term "unbelief" tempt us into telescoping skepticism and atheism. The skeptic does not know how the uni-verse is constituted and doubts the possibility of knowing; the atheist is very sure that he does know, and it is precisely this sort of certainty that the Enlightenments mistrusted and saw as a possible source of fanaticism and even enthusiasm. "These atheist fathers have a bigotry of their own," wrote Burke (or his son for him), "and they have learned to write against monks with the spirit of a monk."[31] The skeptics who lived to see the Revolution—among them Gibbon and several of the *coterie holbachique*—were not uncom-monly to reject it.

It is implicit, however, that enthusiasm could arise both within a frame-work continually more or less Christian, and within one defiantly deist or even atheist. Burke was to diagnose the former variety before he turned his atten-tion to the latter. In his *Speech on Conciliation with the Colonies* (1775), he spoke of the kind of religion developing in the American colonies, and it was there that he identified "the dissidence of dissent, the Protestantism of the Protestant religion. . . . agreeing in nothing except the principles of liberty,"[32] which was converting belief into the inquiry after belief and identifying the experience of God with the liberty of inquiry concerning him. This spirit lay deep within the history of Protestantism; it was that of the Seekers, of William Walwyn the reader of Montaigne,[33] of the Dutch Collegiants,[34] and of the free-thinking Quaker Benjamin Furley; and it is the direct ancestor of Maurice Gee's George Plumb. It was well established within the Congregationalism of New England and the always rather residual Anglicanism of Virginia; but in 1775 it had been represented in England for some years by vigorous move-ments—which assumed some of the character of popular petitioning—against

29. Edward Gibbon, *Memoirs of My Life,* ed. Georges A. Bonnard (New York, 1966), 127.
30. Edward Gibbon, *History of the Decline and Fall of the Roman Empire*, ed. David Womersley (London, 1993), 3:916 (chap. 67, n. 13).
31. Edmund Burke, *Reflections on the Revolution in France*, ed. J. G. A. Pocock (Indianapolis, 1987), 97 and note.
32. Edmund Burke, *Pre-Revolutionary Writings*, ed. Ian Harris (Cambridge, 1993), 224.
33. See Jack R. McMichael and Barbara Taft, eds., *The Writings of William Walwyn* (Athens, Ga., 1990).
34. Andrew Fix, *Prophecy and Reason: The Dutch Collegiants in the Early Enlightenment* (Princeton, N.J., 1991).

required subscription to the Thirty-Nine Articles for Anglicans and the restricted civil rights of Dissenters. Collectively known as Rational Dissent after some of the leaders resolved to leave the Anglican communion, it originated with the Socinian wing of Anglicanism and the Arian wing of Presbyterianism, and was led by those whose Arminian, Lockean, and in some cases paradoxically Platonist inquiries into the history of theology had moved them beyond adherence to any of the ancient alternatives to Nicene orthodoxy and into the spirit of antidogmatic openness that Burke described. This was the point at which rationalism joined hands with pietism, and gave grounds for the Enlightened belief that enthusiasm was capable of secularizing itself.[35]

Rational Dissent was for some years an active political movement with a highly visible potential for subversion; it contained many active sympathizers with the American Revolution and most of those who approved of the French Revolution or disapproved of the war against it.[36] Since it entailed a fairly direct assault on the unity of church and state that was the essence of the English ancien régime, democratic radicalism in the English-speaking world originated, it can be argued, as an attack on the doctrine of the Trinity and the concept of the church that went with it—and Benjamin Franklin's demographic predictions moved Josiah Tucker to ask Edmund Burke why he was being lured into keeping American Unitarians within the empire until they and their English allies were numerous enough to take it over altogether.[37] Insofar as there is justification for Burke's later belief that English Dissent had become a hotbed of Jacobin sympathies, it is to be found in the fact that much of what philojacobinism there was resided here. It was also clear that the movement possessed a measurable potential for enthusiasm. The search for a God whose nature defied definition could easily be identified with the experience of that God's being, and he himself might be identical with that questing spirit in the mind that joined it with reason immanent in the universe. From such a starting point it was possible to proceed in a variety of directions. It has been argued that the outspokenly antibiblical deism of Thomas Paine was at bottom a religion of nature, a doctrine of God and creation joined in one, perhaps originating in a popularized Spinozism or something older still, dating from the Interregnum sects;[38] and in turn, not so far removed from the Behmenism and Swedenborgianism apparent in William Blake, the last and greatest poet of English

---

35. See Knud Haakenssen (ed.), *Enlightenment and Religion: Rational Dissent in Eighteenth-Century Britain* (Cambridge, 1996).

36. J. E. Cookson, *The Friends of Peace: Anti-War Liberalism in England, 1793–1815* (Cambridge, 1982).

37. J. G. A. Pocock, "Josiah Tucker on Burke, Locke, and Price: A Study in the Varieties of Eighteenth-Century Conservatism," in *Virtue, Commerce, and History* (Cambridge, 1985), 157–91, esp. 162–64.

38. Jack Fruchtman, *Thomas Paine and the Religion of Nature* (Baltimore, 1993).

enthusiasm. The Unitarianism of Rational Dissent might evolve into the athe-ist idealism of Godwin and Shelley, or into the revived Platonism that would conduct Coleridge back to the Church of England and a rewriting of its his-tory.[39] In all these instances we may detect variations on the theme that the uni-verse was in one way or another immanent in the mind, which we have found to be the philosophical component of enthusiasm as Enlightenment perceived it, but at the same time a product of Enlightenment itself in its Protestant and English form.

✐ ✐

Such, then, was the history of both enthusiasm and the diagnosis of enthusi-asm, in an England whose Enlightenment remained religious even where irre-ligious, firmly contained within the matrix of Establishment and Dissent; a history that can be prolonged into the nineteenth century. We have arrived at a definition of enthusiasm as the mind's identification with the ideas in it, these in turn defined as correspondent or identical with the substance of real-ity. Karl Popper would instantly have seen why it must produce non-falsifiable propositions, and would very likely have considered historicism as he used the term a source of enthusiasm as Enlightened minds defined it. The mind would be knowing itself as history, and history as its own workings—an error big with mischief. But the more the definition of enthusiasm is removed from the prophetic to the philosophical, the more it ceases to be merely a phenome-non of that spirituality that Enlightenment set out to displace, and becomes instead a phenomenon of Enlightenment itself. The mind, which in the first place set limits to its own powers in the hope of ending fanaticism, becomes the object of its own worship, and several species of rationalist messianism make their appearance. Was there a rebirth of enthusiasm as Enlightenment became revolutionary? Can the definition of enthusiasm assist us in under-standing what happened?

Here the re-entry of English into European history—now going on, if not always in the forms most demanded—creates both problems and opportuni-ties. In England, Enlightenment remained within a religious matrix, and nei-ther Jacobins nor historicists made significant appearance; the nearest we come to a revolutionary rationalist seeking to remodel society is that least Jacobin of

---

39. John Morrow, *Coleridge's Political Thought: Property, Morality, and the Limits of Traditional Discourse* (London, 1990).

figures Jeremy Bentham. For this reason England has long been excluded from the historiography of Enlightenment; where no *philosophes* give birth to either revolution or counterrevolution, it has been hard to speak of *lumières* or *Aufklärung*. But the revisionist move—linked with that of making Hanoverian England an ancien régime[40]—of declaring both the English and the Scottish Enlightenments clerical, intended rather to conserve a regime than to reform or replace it,[41] has enabled us to see how it was that Hanoverian Britain—an ancien régime where most such regimes were Enlightened—experienced the French Revolution by waging war against it for twenty years. Edmund Burke, essentially a defender of Enlightenment in its Montesquieuan form in Europe and its Anglican and Moderate forms in Britain, lost no time in diagnosing revolutionary zeal as a form of enthusiasm, no less deserving of the term for being atheist, and went on to diagnose revolution itself as that political condition in which "nothing rules except the mind of desperate men." Once again, the spirit had revolted against the law, "the enterprising talents of a country against its property,"[42] and the mind must be induced or compelled to return to seeing itself as contained within the conditions that law, economy, and history provided, enabling it to work on something other than itself. Burke, an Anglican because he thought the social order must possess a dimension of sacrality, was no friend to Hume and Gibbon because he thought their irreligious skepticism was corrosive of the sacred. But they too had hoped to see the mind readjust itself to the disciplines of society and would have waited—had they lived so long—for the fires of revolution to burn themselves out and recognize a history that was still going on and could not be divined as the action of Spirit, as it was by German historicism—enthusiasm in yet another new form.

For this to happen, however, property and labor must be recognized as actual forces, bringing into existence a society and history possessed of a certain solidity. Even in the high Enlightenment of the eighteenth century, it was possible to doubt the continued existence of social reality. Hume, in the essay *Of Public Credit,*[43] had pointed out that a society totally mortgaged to an international credit mechanism would be unable any longer to generate government out of the social relations between its members, since these no longer

40. See J. C. D. Clark, *English Society, 1688–1832* (Cambridge, 1986).
41. J. G. A. Pocock, "Clergy and Commerce: The Conservative Enlightenment in England," in R. Ajello et al., eds., *L'Età dei Lumi: Studi storici sul settecento europeo in onore di Franco Venturi* (Naples, 1985), 1:523–62; and "Conservative Enlightenment and Democratic Revolutions," *Government and Opposition* 24 (1989): 81–105.
42. *The Writings and Speeches of Edmund Burke*, vol. 9, pt. 2, *Ireland*, ed R. B. McDowell (Oxford, 1991), 241, 189.
43. *Essays Moral, Political, and Literary*, 349–65.

generated either wealth or power. To Burke—who supplied several conjectural explanations for the rebirth of enthusiasm in a world no longer Christian—the French Revolution was largely the work of the state's creditors in alliance with a fanatical intelligentsia, and he explained that as the states of Europe submerged themselves in a bottomless sea of debt, extraordinary and fantastical intellectual conspiracies appeared everywhere on that ocean's surface.[44] The credit mechanism, which is to say the fluidity of capital, eroded property, reality, and history, and exposed the mind to the temptation of worshipping its own fantasies. We recognize an image which could be that of our own world. Revolution was the postmodernism of Enlightenment; but a postmodernism that is also postrevolutionary—the product of a world in which the fluidity of capital is for the present despotically powerful—is capable of neither enthusiasm nor Enlightenment since it cannot worship even itself. This too shall pass; but how and when?

Johns Hopkins University

44. Burke, *Reflections*, 137 and note.

Enthusiasm or Imagination?
Eighteenth-Century Smear Words in
Comparative National Context

— JAN GOLDSTEIN

The words commonly used in any culture as negative epithets or smear words stand in dialectical relation to the most esteemed values of that culture. They represent the detested "other" that must be extruded if a particularly configured self is to be maintained. In the world of the eighteenth-century European Enlightenment, the key esteemed value (still relatively new and hence relatively vulnerable) was rationality, taken to mean the capacity to assess in a neutral register the pros and cons of any situation, to put this-worldly concerns of utility in the fore, to emulate the scientist's procedures of evidence-gathering and inference, to cordon off and remain unswayed by the passions that comprised the inferior part of one's mental makeup. From this high regard for rationality stemmed the role accorded to enthusiasm. In our own day, that term not only carries a positive connotation—we think that an enthusiastic teacher is likely to be effective in the classroom and that an enthusiastic colleague is an asset in the workplace—but it is also so casually and routinely employed as to have lost any real rhetorical force. By contrast, "enthusiasm" functioned in the eighteenth century as a powerful term of opprobrium. It conjured up everything antithetical to, and rejected by, enlightened rationality.[1]

The question that I wish to raise and to explore in a preliminary fashion is whether "enthusiasm" enjoyed the same lexical status in eighteenth-century France that it did during the same period in Britain and Germany, the other countries treated in detail in this volume. I certainly do not wish to contest the fact that the term carried a primarily negative valence in all three national settings. Nor do I wish to contest what seems equally patent: that it was in all

---

1. At the Clark Library conference on which this volume is based, Anthony La Vopa suggested that "enthusiasm" was an all-purpose eighteenth-century epithet or smear word, at least in Germany. His comments form the starting point of this essay.

three a polyvalent term, with praise being reserved for those instances of enthu-siasm (the distinct minority) that resulted in artistic creation. What I wish to question is whether "enthusiasm" was the smear word of choice, the epithet that came most readily to mind when "enlightened" people in France felt moved to disparage the unenlightened attitudes and behavior of their fellows. My educated guess at this moment—and I should stress that I am making no stronger claim—is that it was not.

My own hunch is that "imagination" played that premier role. As I have argued at length elsewhere, imagination was viewed in eighteenth-century France as the least protected part of the mental apparatus. Situated at the point of intersection between mind and body, it was believed to be the principal entryway for error and disorder, the potential site for the capture of the will and the consequent loss of self-control. Hence the frequent eighteenth-century use of a locution that contrasted people who were "masters" of their imagina-tion with those who ceded their authority to it and became its "dupes"—or, alternatively, the dupes of others who had assumed dominion over them by cleverly manipulating their imagination. The dangers of imagination had already been underscored by the Cartesian psychology of the seventeenth cen-tury. But the sensationalist psychology of the eighteenth century reiterated those dangers and, more important, gave them a new inflection. Because, in the sensationalist account, the environment impinged decisively on the men-tal apparatus, proponents of that psychology could, they thought, identify the environments and practices most liable to cause imagination to go astray and could thus call for preventive hygienic measures. The dangerous environments cited were almost always solitary ones where, in the absence of the consensual force of the community, the distinction between a publicly ratified reality and a personal imaginative fiction might easily be blurred. (The converse was also true: crowds harbored danger because they encouraged imagination's potential for contagion.) The dangerous practices, all of which purportedly overstimu-lated imagination and caused it to generate fictions of a vividness that could plausibly compete with reality, included reading novels, masturbating, pursu-ing one's trade outside the supervision of a guild, and speculating on the stock market. In its sensationalist more than in its Cartesian guise, then, the dis-course on imagination overflowed the bounds of the technical philosophical psychology that had originally shaped it and acquired a relevance to the every-day stuff of eighteenth-century life. Simply to say that imagination was involved in an attitude or activity was—except in rare, artistic contexts—to damn that attitude or activity, to declare it contaminated by irrational forces.[2]

2.   See "Imagination and the Problematization of the Self at the End of the Old Regime," chapter 1 of my book *The Post-Revolutionary Self: Competing Psychologies in Nineteenth-Century France* (Harvard Univer-sity Press, forthcoming).

Imagination and enthusiasm were closely linked terms in France in this period, which is why the one might serve as a functional substitute for the other. Their intimate affiliation is evident in two representative Enlightenment texts, the articles "Enthusiasm" in the *Encyclopédie* (1751–65) of Diderot and d'Alembert, and in the *Dictionnaire philosophique* (1764) of Voltaire.

In an *Encyclopédie* article not remarkable for its analytic rigor, Jean-Louis de Cahusac postulated a near but incomplete equivalence between our two key terms.[3] Enthusiasm was, he implied, a transient mental event while imagination was a lasting mental structure; yet the two habitually operated in tandem, with the former stimulating the latter and/or deriving from it. Thus Cahusac presented the prevailing wisdom on the subject (from which he would, later in the article, personally dissent): "Commonly one understands by *enthusiasm* a kind of furious fit that grabs hold of the mind and overpowers it, that inflames the imagination, elevates it and renders it fertile." A few paragraphs later he reversed the causal arrow in this putative commonplace: "imagination [is] commonly believed to be the unique source of enthusiasm." Yet, whatever the cause and whatever the effect, Cahusac was intent upon removing the stigma attached to both enthusiasm and imagination. He insisted that enthusiasm not be likened to madness but rather that it be regarded as the "masterwork of reason," a "rapid operation of reason [producing] that mutual accord between the soul and the senses from which swift expression is born." Attempting in parallel fashion to rescue imagination from ill repute, he spoke of a future time when "persons of genius . . . will have discovered that reason, and not imagination, is the primary motor of their soul" and when imagination itself will be regarded as one of the "operations of reason."[4]

Voltaire offered a variation on the Encyclopedist's theme. Accepting as true the common opinion that Cahusac contested, he portrayed enthusiasm as a "madness, fury, rage," even a "disease." He stressed its physiological nature (tumult in the blood vessels, violent vibrations in the nerves) and was apparently inclined to lend credence to what he took, erroneously, to be the Greek etymology of the term as a "convulsion of the entrails."[5] But like the Encyclopedist, he believed that reason could purify both enthusiasm and imagination—

3. On the identity of the author, a scion of the provincial robe nobility who came to Paris in the 1730s and signed his numerous *Encyclopédie* articles only with the initial "B," see John Lough, *The Contributors to the Encyclopédie* (London, 1973), 76.

4. "Enthousiasme," *Encyclopédie, ou dictionnaire raisonné des sciences, des arts at des métiers*, 17 vols. (Paris and Neufchâtel, 1751–65), 5:719–22.

5. "Enthousiasme," *Dictionnaire philosophique* in *Les Oeuvres complètes de Voltaire/The Complete Works of Voltaire*, 132 vols. (Oxford, 1968), 36:58–61. See 58 n. 2 for a discussion of Voltaire's incorrect etymology. My English renderings of the text are drawn from Voltaire, *Philosophical Dictionary*, trans. Peter Gay, 2 vols. (New York, 1962), 1:251–53.

although, significantly, he conceptualized such a purification as a merely temporary collaboration between reason and a conjoint enthusiasm-imagination for
artistic purposes rather than as a permanent recategorization of enthusiasm and
imagination under the rubric of reason. According to Voltaire, "reasonable enthusiasm is the characteristic of great poets." Reason succeeds in governing enthusiasm when it lays down the basic framework of an artistic composition, which is
subsequently animated when the artist lets "imagination kindle" and "enthusiasm
take effect [*agir*]"; under those optimal conditions, Voltaire went on to say, imagination and enthusiasm could be metaphorically identified as a single racehorse
speeding headlong through a predetermined course. Thus Voltaire seemed to
obscure Cahusac's distinction between enthusiasm and imagination, depicting
both as mental events of a quite similar sort and neither as a mental structure. But
much like the Encyclopedist, Voltaire seems simply to have taken for granted the
habitual partnership of enthusiasm and imagination.

If the terms were as closely associated as these representative texts suggest,
is anything really at stake in arguing, as I will do here, that the French preferred
"imagination" as an all-purpose epithet? Obviously, I have an interest in
mounting such an argument because it reinforces the centrality that I have
attributed to eighteenth-century imagination in the context of my other work.
But apart from that, demonstrating a French partiality for "imagination" over
"enthusiasm" as a term of opprobrium would, I believe, show the local factors
at work in the evolution of the latter term. It would reveal that the overridingly
negative meaning attached to "enthusiasm" in certain eighteenth-century settings had as its prerequisite the historical experience of living amidst radical
Protestant sects and living through the unsettling public controversies that
they provoked. As inhabitants of a country that had for the most part repelled
the Protestant Reformation, the French had never had their word *enthousiasme*
so thoroughly saturated with the particular set of pejorative connotations that
derived from hostility to the religious claims of Protestant sectaries. As a result,
the French generally used the term "imagination" and its cognates to do the
work—or dirty work—that "enthusiasm" performed for their British and German contemporaries.

THE LEXICOGRAPHICAL EVIDENCE

As a first step toward supporting this contention, I will confine myself to the Franco-British case and compare the entry for "enthusiasm" in the *Oxford English Dictionary* with that for "enthousiasme" in two similarly reliable French historical dictionaries, the *Grand Robert de la langue française* (2d ed., 1985) and the *Trésor de la langue française* (1971–85).

    The degree of transnational congruence among the entries is striking. All three dictionaries offer as their initial definition of the term its etymological, ancient Greek sense—that is, possession by a god. All end with its current watered-down and secularized sense: "rapturous intensity of feeling in favour of a person, principle, cause, etc.," according to the *OED;* "very intense joy which tends to be externalized and expressed in the form of total adherence and complete approbation," according to the *Trésor.* All three, moreover, include an artistic meaning. But here a difference in emphasis is evident. The *OED* gives short shrift to artistically fertile enthusiasm, incorporating it into the core etymological meaning by listing "prophetic or poetic frenzy" alongside "possession by a god." The two French dictionaries, by contrast, reserve separate subentries for the artistic dimension of enthusiasm and take the opportunity to expatiate on it. The *Robert* presents "transport, exaltation of the poet under the influence of inspiration" and "the force that pushes man to create" as extensions of the core etymological meaning, noting that they have been used in French since the sixteenth century. The *Trésor* likewise sees a "state of exaltation of the soul in a poet or painter in the prey of inspiration" as an extension of the core meaning, noting that the original religious coloration is often retained in this usage, which conceptualizes enthusiasm as a divine gift.

    But the most conspicuous divergence between the English and French dictionaries is the presence in the former of a meaning that is completely lacking in the latter: enthusiasm as "fancied inspiration," or what Samuel Johnson called "a vain confidence of divine favour or communication." The *OED* notes that this meaning often mutated in the eighteenth century into the "vaguer" one of "ill-regulated or misdirected religious emotion, extravagance of religious speculation." And it cites in support of its main point a bevy of famous users of English. Henry More (1660): "If ever Christianity be exterminated, it will be by Enthusiasme." Joseph Priestley (1772): "Enthusiasm [makes us] imagine that we are the particular favourites of the divinity." Or the particularly direct and hard-hitting formulation of the third earl of Shaftesbury (1711): "Inspiration is a real feeling of the Divine presence, and Enthusiasm is a false one." In the period under consideration, then, the English could build the self-deception of enthusiasts and the falsity of their mental state into the very definition of "enthusiasm." Whereas the French dictionaries abstain from judgment about the validity of an enthusiasm defined as (in the words of the *Trésor*) a "state of religious fervor, of intense religious emotion providing intuition of religious verities or supernatural realities," the *OED*, presumably reporting on the empirical state of the English language in past centuries, allows a massive intrusion of judgment into definition. It lists two different meanings of religious enthusiasm that are distinguished from one another precisely by the evaluations they contain: one is the entirely neutral and descriptive "supernatural inspiration," the other, ascribed to seventeenth- and eighteenth-century usage, the prejudged and pejorative "fancied inspiration."

The relative accents placed by the *OED*, the *Grand Robert,* and the *Trésor de la langue française* on an esteemed artistic enthusiasm and a maligned religious one shed light on the "national" characteristics of the representative texts by Cahusac and Voltaire discussed above. I earlier examined those texts for evidence of the connection between enthusiasm and imagination; but the results of my foray into the late-twentieth-century historical dictionaries provide a second, equally relevant interpretive grid through which to read them. Through such a grid, Cahusac appears very French. An author of plays, opera libretti, and ballet scenarios,[6] he construed the "enthusiasm" about which he had been commissioned to write for the *Encyclopédie* in an artistic sense only. Thus his article begins: "We have no entirely satisfactory definition of this word; however I believe it useful to the progress of the fine arts that we seek and, if possible, fix its true meaning."[7] Indeed, in Diderot and d'Alembert's famous compendium, the virtually exclusive attention lavished on the aesthetic meaning of "enthusiasm"—both by Cahusac himself and by the cross-references to his article supplied by the editors, including one to a lengthy digression in Diderot's article "Eclecticism"[8]—is quite striking. It is broken

---

6. Lough, *Contributors*, 76.
7. The article does briefly discuss, as the earliest meaning of enthusiasm, the "prophetic furor" of pagan antiquity, manifested by the grimaces and contortions of the priests who allegedly experienced it. But Cahusac makes clear that he has introduced this material only for the purpose of explaining why intimations of madness still cling, erroneously in his view, to the modern concept of artistic enthusiasm ("Enthousiasme," *Encyclopédie*, 5:719).
8. To such predictable cross-references as "Expression," "Music," "Genius," and "Elocution" is added a quite extraordinary one to a particular page (p. 276) of the article on the philosophical school, or non-school, "Eclecticism" (5:270–93), a generic name for those philosophers refusing to adhere strictly to any doctrine; since Diderot was its author, he knew that an article on this apparently unpromising subject contained material relevant to Cahusac's "Enthusiasm." In the passage cited, Diderot is recounting the biography of Porphyry, whose intense and unrelieved study of philosophy in Rome with Plotinus at the age of twenty gave his temperament an enthusiastic and melancholic cast. This chance remark prompts a long digression on enthusiasm. Says Diderot: "I will observe here in passing that it is impos-

only by an abrupt reminder of another lode of contemporary signification. In the very brief (two-sentence) entry for "Enthusiast" by the abbé Mallet (who had the distinct advantage in this situation of being an expert both in the arts and in theology)[9] we find: "Separate from the meaning that one gives to it in the fine arts, this word [enthusiast] is often construed in a negative sense [*se prend souvent en mauvaise part*] to designate a fanatic." Significantly, Mallet depicts the pejorative religious meaning of the term as derivative, a corruption of the fundamental aesthetic meaning.[10]

Voltaire's article "Enthusiasm" in his *Dictionnaire philosophique* is more ecumenical; in the roughly equal attention that it pays to the artistic and religious modalities of enthusiasm, its sensibility might well be deemed Anglo-French. As noted above, the article concludes with a discussion of the necessary marriage of reason and enthusiasm in great poets and painters. Another passage on the aesthetic dimension of enthusiasm describes different audience reactions to a performance of a "moving tragedy," observing that the spectator who is so carried away that he decides to write a tragedy himself "has caught the disease of enthusiasm." But the article also betrays a vivid awareness of the negative religious meaning of enthusiasm—an atypical awareness for an eighteenth-century Frenchman, if we are to judge from the *Grand Robert* and the *Trésor,* whose silence concerning this usage suggests that it occupied a liminal zone in the French of the period, never acquiring sufficient currency to leave its mark for latter-day lexicographers. Thus Voltaire opines that "enthusiasm is *above all* the characteristic of misdirected piety" (italics added), citing the hypothetical example of a young fakir who believes that self-inflicted pain will leave "the supreme Being . . . deeply obligated to him."

---

sible to produce anything sublime in poetry, painting, eloquence or music without enthusiasm. Enthusiasm is a violent movement of the soul transporting us amidst objects that we have to represent; we see an entire scene occurring in our imagination, as if it were outside ourselves; in fact it is outside ourselves, for while this illusion lasts, all actually present entities are annihilated, and our ideas acquire reality in their stead." This digression on enthusiasm continues for more than a full column and includes statements similar to those of Cahusac and Voltaire on the need to combine enthusiasm with reason: "If that state is not itself madness, it is very close to madness. That is why much good sense is needed to balance enthusiasm." When allowed to spread unchecked throughout an artistic work, enthusiasm deforms it, producing "I don't know what kind of oversized and unbelievable thing."

9. The article is signed "G," the code name in the *Encyclopédie* for the abbé Edme Mallet who, like Cahusac, was a prolific contributor of articles to that compendium. See Lough, *Contributors*, 90–91.

10. "Enthousiaste," *Encyclopédie,* 5:722. Oddly enough, the article on "Enthousiastes" in the plural, only slightly longer than that on "Enthousiaste" in the singular, is totally religious in content. The term, we are told, belongs to ecclesiastical history and refers to ancient sects who were agitated by the Devil but believed themselves truly inspired. It is used in the mid-eighteenth century to refer to Anabaptists and Quakers, "who believe themselves filled with a divine inspiration and maintain that the Holy Scripture ought to be interpreted in light of this inspiration." Nothing is said about the truth or falsity of this modern belief.

Of course, Voltaire's atypical embrace of this "English" understanding of enthusiasm presents the historian with no special puzzle. Voltaire spent more than two years in England in the late 1720s. During this intellectually formative sojourn he was so attuned to the religious complexion of the inhabitants that he famously characterized the land across the Channel as the "country of sects," where each man "goes to Heaven by whatever road he pleases."[11] The first four of his *Lettres philosophiques* (1732), which recorded his English experiences, were devoted to the Quakers. And, while Voltaire evinced a much higher regard for this sect than did most of his contemporaries, the task of describing their conduct still gave him the opportunity to utilize the negative religious language of enthusiasm. In the first letter, Voltaire gets into a nasty quarrel with a Quaker about whether baptism is an original and essential element of Christianity. After a few parries, he decides to hold his tongue, explaining to the reader as follows: "I took care not to dispute anything he said, for there's no arguing with an *Enthusiast*. Better not take it into one's head to tell a lover the faults of his mistress, or a litigant the weakness of his cause—or to talk sense to a fanatic."[12] In the third letter, he recounts the history of the seventeenth-century Quaker preacher Richard Fox, sent to a lunatic asylum to be whipped. Perversely, Fox arranges for the men flogging him to double the punishment, declaring it good for his soul. When he begins to preach, these same men laugh derisively but, since "the disease of Enthusiasm is catching," their mood quickly changes, and some are even converted.[13]

Yet, while Voltaire the Anglophile and observer of English sects deploys the negative religious language of enthusiasm in both his *Lettres philosophiques* and his *Dictionnaire philosophique,* he falls short of articulating the most barbed English meaning of that term. He never uses the term to mean the erroneous belief that one is suffused with divine inspiration. Instead, he confines himself to the more moderate and what the *OED* calls the "vaguer" meaning of misdirected religious emotion, as well as to the identification of enthusiasm with fanaticism, or a blindly unreasoning insistence on the correctness of one's position—a usage common in mid-eighteenth-century

11. Voltaire, *Lettres philosophiques*, ed. Gustave Lanson, 2d ed., 2 vols. (Paris, 1915), 1:60. My English renderings of this text come from Voltaire, *Philosophical Letters,* trans. Ernest Dilworth (New York, 1961). The quoted passage is the opening of Letter 5; see p. 22.

12. Voltaire, *Philosophical Letters*, 5 (italics added). The word here translated as "fanatic" is actually *illuminé*; see Voltaire, *Lettres philosophiques,* 4.

13. Voltaire, *Philosophical Letters,* 12. Voltaire's labeling of the Quakers as enthusiasts (coupled with an otherwise favorable portrait of them as people of simple piety and natural nobility) seems to have become quasi-canonical among French *philosophes*. The *Encyclopédie* article "Enthousiastes" (5:722) was cross-referenced to the article "Quaker" (13:648–50), whose author, the Chevalier de Jaucourt, credited Voltaire with having furnished him with most of his material (13:650).

France, according to the abbé Mallet.[14] In the *Lettres philosophiques*, Voltaire does, to be sure, mention the Quakers' belief in personal divine inspiration, the physical contortions accompanying such intensely heightened states, and the uncertainty about whether their source is truly divine. He describes crowds mimicking the Quakers, "trembling, having convulsions . . . and fancying that the Holy Ghost was in them." But he does not associate the word "enthusiasm" with this particular cluster of issues.[15] One might say that his command of the English vocabulary of enthusiasm, however impressive for a Frenchman, had its limits.

It is the derogatory religious meaning of enthusiasm, especially in its strongest, most polemical form—a meaning developed to express scorn for certain key claims made by Protestant sectaries—that, I would argue, accounts for the salience of "enthusiasm" as a negative epithet in countries, such as Britain, whose recent histories had been marked by the activities of those sectaries. It is thus this meaning of enthusiasm on which J. G. A. Pocock focused when he brilliantly traced the transformation of the language of enthusiasm in Britain, its replacement of a religious referent with a political one.[16] As Pocock shows, this bit of discursive magic was performed by Edmund Burke in the course of his precocious condemnation of the French Revolution. In *Reflections on the Revolution in France* (1791), Burke played upon the familiarity of his British audience with the seventeenth-century controversies over Protestant religious dissent and their intertwinement with Britain's own experiment in political revolution during that same era. He suggested a striking formal analogy between the old-style Protestant religious enthusiast and the new-style Revolutionary political enthusiast across the Channel.[17] Just as the former mistakenly believed in personal divine inspiration and appealed to the Spirit's immediate presence within him as grounds for rejecting all other authority, so the latter just as mistakenly believed in what Pocock calls the "sovereignty of self-creating discourse," the possibility and indeed necessity for people to "reshape

14. See "Enthousiaste," *Encyclopédie*, as discussed above (note 10). The eighteenth-century French enthusiasm-fanaticism identification, apparently not commonplace enough to be recorded in either the *Grand Robert* or the *Trésor*, is also noted in the posthumously published work of the abbé Pluquet, *De la superstition et de l'enthousiasme* (Paris, 1804), 109.

15. Voltaire, *Philosophical Letters*, 8–9, 13.

16. J. G. A. Pocock, "Edmund Burke and the Redefinition of Enthusiasm: The Context as Counter-Revolution," in François Furet and Mona Ozouf, eds., *The Transformation of Political Culture, 1789–1848* (Oxford, 1989), 19–36.

17. The formalism of this analogy must be stressed; neither Burke nor Pocock postulate that the French revolutionaries of 1789 were influenced by the Protestant sectaries of the previous century. Indeed, Pocock asserts that the source of the revolutionaries' belief system was in classical antiquity: an "already available . . . rhetoric, based on a cult of republican rhetoric in the ancient world" (ibid., 20).

their political universe, and in so doing to reshape themselves" through the simple affirmative device of "public speech in a public place."[18] The denotation of "enthusiasm" that Burke found readily at hand and that he enlisted in his attack on the spirit animating the French Revolution was just the denotation that is conspicuously absent both from the standard French historical dictionaries and from our two representative eighteenth-century French texts: human self-deification, or the false (and, inevitably, socially disruptive) belief that one has within oneself a supernatural presence enabling one to challenge, solo, all other forms of authority.

Interpreting the Saint-Médard Convulsionaries (I): Dr. Hecquet

In order to illustrate my claim that the eighteenth-century French were likely to use the term "imagination" to interpret and disparage phenomena that would probably have been labeled "enthusiasm" in a British (or German) setting, I will look at some of the voluminous literature generated in France in the 1720s and 1730s by the episode of the so-called convulsionaries of Saint-Médard.[19] This episode was one of the most conspicuous sequelae to the papal bull Unigenitus (1713), which condemned the major tenets of Jansenism as heretical. Intended to deal the final blow to a Jansenist movement already weakened by the destruction of Port-Royal, the bull had the opposite effect, galvanizing the remnants of that Catholic sect into an obdurate and vocal resistance. In 1727, in the midst of the controversy over the bull, the revered Jansenist deacon François de Pâris died and was buried in the cemetery of the Saint-Médard church on the rue Mouffetard, in what was then a poor and overcrowded *faubourg* of Paris populated primarily by artisans. A new and defiant Jansenist cult soon declared the spot sacred. Its adherents were seized by convulsions, frenzied paroxysms, and screams and swoons so uncontrollable and violent that their coreligionists placed mattresses and cushions around the gravesite to prevent injuries. Initially only those who touched the deacon's tomb were convulsed; later the geographical range widened, so that individuals

18. Ibid., 20, 25.
19. For historical accounts of this episode, see B. Robert Kreiser, *Miracles, Convulsions, and Ecclesiastical Politics in Early Eighteenth-Century Paris* (Princeton, N.J., 1978); and Catherine-Laurence Maire, ed., *Les Convulsionnaires de Saint-Médard: Miracles, convulsions et prophéties à Paris au XVIIIe siècle* (Paris, 1985). I wrote about this episode from a different viewpoint in "'Moral Contagion': A Professional Ideology of Medicine and Psychiatry in Eighteenth- and Nineteenth-Century France," in Gerald Geison, ed., *Professions and the French State, 1700–1900* (Philadelphia, 1984), 181–222. Most of the following paragraph comes from this article (pp. 185–86).

throughout the cemetery, in the church, in nearby houses, and even in the streets were affected.

The physical convulsions brought forth in their turn what one historian has called a "convulsion of interpretations,"[20] a polemical outpouring attempting to make sense of the bizarre behavior and in particular to assess the accuracy of the participants' own interpretation of it as a divine miracle working through the intercession of M. de Pâris. If ever there was an opportunity seemingly tailor-made for the invidious employment of the term enthusiasm, this was it. And yet the individual who most forcefully advanced a naturalistic, enlightened understanding of the events, the eminent physician and former dean of the Paris Faculty of Medicine Philippe Hecquet, relied primarily on the term imagination as his interpretive—and debunking—tool. The author of the unambiguously titled 1733 treatise *Le Naturalisme des convulsions dans les maladies de l'épidémie convulsionnaire*, Hecquet (himself a Jansenist and hence a decidedly reluctant debunker of the sectaries) subsequently wrote several pamphlets responding to the attacks on this initial statement of his position. In all of these writings, the word imagination was pivotal.

Hecquet struck this note in the opening pages of *Le Naturalisme des convulsions* when, in his central strategic gambit, he converted the epidemic convulsions from an alleged miraculous phenomenon into "hysterical vapors, perhaps truly uterine in nature, [but] caused and sustained by passions of the soul, as philosophical physicians speak of them, or [in other words] by those movements excited by objects that trouble the *imagination,* which in women is all the easier to rattle and unhinge."[21] With respect to the young female convulsionaries, the animating or "inflaming" passion, the imagined object sought, was precisely that God use them as the instrument of a miracle and, as such, that they receive the approbation of their fellows.[22] That imagination could produce a complex muscular event like a convulsion was, in Hecquet's view, entirely explicable, for the imagination had much more thoroughgoing power over our corporeal nature than did the will:

> If the simple will of the soul is a commandment executed on the
> spot by the [animal] spirits which, like runners, go to the places
> in the body where the soul sends them, how are we to conceive
> of [imagined] objects which by their activity remove the soul

20. Maire, *Convulsionnaires de Saint-Médard*, title of chap. 5.

21. [Philippe Hecquet], *Le Naturalisme des convulsions dans les maladies de l'épidémie convulsionnaire* (Soleure, 1733), 12–13 (italics added).

22. Ibid., 13–14.

from its ordinary condition and oblige it to heat up the animal spirits with impetuosity in the direction of certain organs? However the will of the soul alone sends the spirits simultaneously to three hundred different muscles when a guitar player touches his instrument while crooning and tapping his feet. How many muscles and muscular fibers, then, are strongly agitated in the body of a young girl whose brain is inflamed by the desire to see herself a miraculous convulsionary?[23]

To clinch this argument (and, from our vantage point, to underscore his reliance on the concept of imagination), Hecquet made reference to a staple element in the early modern discourse of imagination, one supported by both Cartesian and sensationalist epistemologies and possessing currency in both scholarly and popular milieux: the alleged capacity of the pregnant woman's imagination to imprint the bodily form of her gestating child.[24] "Very real proof" of his contention that an unaided imagination could produce the particular muscular pattern of a convulsion was, he said, found in the "signs that mothers impress on the bodies of the infants that they carry in their wombs" as a result of their "strong imaginations."[25]

Throughout this treatise, Hecquet was overtly engaged in a professional boundary dispute. Trying to temper his polemical purpose by assuring his readers that his intervention in the debate smacked neither "of supererogation nor of indiscreet and presumptuous enterprises of Medicine against Theology," he was nonetheless intent on asserting that the convulsions fell within the purview of medicine rather than theology—that physicians rather than church doctors possessed the competence both to interpret and to treat them.[26] Might Hecquet's training and self-representation as a physician, then, explain his preference for the term imagination over the term enthusiasm in his analysis of the convulsions? Might the embeddedness of the former term in an

---

23. Ibid., 14–15.
24. The sheer longevity of this belief is striking. For the classical, late-seventeenth-century Cartesian statement of it, see Nicholas Malebranche, *La recherche de la vérité* (1675), bk. 2, pt. 1, chap. 7, sec. 3. Even at the beginning of the nineteenth century, the *Idéologue* P.-J.-G. Cabanis asserted that there was much empirical evidence in support of it; see his *Rapports du physique et du moral de l'homme* (1802), Mémoire XI, in *Oeuvres philosophiques de Cabanis*, ed. Claude Lehec and Jean Cazeneuve, 2 vols. (Paris, 1956), 1:605. Three years later, a revised edition of a text of 1788 reaffirmed the traditional belief; see Benjamin Bablot, *Effets prodigieux de l'imagination des femmes enceintes, prouvés par les faits les plus curieux* (Paris, 1805). See also Marie-Hélène Huet, *Monstrous Imagination* (Cambridge, Mass., and London, 1993), on the career of this trope from the Renaissance through the Romantic period.
25. Hecquet, *Naturalisme*, 14–15; see also Hecquet's return to this motif and mode of argumentation (p. 37).
26. Ibid., 21.

eighteenth-century biomedical language of nerves, muscles, and animal spirits have determined his choice, thus negating the value of his text as a testing ground for my hypothesis?

While such an argument has an apparent cogency, it is belied by the fact that "enthusiasm," too, was at this date a thoroughly medicalized term. Michael Heyd's recent study of anti-enthusiasm discourse has shown that the firm association of enthusiasm with the pathological condition of melancholy went back to Greek antiquity and survived into the early modern period. In this traditional formulation, melancholy was understood according to the Galenic theory of humors as an excess of black bile. But, more important, with the decline of the humoral paradigm in the late seventeenth century and its replacement by a mechanistic and corpuscular model of the human body, the age-old affiliation of melancholy and enthusiasm got a new lease on life. Melancholy was reconceptualized in terms of "animal spirits," which were also, as we have seen, the linchpin in Hecquet's concept of imagination. Clerical critics of enthusiasm in Britain and Geneva then made extensive use of the newly overhauled and fashionable enthusiasm-melancholy equation to disparage the sectaries. (Although Heyd depicts his study as pan-European, all the authors he cites as using the newly medicalized melancholy in fact come from those two geographical areas, which were, not coincidentally, also predominantly Protestant.) Reliance on medical vocabulary even led British clerics to make, with respect to religious enthusiasts, a claim fully analogous to the one that Hecquet made in the name of his own profession with respect to the hysterical and overly imaginative convulsionaries of Saint-Médard. Given the corporeal nature of enthusiasm, they said, the treatment of so-called enthusiasts ought to be relegated to physicians rather than divines.[27] In other words, the term enthusiasm was in the early eighteenth century as amenable to a medical gloss as the term imagination was. Hecquet's choice of the latter, it seems fair to say, derived from his participation in the French national discursive community rather than from the intrinsic lexical resources of the two terms in question.

The language of enthusiasm of the English and Swiss clerics cited by Heyd was, moreover, very much entwined with the language of imagination. For example, the anonymous author of *A Dissuasive against Enthusiasm* wrote that "a Delirium, or natural Enthusiasm, arising from a disorder'd Brain, occasion'd by great Fervency of Temper, or violent Agitations of the animal Spirits, will necessarily impregnate the Fancy, cause the Images of Things to Come into it very

---

27. Michael Heyd, *"Be Sober and Reasonable": The Critique of Enthusiasm in the Seventeenth and Early Eighteenth Centuries* (Leiden, 1995), chaps. 2 and 7, esp. 193–203.

fast."[28] But while Englishmen of Hecquet's era freely admixed the language of enthusiasm with that of imagination—Heyd goes so far as to speak of a generally accepted "circular mechanism between 'animal spirits' on the one hand, and passions and imagination on the other"[29]—Hecquet's discourse of imagination was far purer, peppered only on rare occasions with references to enthusiasm.

Thus, even when Hecquet turned to the more specifically theological allegations of the convulsionaries, allegations whose content could be most appropriately and literally described by the epithet "enthusiasm," his choice of vocabulary did not waver. The Saint-Médard cultists claimed that through their spasmodic movements the Divinity had revealed "figures"—that is, symbolic representations or prefigurations—setting forth "God's plan in the conduct of His Church," and that they alone had been endowed with the capacity to interpret these figures. Hecquet lent no credence to this self-aggrandizing assertion. Given his position on the matter, he might well have accused the convulsionaries of "enthusiasm" in the invidious English sense, of being puffed up by false inspiration or false prophecy. But, significantly, he cast substantially the same accusation in the language of imagination. Sarcastically calling those who had made the arrogant claims "convulsionary [Church] Doctors," he stated categorically that their "revelation . . . cannot be from God because He wants all the figures concerning the Church to be within the grasp of every one of his faithful." The assertions of the convulsionaries were thus "inventions growing out of the human mind, sustained by overheated imaginations whose fire comes from a source other than divine inspiration. . . . The figures of the convulsionaries are ingenious imaginings."[30]

The very last page of the 1733 treatise reiterated the central theme of imagination. What could be done, Hecquet asked, to end the convulsions? The young girls in question had to be removed from the nefarious influence of several groups: the churchmen who championed their high-flown religious claims; the laymen who came to their aid by touching their contorted bodies in a too familiar and covertly erotic manner; and the crowds of bystanders who sang their praises. Once the impressionable girls had been placed in infirmaries under the eyes of physicians, once they had been deprived of social approval for

28. Quoted in ibid., 200–201. The book was published in London in 1708. Its subtitle reads: *Wherein the Pretensions of the modern Prophets to Divine Inspiration, and the Power of Working Miracles, are examined and confuted by Scripture and Matter of Fact.*

29. Ibid., 196. Heyd also remarks: "The imagination could excite the passions and disturb the [animal] spirits which in turn rendered the imagination more confused and intense" (p. 199). This circular relationship would seem to explain and clarify Cahusac's more dispersed and hence more muddy assertions that enthusiasm both inflamed imagination and was derived from it; see my discussion, above.

30. Hecquet, *Naturalisme*, 133, 135.

their grandiose fantasies of being God's chosen instruments, once (to rephrase the point in Freudian terms) they ceased to derive secondary gain from their pathological behavior, Hecquet was certain that "all the convulsions will vanish because imagination will have changed its object."[31]

To be sure, Hecquet did on one occasion explicitly invoke the concept of enthusiasm in this treatise. Bemoaning the "base, childish, and indecent things" that were passing for miracles in the Saint-Médard churchyard, he exclaimed: "But what is the enthusiastic [spelled *enthusiaste*, not *enthousiaste*] brain of a convulsionary not capable of imagining?"[32] Yet not only was this single use of a potential keyword massively outweighed by Hecquet's repeated references to imagination, it was itself diluted in several ways: it was used together with imagination; it was used adjectivally rather than being assigned the causal role more often inhering in a noun; and it was spelled in a quasi-English manner, as if to indicate that it had been found on the other side of the Channel and pressed into service and that, as a somewhat exotic import, it carried less authority.

In the shorter pamphlets written in response to the attacks that his original treatise elicited, Hecquet displayed a slightly greater tendency to avail himself of the language of enthusiasm. In one such pamphlet, dated May 1733, it was again the adjective "enthusiastic" and the noun derived from that adjective, "enthusiast" (the two words are identical in French) that were employed, not the noun "enthusiasm." Once again the spelling of enthusiast/enthusiastic was unusual (although this time the word appeared as "anthousiast"), as if to indicate through orthographic instability a foreign provenance and hence a merely tentative authority.[33] Moreover, in this same pamphlet "imagination" continued to be marshaled wherever a causal explanation for the phenomenon of the convulsions was advanced. For example, arguing that the convulsions were "bodily and mechanical" rather than "divine and spiritual," Hecquet observed that "nothing in the world is so mechanical—that is, so sensitive to

---

31. Ibid., 198.
32. Ibid., 130–31. The older French spelling of the term, "entousiasme," which is given in the *Dictionnaire universel* of Antoine Furetière (1690), omits the "h" and not the "o," leading me to suspect that Hecquet's spelling here may be influenced by English.
33. [Hecquet], *Réponse à la lettre à un confesseur touchant le devoir des médecins et des chirurgiens, au sulet des miracles et des convulsions* (Paris, 15 May 1733). The noun "Anthousiastes" can be found on p. 10 ("Ce sont donc des impostures, de quelque sorte qu'elles soient, que cachent ordinairement les scènes des *Anthousiastes*"); and p. 15 ("la fourberie des *Anthousiastes* de l'un et de l'autre sexe"); the adjective "anthousiastes" on p. 10 ("Il ne faut pas même être bien sçavant dans l'Histoire ou dans les affaires du monde, pour sçavoir combien des scènes étonnantes se sont données au Public dans tous les tems, par des filles ou des femmes hystériques ou vapoureuses, dont les opérations *anthousiastes* ont paru si extraordinaires, que les uns les attribuent à Dieu, les autres au diable"); italics in original.

the animal machine—as the nervous sort of person, and especially the Imagination, which is commanded by the animal machine in the bodies of girls."[34]

In an occasional pamphlet of 1736—the controversy over the convulsionaries had still not abated—Hecquet left his most suggestive clue about his personal relationship to the debunking language of enthusiasm. That clue came
not in the text itself, which makes no mention of the term, but in a footnote
to Shaftesbury's *A Letter concerning Enthusiasm,* published in English in 1708
and in French translation a year later. "See *Lettre de l'Antousiasme,*" wrote Hecquet on the very last page of this pamphlet, offering yet another variation on
the spelling.[35]

At this point in the text, Hecquet was summing up his argument, reiterating that the convulsions were a natural and not a supernatural phenomenon,
accusing those who persisted in maintaining their miraculous nature of
enveloping the issue in fog. Suddenly, he had an idea: the French should emulate the way the English handled a similar problem—that of the so-called
French prophets, the Huguenot émigrés from the Cevennes and their English
followers, whose millennial outbursts attracted attention in London in 1706
and 1707.[36] As his footnote suggests, Hecquet's awareness of this parallel inci-
dent probably came from his reading of Shaftesbury's *Letter,*[37] which devoted
two paragraphs to the "*French* Protestants lately come amongst us," readily
identifiable by their "strange voices and involuntary agitations." With mordant
irony, Shaftesbury noted that these religious refugees had been frustrated in
their efforts to provoke their English hosts to persecute them bodily. "We *English* men," he said, "who . . . will not suffer the Enthusiasts to be thus us'd,"
had instead dealt with them by the nonviolent and humorous "Bart'lemy Fair
Method"—that is, by using puppets to mimic their awkward movements.[38]

34. Ibid., 9.

35. [Hecquet], *Le Naturalisme des quatre requestes, montré dans le faux de ces pièces, dans la fausseté des reguer-
antes et dans la physique des opérations qu'on y donne pour des miracles* (Paris, 1 March 1736), 83, note a.

36. On the French prophets, see Hillel Schwartz, *Knaves, Fools, Madmen, and That Subtile Effluvium: A
Study of the Opposition to the French Prophets in England, 1706–1710* (Gainesville, Fla., 1978), esp.
chap. 1. On Shaftesbury's *Letter concerning Enthusiasm*, see ibid., 53–54; and Lawrence E. Klein,
*Shaftesbury and the Culture of Politeness: Moral Discourse and Cultural Politics in Early-Eighteenth-
Century England* (Cambridge, 1994), 18–19, 166–67.

37. Shaftesbury was relatively well known to French readers after the 1709 appearance of the first translation of the *Letter concerning Enthusiasm*. See E. Casati, "Hérauts et commentateurs de Shaftesbury en
France," *Revue de littérature comparée* 14 (1934): 615–45, esp. 616–17: "From [1709] to the middle of
the century and beyond. . . . French literary periodicals whose goal was to inform their readers about
what was happening outside French borders, devoted articles to Shaftesbury and his work."

38. Shaftesbury, *A Letter concerning Enthusiasm*, sec. 3. I have used the text in Richard Bowen Wolf, "An
Old-Spelling, Critical Edition of Shaftesbury's *Letter concerning Enthusiasm* . . ." (Ph.D. diss., University
of Chicago, 1976), 65–67; italics in the original.

Following Shaftesbury's lead, Hecquet makes his own modest, perhaps tongue-in-cheek, proposal:

> The English were successful in arresting a [moral] contagion that was overtaking the common people. They had marionettes at the [Bartholomew] fair act out the scenes of fanaticism of the [refugees from] the Cevennes. A worthy subject for the Saint-Germain Fair [in Paris]! Thus will end the triumph of convulsionism and its miraculous operations.[39]

In other words, Hecquet proposed adopting both the particular concrete remedy employed by the English and the general remedy for extreme religious behavior that Shaftesbury had advanced in his *Letter:* good-natured public ridicule. Broad satire in the manner of the puppet-booths of Bartholomew Fair—which he fancifully proposed to stage in its Paris analogue, a fairground open three months a year and drawing people of every social rank[40]—would restore the convulsionaries to their senses, thus offering a more effective solution to the problem than police repression.[41] What is important for our purposes is that, while Hecquet apparently believes the phenomenon of the Huguenot prophets in London to be entirely parallel to that of the Jansenist convulsionaries in Paris, and while he knows, if only from the title of Shaftesbury's work, that Shaftesbury has discussed the former under the rubric of "enthusiasm," he nonetheless places the latter primarily under the rubric of "imagination." He thus implicitly acknowledges that the English have not only different tactics for dealing with such troublesome religious phenomena but also a different vocabulary for speaking about them.

---

39. Hecquet, *Quatre requestes*, 83.

40. On the Saint-Germain Fair, see Thomas E. Crow, *Painters and Public Life in Eighteenth-Century Paris* (New Haven, Conn., 1985), 45–47.

41. Shaftesbury, not Hecquet, makes explicit the superior efficacy of comedy over repression as a strategy for managing extreme religious behavior; but very likely Hecquet was attracted to Shaftesbury's text precisely because repression had just been used in the affair of the convulsionaries: the Saint-Médard cemetery was closed by royal ordinance in 1732 and, when the adherents of the cult subsequently moved to private conventicles, the royal government responded with sporadic police harassment and then banned all convulsionary activity in 1733. See Kreiser, *Miracles, Convulsions, and Ecclesiastical Politics*, 213, 279–83.

INTERPRETING THE SAINT-MÉDARD CONVULSIONARIES (II): THE CLERICS

The physician Hecquet was hardly alone among his contemporaries in rejecting the self-interpretation of the Saint-Médard convulsionaries. Even within the Jansenist religious camp, opinion about the meaning of the convulsions was decidedly mixed, sowing internal discord in a group already beleaguered from without. Some decades after the fact, the *Encyclopédie* article "Convulsionnaire" described the warring parties of "anti-convulsionists" and "convulsionists" that the events of Saint-Médard had generated within the Jansenist fold. And one contemporary clerical participant in the debate, Louis-Bernard de La Taste, who regarded the convulsions as the work of the Devil rather than of the Divinity, held that the terrible state of divisiveness into which they had immediately plunged the Jansenists was ample proof of his position.[42] The interpretations of the convulsions by hostile *religious* commentators have a less clear relevance to the argument I am putting forth here than do those of "enlightened" commentators like Hecquet. After all, I have predicated the popularity of "enthusiasm" as an eighteenth-century smear word on a prior acceptance of the enlightened value of rationality, and it is by no means evident that a religious dismissal of the convulsions would be made on rational grounds. Nonetheless, it will be interesting to take a brief look at the vocabulary of some of these religious texts.[43]

The aforementioned La Taste, who regarded the convulsions at the metaphysical level as engineered by the Devil to weaken the Jansenists through internal division, also offered a variety of naturalistic explanations to account for those same convulsions at the humbler level of the afflicted individuals. The convulsionaries had been "thrown into enthusiasm" and were "entirely beside themselves" (*tout hors de vous-mêmes*); the figural meanings that they purported to see in their spasmodic movements were "productions of wounded brains."[44] They were people who had "abandoned the duties attached to their social condition [*état*] in order to follow the strangest and most scandalous chimeras."[45] The abbé d'Asfeld, an early architect of the figurist interpretation of the convulsions, abandoned his initial position on the matter once he became convinced that excessive fascination with the convulsions was harming

---

42. See Maire, *Convulsionnaires de Saint-Médard*, 155, discussing Louis-Bernard de La Taste, *Lettres théologiques aux écrivains défenseurs des convulsions et autres prétendus miracles du tem*s, 2 vols. (Paris, 1740).

43. My choice of the texts of Asfeld, Bonnaire, and La Taste has been guided by the selections in Maire, *Convulsionnaires de Saint-Médard*, chap. 5.

44. La Taste, *Lettres théologiques aux écrivains défenseurs*, 1:786, 788.

45. Ibid., Letter 19, reprinted in Maire, *Convulsionnaires de Saint-Médard*, 176.

the Jansenist movement by diverting its energy from more urgent matters, notably the doctrinal and constitutional issues related to the bull Unigenitus. In his post-figurist phase, Asfeld stigmatized the convulsionaries on social grounds as "that lowlife emerging from the dust of the streets."[46] And, like La Taste, he invoked without apparent preference a variety of pejorative terms to characterize the psychological forces driving the convulsionary rabble: enthusiasm, illusion, fanaticism, fantasy, imagination.[47]

A third commentator, the abbé Louis de Bonnaire, belonged to the group of anti-convulsionary Jansenists who focused their attention not on the immediate ecclesiastical politics surrounding Unigenitus but on the eventual return of the prophet Elijah, believing that the era of renewed spirituality that would then commence would eradicate doctrinal deviance of the convulsionary sort.[48] Bonnaire advanced an analysis of the convulsionaries in which, for purposes of debunking, the term imagination occupied pride of place. According to one historian, he "placed the blame for the convulsionary madness squarely on figurist exegesis, which . . . had given free rein to the extravagances of the imagination."[49] And perusing his most famous work, one finds Bonnaire speaking of the system of figurist exegesis as having "inflamed the imaginations [of the convulsionaries] to the point of fanaticism" and, reciprocally, of the figurists as having been "charmed" by the convulsions because they "believed to see realized in this new phenomenon the chimera of their old imaginations."[50] Indeed, Bonnaire contended more generally that, while the Gospel contained eschatological predictions, these were of the concrete sort that properly inspired vigilance rather than anxiety. Expressly forbidden by Christianity on the other hand was that anxious curiosity about the end of time that led, in the manner of the figurists, to arcane interpretive practices and the ferreting out of hidden

---

46. Joseph Dedieu, "L'Agonie du jansénisme (1715–1790)," *Revue d'histoire de l'église de France* 14 (1928): 161–214. See p. 196 for the quotation, which reads in French "cette canaille sortie de la poussière."

47. Abbé [Jacques Bidal] d'Asfeld, *Vains efforts des mélangistes ou discernans dans l'oeuvre des convulsions pour défendre le système du mélange* (n.p., 1737), 155–57, 187. Attacking the so-called *Mélangistes,* who held that the convulsions were a mixture of divinely and demonically inspired acts, Asfeld at one point zeroed in on the classical problem of enthusiasm *à l'anglaise.* The *Mélangistes,* he said, gave comfort to "enthusiasts" and "authorize[d] every conceivable sort of illusion," because their method "remov[ed] the force of the principal proofs that the Church has successfully employed until now against those who falsely present themselves as men extraordinarily inspired by God." But the point here is that enthusiasm as false inspiration is just one string in Asfeld's bow. His argument does not turn on this concept.

48. On this current in the Jansenist thought of the period, see Kreiser, *Miracles, Convulsions, and Ecclesiastical Politics,* 288. Kreiser does not specifically mention Bonnaire.

49. Maire, *Convulsionnaires de Saint-Médard,* 178.

50. Bonnaire, *Traités historiques et polemiques de la fin du monde, de la venue d'Elie, et du retour des Juifs, dans lesquels on examine le Système des nouveaux Figuristes sur ces trois questions,* 3 vols. (Amsterdam, 1737–38), description of chap. 3 in "Table des chapitres" (vol. 1), and 1:149.

meanings, that overstimulated imagination and produced nothing but "dangerous illusions" and "chimerical prognostications."[51]

Of these three religious polemicists, then, Bonnaire uses a vocabulary most similar to Hecquet's. But what is most significant for our purposes is that, presented with religious behavior that, in an eighteenth-century British context, would almost certainly have received the label "enthusiastic," none of these Jansenist religious commentators privileged that particular word. All gravitated equally or by preference to "imagination."

❧ ❧

The argument of this essay can be summed up by citing some remarks of the second French translator of Shaftesbury's *Letter concerning Enthusiasm*. In his preface to his rendering of that text, which appeared in 1761, Monsieur Lacombe complained:

> Several French authors have written on poetic enthusiasm. They all seem to have preceded the English philosopher [i. e., Shaftesbury]. Their descriptions are lively and picturesque. Shaftesbury does not speak of them; his silence surprises me. He cites frequently and with an arrogant servility all the Latin authors who had something to say about enthusiasm and divine inspiration. It would no doubt be pleasurable to see the views of some French writers on this interesting subject.[52]

The translator's complaint is a nationalist, or proto-nationalist, one: an English author has predictably failed to recognize French contributions to the literature on his topic. But Lacombe's sense of the French contribution in this case is strikingly specific. The Gallic authors rudely overlooked by Shaftesbury wrote, he observes, on *poetic* enthusiasm. No claim is made that they wrote on *religious* enthusiasm, although the most celebrated portions of Shaftesbury's text treated that aspect of the topic. Lacombe's implicit grasp of the situation thus accords with what I have tried to advance explicitly here: that, for eighteenth-century Frenchmen, the problem of enthusiasm was primarily an aesthetic one, a concern about the conditions under which enthusiasm produced good or bad art.

---

51. Ibid., 1:90–100, esp. 98–99.
52. *Lettres sur l'enthousiasme de Milord Shaftesbury avec sa vie, traduites de l'Anglois par M. Lacombe* (London, 1761), preface.

In this essay, I have also drawn out some of the ramifications of that priority. The most pungent and pejorative language of enthusiasm, which arose as a response to the extreme religious manifestations of that mental state, was far less developed in France than in Protestant countries. As a result of this low linguistic profile, "imagination," and not "enthusiasm," was probably the enlightened Frenchman's smear word of choice.

University of Chicago

Passionate Spectators: On Enthusiasm, Nymphomania, and the Imagined Tableau

—————————————— Mary D. Sheriff

Aesthetics and myth bound them in loose relations; moral philosophy knotted them up; and science secured them in complicated patterns of its own invention. By the end of the eighteenth century, the enthused artist and the nymphomaniac had become France's most impassioned spectators. Each held a place in a matrix of types given to imaginative vision; devout *convulsionnaires*, notorious ladies, monstrous fathers, and mythical artists also twisted in the loops of this peculiar interlace. The various discourses of enthusiasm implicitly positioned the artist and the nymphomaniac in relation to these types, but their particular subjectivities emerged in irresistible desires ignited by acts of spectating. What they looked at, however, was not always visible, nor was their object other than themselves. Each was moved, aroused, and touched by the spectacle of a self-generated tableau. Although both experienced self-arousal, what followed was different in each case. Moved by her projection, the nymphomaniac touched herself in a literal gesture of onanism. Hers was an enclosed and nonproductive circuit of self-gratification; her desire had no proper aim, although it could lead to insanity, death, or social disorder. In contrast to the nymphomaniac, the artist was fecund. When aroused by his idea, the enthused artist touched his instrument—pen, chisel, brush, lyre—and a new creation came to life.

My purpose here is to unravel and redraw the interlace that bound artist to nymphomaniac and situated both types within the discourses of enthusiasm, sexuality, and creativity. At the center of my enterprise is the story of Pygmalion and Galatea, whose textual, visual, and dramatic versions ostensibly worked to secure distinct male and female roles in the drama of creativity. In Pygmalion's story, the active role of desiring subject is predictably given to the male creator, who is also endowed with the power to bring forth a living being. At the same time, the tale emphasizes the sculptor's narcissism, his obsessive fixation on a single object, his attachment to sensory perceptions, and his confounding of

ᴥ 51

fantasy and reality. By attributing these qualities perceived as irrational and "feminine" to the male creator, the story compromised attempts to locate the artist's enthusiasm (and hence his particular creativity) in the realm of reason, and hence to gender it as masculine. These thwarted attempts are exemplified here by the *Encyclopédie*'s entry for "enthusiasm, philosophy and belles lettres," written by J.-L. de Cahusac, who also authored the libretto for Rameau's *Pygmalion*. Although his entry figures enthusiasm as "reason's masterpiece," Cahusac cannot keep the mythical sculptor from invading his account.[1] When read in conjunction with those strands of the discourse that tie enthusiasm to reason, the Pygmalion story seems not so much to secure the male and female positions as to confuse them. In many retellings of Ovid's tale, gendered attributes are detached from their proper bodies and worn by the other sex.

If the Pygmalion story encodes an impropriety that has at one time or another rendered all artists suspect, the impact of this impropriety on the woman artist has been more acute. During the eighteenth century, for example, laudatory accounts of artistic enthusiasm were written only about the male artist and were aimed, in one way or another, at reaffirming his masculinity. That this affirmation could never be definitive—and this is my central point— actually weakened women's claims on the position of artist. In general, women artists were not able to (re)appropriate for themselves the feminine aspects of the male creator. Attributing "feminine" properties to the male artist made it imperative that woman's incapacity for making (great) art be constantly re-affirmed. Once the feminine properties were detached from female bodies, such properties could be seen as positive and then claimed by male creators with minimal loss of masculinity. Whereas the obsessive man might give himself over to writing or painting, the obsessive woman, unable to do the same, would fall prey to the vapors or to melancholia. Even though women could never be entirely separated from the feminine properties positively associated with art-making, in theory women could be disconnected from such properties if the capacity to produce art was put firmly out of their reach.

My unraveling of Pygmalion's story stresses its presentation of male creative power as generated by both a female sexuality that is condemned and a femininity that is desired and mimicked. I conclude my story by turning to Galatea, or more precisely to the actress—Mlle. Raucourt—who in 1775 rep-

---

1. Jean-Louis de Cahusac, "Enthousiasme," in Denis Diderot and Jean Le Rond d'Alembert, *Encyclopédie, ou Dictionnaire raisonné des sciences, des arts et des métiers, par une société de gens de lettres,* facsimile of 1751–80 edition, 17 vols. (Stuttgart, 1967), 5:720. Subsequent references to this work are given in parentheses in the text. For another discussion of this entry and the problem of enthusiasm, see Mary Sheriff, *J. H. Fragonard: Art and Eroticism* (Chicago, 1990), 138–42.

resented her in Jean-Jacques Rousseau's popular *scène lyrique*. Raucourt provides one very visible example of how the discourses of enthusiasm, which appropriated so much of the feminine to the male creator, helped position the female artist as unnaturally donning the attributes of masculinity while at the same time retaining all the irrational behaviors typical of the "normal" woman.

REASON'S MASTERPIECE: ENTHUSIASM IN THE "ENCYCLOPÉDIE"

Appearing in a publication that embodied the French Enlightenment, Cahusac's entry for "enthusiasm, philosophy and belles lettres" engages and rewrites notions of enthusiasm current in the national tradition throughout the seventeenth and eighteenth centuries and exemplified in the writings of the art theorist Roger de Piles. In 1709 de Piles cast enthusiasm as a transport that could be cultivated through beholding masterpieces of art.[2] In defining enthusiasm, Cahusac adjusts this notion so that contemplating an actual painting is initially cast as a mere analogy for contemplating a mental tableau. He likens the two experiences in a passage that asks readers to imagine themselves as art lovers: "Without expecting it, you see in the best light an excellent painting. A sudden surprise arrests you, you experience a pervasive emotion. Your gaze, as if absorbed, remains in a kind of immobility. Your entire spirit focuses on a mass of objects that occupy it all at once." The rush of emotion experienced before the painting is "the image of what passes in the mind of the man of genius when reason, by a rapid process, presents him with a striking and new picture, which arrests him, moves him, ravishes him, and absorbs him." The comparison gives onto the first definition of enthusiasm as "a lively emotion of the mind produced by the sight of a new and well ordered image which strikes it and that reason has presented to it" (5:720).

Enthusiasm is thus that emotion which excites the artist at the sight of the invisible mental image. Unlike de Piles, who held enthusiasm as equally accessible to both artist and spectator, Cahusac establishes a hierarchy of responses in which beholding a real painting is an "image" of the contemplation of an image. His construction not only privileges artist over spectator, but it also elevates the conceptual over the sensory, form over matter, and, by tradition, masculine (form) over feminine (matter).[3] The artist usurps the godlike function of

2. Roger de Piles, *Cours de peinture par principes* (Paris, 1709; reprint, Nîmes, 1990), 74–75.
3. This long-standing gendering of form and matter is discussed by Luce Irigaray in *Speculum of the Other Woman*, trans. Gillian Gill (Ithaca, N.Y., 1985); Judith Butler in *Bodies that Matter* (London, 1993); and Elizabeth Grosz in *Volatile Bodies* (Indianapolis and Bloomington, 1994), among others.

creating "ideas" or "ideals"; he does not content himself with the degraded one of copying copies. For Cahusac, an idea—new, well ordered, and original—is the reality to be represented; it neither mirrors nor distorts objects in the natural world. Thus Cahusac appears to cleave the formulation of ideas from the physical perceptions in which prevailing accounts grounded mental processes.

Although we might term Cahusac Neoplatonic because he privileges mental visions over objects of sensation, he distances himself from the notion of enthusiasm put forth in Plato's *Phaedrus*. In that text Plato likened the poet gripped by enthusiasm to the madman, and this analogy dominated the French tradition in both poetic theory and writing about the visual arts. The Encyclopedist separates himself from this tradition, rejecting the idea of enthusiasm as either "a kind of furor" or "a transport." Rather, Cahusac argues that "a furor is only a violent onset of madness and madness is an absence or a disorder of reason. So when enthusiasm has been defined as a furor, a transport, it is . . . consequently incompatible with reason. It is from reason alone, however, that enthusiasm is born" (5:719). Enthusiasm has only one parent—reason—and that parent his century viewed as masculine. Enthusiasm is a motherless child.

By firmly grounding enthusiasm in reason, Cahusac also diminishes the role of combinatory imagination in the creative process and carefully limits the function of imagination to that of the screen, or "toile," on which the brush of genius painted the picture.[4] By defining imagination as a visualizing power, and by fixing the idea that ignites enthusiasm in the realm of reason, Cahusac keeps in his picture those mental powers—judgment, for example—that control a wanton imagination. Indeed, he spells out in his comparison how pow-

---

4.   In tracing the "development" of imagination, Condillac charted a course leading first to a primitive or instinctual imagination whose operation is tied to the perception of some bodily sensation. A more developed power evolves from instinct, but this evolution is an "adding to" more than a "transforming of." When memory is added to the arsenal of mental powers, the imagination can take on another function—that of operating apart from sensations or perceptions. Memory Condillac defined as the process by which the mind both retains and retrieves the *signs* for perceptions, and it presumed society: "Since people can make up signs only through living in society, it follows that as their minds begin to develop, the source of their ideas is in their mutual intercourse"; Étienne Bonnot, Abbé de Condillac, "Essay on the Origin of Human Knowledge," in *Philosophical Writings of Etienne Bonnot, Abbé de Condillac*, trans. Franklin Philip, 2 vols. (Hillsdale, N.J., and London, 1987), 2:503. Subsequently, this socialized imagination can conjure from signs stored in memory the perception or simple idea associated with that sign. Once memory and imagination are working together, the stage is set for the most important of imagination's powers—that of combining simple ideas to form more complex ones. In explaining how imagination can be a source of knowledge, Condillac writes: "Up to now I have taken the imagination to be merely the operation that revives perceptions in the absence of objects. But now that I am considering the effects of this operation, I see no reason not to conform to standard usage, and I am even

ers of reason operate. After the amateur has been struck by the painting (and by analogy, the man of genius by a new idea), he begins to analyze: he looks at the details, compares the poses of the figures, notices the contrasts, the light effects, the artist's touch. Attending to the features of the characters, he identifies their emotions and correlates them to the action represented (5:720). Here the author articulates how reason is called into action through the mental processes particular to it: comparison, contrast, judgment. Moreover, he insists that the spectator will observe that his inspiration will be "more or less lively, according to the different degree of previous knowledge" and according to his taste, delicacy, and judgment. Associated with reason, enthusiasm here is also tied to experience and learning (5:720). Locke's definition of enthusiasm as the state in which a person assumes for the basis of opinion and conduct the ungrounded fancies of his own brain is thus also contradicted by the Encyclopedist who deems enthusiasm "reason's masterpiece."

In aligning enthusiasm with reason, Cahusac disconnects it from imagination, that property of mind often gendered feminine. In Condillac's sensationalist philosophy, for example, combinatory imagination is the basis for making poetry and art, and, although it operates for the male creator, it is conceived of as feminine. In his *Essay on the Origin of Human Knowledge* (1746), imagination is a flirtatious woman "whose only desire is to please." As woman, the imagination is "*mobile,*" unstable, ever changing.[5] This combinatory imagination is the only part of the mind that bears the mark of sex; and, even as he gives imagination an important aesthetic function, Condillac writes in tandem with older conceptions that regarded imagination with deep suspicion, associated it with the sin of Eve, and opposed it to truth.[6]

---

obliged to do so. That is why in this chapter I take imagination to be an operation that, by reviving ideas, freely makes new combinations. So from here on, the word *imagination* will have two different meanings" ("Essay on the Origins," 2:472). In practice, however, Condillac gives imagination more than two meanings, for combinatory imagination is the basis not only for forming complex ideas but for artistic achievement. For a discussion of Condillac's concept of imagination, see Jan Goldstein, *Console and Classify: The French Psychiatric Profession in the Nineteenth Century* (Cambridge, 1987), 91–93. A specific discussion of the problematics of gender in Condillac's notion of imagination can be found in Mary D. Sheriff, *The Exceptional Woman: Elisabeth Vigée-Lebrun and the Cultural Politics of Art* (Chicago, 1996), 20–23.

5. Condillac, "Essay on the Origin," 2:478.
6. See Blaise Pascal, *Pensées,* trans. A. J. Krailsheimer (Harmondsworth, England, and New York, 1966), 38–42. See also Marion Hobson, *The Object of Art: The Theory of Illusion in Eighteenth-Century France* (Cambridge, 1982), 1–32.

FUROR PROPHÉTIQUE: ENTHUSIASM AND FEMALE SEXUALITY

A second turn against the feminine and against a wanton imagination can be read in the Encyclopedist's rejection of prophetic enthusiasm. Cahusac again distances himself from the Platonic tradition, separating enthusiasm from *furor prophétique*, which he associates not with true revelation but with false prophecy. Through such prophecy the priestly class, he argues, kept the multitude in thrall (5:719). Although Cahusac levels a political critique against *furor prophétique*, also notable is his deviation from the *Phaedrus* and from related traditions in which prophecy is not primarily associated with wily, manipulative priests but with madwomen. Indeed, Plato cites as those blessed with this madness the prophetess at Delphi, the priestesses at Dodona, Cassandra, and the sibyl.[7]

While it is true that condemnation of religious enthusiasm throughout eighteenth-century Europe was aimed at both men and women, such enthusiasm came, at least by the end of the century, to have a particular association with women's health and sexuality. These associations were wide ranging. Louis-François Lignac, in his *De l'Homme et de la femme considerés physiquement dans l'etat du mariage* (1772), noted that the ancient sibyls delivered their prophecy through their vaginas, and the sculptor Falconet suggests that they received them through the same organ as they sat nude at the opening of the sacred cave, straddling a tripod on which was mounted a globe-shaped vessel pierced with a hole or, as Falconet put it, a "belly button." In this position nothing could hinder their inspiration when through the belly button "the spirit of the god plunged itself into the entrails of the priestess."[8] Physiologist Pierre Roussel and psychologist Philippe Pinel made more scientific claims. Although Roussel and Pinel actually debunked the idea that women had more rapport with divinity and so were its chosen interpreters, they did so by observing a similarity between the actions of those reputed to be prophets and symptoms of "maladies convulsive."[9] From this similarity they concluded that women, far from being more inspired, were simply more given to these sorts of diseases.

7. Plato, *Phaedrus,* trans. W. C. Helmbold (Indianapolis, 1956), 25. Irigaray argues that it is from the position of prophet or mystic that women have historically been allowed to speak publicly, a right generally denied them (or to which they have been given limited access) in other areas of life; see *Speculum of the Other Woman*, 191–202. During the eighteenth and early nineteenth centuries, women who had creative ambitions often had themselves represented as sibyls, giving a positive valence to this form of female enthusiasm and appropriating it for themselves. I take up this issue in *The Exceptional Woman*.
8. Maurice-Étienne Falconet, *Oeuvres Complètes,* 3 vols. (Paris, 1808; reprint, Geneva, 1970), 1:59.
9. Pierre Roussel, *Système physique et moral de la femme* (Paris, 1775), 46–47; and Philippe Pinel, *Nosographie philosophique ou la méthode de l'analyse appliquée à la medicine,* 3 vols. (Paris, 1813), 1:103–4.

In eighteenth-century France, the case that most closely associated women with enthusiasm and linked their nervous disorders—these "maladies convulsives"—with religious fanaticism was that of the *convulsionnaires* of St. Médard.[10] Nearly three-quarters of the *convulsionnaires* were women, and these women drew much attention since in the course of their performances they had themselves shaken, pulled about by men, suspended upside down in the air, and placed in lascivious postures. As Lindsay Wilson explains in her study of women and medicine in the Enlightenment, many conservative Jansenists doubted the divine charge of the *convulsionnaires*, wondering why God would have chosen as his prophets women who seemed to be in a trance and incapable of reason when they described their visions.[11] The medical profession was drawn into the controversy, and doctors concluded that the convulsions were likely the effects of a premeditated deception, an overactive imagination, or the devil's malice.[12] Thus, three sources of "illusion" were imagined: one consciously staged to gain a sort of publicity or power usually denied women; the second produced by the ungrounded fancies of the female imagination; and the third crafted by the devil and hence associated with witchcraft. Some doctors, including Philippe Hecquet, opted for the second explanation, and believed the convulsions rooted in an overactive imagination and uncontrolled eroticism. These two properties, as we shall see, figured as the salient traits of *furor utérine*, or nymphomania, as that disease was defined in the *Encyclopédie* and elsewhere. Thus it was the taint not only of irrationality but also of sexual immorality that surrounded these *convulsionnaires*. Far from praising their devotion, physicians called these women "shameful" and "criminal."

The medical profession, moreover, generally regarded convulsions as symptoms of the vapors or hysterical affections, disorders peculiar to women and caused by their overly sensitive nervous systems and easily deranged imaginations.[13] These diseases often had a sexual base, and convulsions could be

10. Lindsay Wilson, *Women and Medicine in the French Enlightenment* (Baltimore, 1993), 32. Wilson discusses this case at length and notes that Diderot was drawn repeatedly to the image of the *convulsionnaires* in his *Pensées philosophiques*. These women came to embody the link between nervous disorders in women and religious fanaticism. The most thoroughgoing study of the *convulsionnaires* is B. Robert Kreiser, *Miracles, Convulsions, and Ecclesiastical Politics in Early-Eighteenth-Century Paris* (Princeton, N.J., 1978).

11. Wilson, *Women and Medicine*, 19–20.

12. Ibid., 25–29; and Kreiser, *Miracles, Convulsions,* 276–83.

13. For discussion of women's sensitivity, see Roussel, *Système physique;* Pierre Edme Chauvot de Beauchene, *De l'Influence des affections de l'âme dans les maladies nerveuses* (Montpellier and Paris, 1781); Joseph Bressy, *Recherches sur les vapeurs* (Paris, 1789); Pierre-Jean-George Cabanis, *On the Relations between the Physical and Moral Aspects of Man,* trans. Margaret Saidi; ed. George Mora; intro. Sergio Moravia and George Mora, 2 vols. (Baltimore, 1981); Pierre Fabre, *Essai sur les facultés de l'âme* (Paris and Amsterdam, 1785); and Pierre Pomme, *Traité des affections vaporeuses des deux sexes* (Paris, 1760).

brought on by sexual deprivation. Young girls, widows, and spinsters—the same group most likely to suffer from nymphomania—were particularly susceptible. Convulsions, then, were a manifestation of women's sexual frustration, and shameful or immodest because women's fantasies were acted out in public.

The tradition of representing religious mysticism in the visual arts, moreover, made clear the association between women's sexuality and divine visitation. Undoubtedly the most famous example of such representations for the eighteenth century was Gianlorenzo Bernini's *Saint Theresa in Ecstasy* (1652).[14] But Theresa's pose, when attached to the female figure in eighteenth-century France, appeared almost exclusively in erotic or pornographic paintings and prints, such as Pierre-Antoine Baudouin's *La Lecture* (c. 1765; Musée des arts décoratifs, Paris; figure 1). As in Bernini's sculpture, woman's ecstasy is marked on her reclining body—her head is thrown back and to the side, her eyes half-closed roll upward in their sockets. But in Baudouin's image no angels with darts pierce the woman's soul. Rather, her aroused state can be attributed to her own hand, placed in her lap at the point where we can imagine that beneath her skirt her legs are opened. Thus the pose of the saintly Theresa was easily transferred to masturbating women, women in erotic reverie provoked not by religious devotion but by reading novels. This latter activity was thought to stimulate woman's passionate imaginings, thus rendering her more susceptible to masturbation and the various diseases that devolved from self-pollution. If in separating enthusiasm from *furor prophétique*, Cahusac attempted to banish madness and chicanery, he also sidestepped female eroticism by distinguishing enthusiasm from the deceptive practices of the priestly class. Nevertheless, as his English contemporary William Hogarth was to show in his print *Credulity, Superstition, Fanaticism* (1762), deceptive priests, enthusiastic preachers, and overheated devotees were not easily parted.[15]

14. As Jacques Lacan put it, "You only have to go and look at Bernini's statue in Rome to understand immediately that she is coming, there is no doubt about it" ("God and the Jouissance of The Woman," in Juliet Mitchell and Jacqueline Rose, eds., *Feminine Sexuality* [New York, 1985], 147). Here is Luce Irigaray's answer: "In Rome? So far away? To look? At a statue? Of a saint? Sculpted by a man? What pleasure are we talking about? Whose pleasure? For where the pleasure of the Theresa in question is concerned, her own writings are perhaps more telling" ("Cosi Fan Tutti," in *The Sex Which Is Not One* [Ithaca, N.Y., 1985], 91).

15. In Hogarth's print there is a thermometer to the right that registers love, heat, lust, ecstasy, above; and low spirits, sorrow, agony, grief, despair, madness, suicide, below. This "thermometer" grows from a very organic base that looks like some grotesque combination of male and female genitals. The key tells us that this form is the brain of Wesley, and we see that it is this brain from which the mercurial fluid rises. The print includes references to witchcraft, devils, religious enthusiasm, monstrous births, and overheated devotees. These themes were also taken up by Hogarth in the unpublished *Enthusiasm Delineated* (1761). For a discussion of the print and its relation to female sexuality, see Terry Castle, *The Female Thermometer: Eighteenth-Century Culture and the Invention of the Uncanny* (New York, 1995), 21–43.

Figure 1. Pierre-Antoine Baudouin, *La Lecture* (c. 1765); Musée des arts décoratifs, Paris.

CREATIVE ENTHUSIASM, OR PYGMALION PERFORMED

It was not enough for Cahusac to define enthusiasm as an emotion of the mind excited by the sight of a reasoned image. Quite simply, the artist—and it is artistic enthusiasm that concerns Cahusac—is only an artist if enthusiasm moves him to create. The particular sort of emotion the artist feels is recast as a desire or impulse that, although allied to reason, becomes an irresistible motivating force: "Enthusiasm is that impetuous movement, whose effort gives life to all the masterpieces of the arts, and this movement is always produced by an operation of reason as prompt as it is sublime." This prompt and sublime operation of reason, however, is impetuous. It ravishes the artist and brings on a loss of self-control: "The impulse that grabs him, fills him and leads him, is such that everything cedes to it, and it is the predominant sentiment" (7:721).

Cast now as a compulsion, enthusiasm does not seem quite the reasonable state Cahusac argues elsewhere that it is. The artist is grabbed by an impulse, which demands obedience. Nothing stops or distracts him. Here madness in the guise of melancholia returns to characterize enthusiasm. Although I do not intend to review all the theories of melancholia that have characterized creative individuals, I do wish to note that eighteenth-century medical texts (for example, those by Pomme and Bressy; see n. 13 above) describe the melancholic as possessed by a single idea or a series of ideas that dominates him with a more or less extreme passion. Moreover, in his influential treatise *De la santé des gens de lettres et des valétudinaires,* first published in the 1750s, Tissot found this aspect of melancholia useful to creative men (among whom he placed artists), arguing that because melancholics were attached to a single idea, they considered an object under all its aspects and without distraction. This process, he suggested, was beneficial in producing great art.[16] Thus, no matter how much Cahusac wants to secure enthusiasm on the side of reason, the moment of total absorption and compulsion is a mad moment from which the enthused artist will emerge, but to which he must return.

Erotic components of enthusiasm, equally subversive of reason, are also both denied and validated at once in this complex conception. In describing the "natural" actions of enthusiasm, Cahusac turns to the example of the heart, usually viewed metaphorically as the seat of sentiment and love. He reduces that organ to its mechanical operation in an analogy that denies enthusiasm its erotic component: "But it is natural that the mind cannot experience sentiments

16. Samuel-Auguste-David Tissot, *De la santé des gens de lettres et des valétudinaires,* in *Oeuvres complètes de Tissot* (Paris, 1809), 57.

without the quick and lively desire to express them; all its movements are only a continuous succession of sentiments and expressions; it is like the heart, whose machinery continuously opens itself to receive and to send" (5:721).

Yet eroticism, like madness, was so ingrained in the discourse that it slipped into Cahusac's discussion, entering into his description of the artist's compulsion to create: "So without anything able to distract or stop him, the painter seizes his brush and the canvas is colored, the figures arranged, the dead revived; the chisel is already in the hand of the sculptor and the marble comes to life; the verse flows from the pen of the poet. . . . The musician picks up his lyre and the orchestra fills the air with a sublime harmony" (5:721). The particular erotic component here insinuated in Cahusac's entry has an antique pedigree. It invokes the mythological discourse of artistic creation and cites the story of Pygmalion, the sculptor who brings marble to life.

In eighteenth-century France, Pygmalion stood as one prototype for the artist, in general, and the sculptor, in specific. The story poses art making as a male erotic activity that turns on the projection of desire into and onto a work of art. The work of art becomes the mirror of (what the) male desires, and hence inseparable from him. As Ovid relates the story, the Cypriot King Pygmalion falls in love with a maiden he has carved from pure, white ivory, following an ideal conceived entirely in his mind. His maiden is not composed—as was the ideal beauty of Zeuxis—by copying the most perfect features in real women. Pygmalion would never have allowed those lascivious wretches—for that was his opinion of the sex—into his palace, as Zeuxis had invited them into his studio. Detached from the real, his Galatea materializes the sculptor's idea. Pygmalion thus usurps the godlike function not only by animating matter but also by creating the concept, the ideal from which the particular instance is generated. Ovid makes a point of distinguishing Pygmalion's artful creation from her semblables: "Meanwhile he carved his snow-white ivory / With marvelous triumphant artistry / And gave it perfect shape, more beautiful / Than ever woman born."[17] By emphasizing the difference between Pygmalion's sculpture and those creatures "of woman born," Ovid both compares and separates male creativity and female reproduction.

It is the sight of his ideal creation, his brain child, that touches Pygmalion, and Ovid describes how "His masterwork / Fired him with love." Now dependent on an object of sensation, Pygmalion kisses and caresses his masterpiece; he fondles it, speaks to it, and decks it in jewels and finery. He imagines, moreover, that Galatea—as she is called in later versions of the story—returns his affection and enters into dialogue with his own passion, which is reflected back

17. Ovid (Publius Ovidius Naso), *Metamorphoses,* trans. A. D. Melville (Oxford, 1989), 232.

to him through the statue. In Ovid's tale, Venus endows Pygmalion with the confidence he needs to believe in his own ability to animate matter—this is his gift from the gods, his divine inspiration—and when he next kisses the statue and caresses her breast, he feels the ivory softening under his touch, a sensation he had experienced before only in his imagination.

The story of Pygmalion was told and retold in painted, sculpted, and textual versions, many of which are pertinent to the discourses on art and enthusiasm that developed in eighteenth-century France. These include paintings by Jean Raoux (1716); François Lemoyne (1729); Jean-Baptiste Deshays (1749) and Jean-Louis François Lagrenée (1761, 1777, and 1781). Many of the works display the passionate spectatorship long a part of the artist's enthusiasm, for images of Pygmalion inevitably show the sculptor-king rapturously gazing at his creation as it is coming to life. We do not see in these works the moment of Pygmalion's enthusiasm as he contemplates "a new idea" invisible to all others. Rather, we see a later moment of the story, when he is moved by the physical sight of Galatea and sees that through the force of his enthusiasm the image of his desire comes to life. The sculptor Falconet exhibited one of the most interesting treatments of Ovid's tale at the Salon of 1763, a marble sculpture titled *Pygmalion aux pieds de sa statue qui s'anime* (Musée du Louvre, Paris; figure 2).[18]

In Falconet's work, as in other versions of the story, the adoring sculptor kneels before his masterpiece. His hands are clasped in wonder, his mouth drops in awe, his eyes are riveted on the miracle he sees. The figural group is marked off as "sculpture" by the pedestal on which it is framed, but Galatea is also *represented* as sculpture because placed on a round base that itself is further supported by a second dais. Still, we see that she is not just a sculpture, and Falconet achieves this effect cleverly. He places the legs in a very conventional *contrapposto* copied from ancient models and orients them so that the viewer facing the group sees them straight on. In positioning her arms and upper body, however, he avoids any resemblance to an antique model. This deviation marks a "movement" in the sculpture, as we imagine it breaking free of the frozen classical pose the legs still hold. It adds to this effect that we see the upper body from an oblique angle, registering both a change of position and a change from sculpture to woman. The slight twist in her body, the inclination of her head, and the faint smile that plays over her lips further suggest that there has been some change in her state of being. An amour does not merely bring Venus into the story (though Amor is often her agent). Rather, in ravishing Galatea's hand

18. There is a smaller version of this group in the Walters Art Gallery in Baltimore. Louis Réau believed that this smaller version was the one that actually appeared in the Salon; see Louis Réau, *Étienne-Maurice Falconet,* 2 vols. (Paris, 1922), 1:212–15.

Figure 2. Étienne-Maurice Falconet, *Pygmalion aux pieds de sa statue qui s'anime* (1763?); Musée du Louvre.

with kisses, the amour becomes a substitute Pygmalion, reminding us of the affection the sculptor lavished on his work and suggesting that his desire has brought her to life. In coming to life, in moving, Galatea remains Ovid's chaste and modest virgin, the "girl who wished to move but modesty forbade." Her eyes, with lowered lids, can be read both as just beginning to open and as downcast in a traditional expression of womanly modesty.

Unlike Galatea, Pygmalion is not coded as "sculpture." His pose resembles no classical types for that art; indeed, wide-eyed and gaping, he signals naturalness in the awkward expression. His garment falls away at the neck, his elbow protrudes sharply, and his sandaled feet are posed to suggest the effort of keeping his balance. Indeed, the tour de force of this much admired work is not Galatea but Pygmalion, the one Falconet brings to life. Falconet, one might say, was a real-life Pygmalion, and a sculpture of the story of sculpture is undoubtedly a self-referential work: the act of sculpting Pygmalion's story proclaims Falconet's ability (metaphoric though it may be) to animate sculpture. The self-referentiality of the work is further signaled by Falconet's reliance on his earlier *Bather* (1757; Musée du Louvre, Paris) for the face and body type of Galatea.[19]

Diderot's Salon criticism also figured the work as both self-referential and a discourse about artistic creation. He invokes the core event of the Pygmalion tale, the moment when marble turns to flesh, in praise of Falconet's handling of the material: "What softness in the flesh! No, it is not marble; press it with your finger and the material which has lost its hardness will yield to the pressure." But this pretty reference to Ovid's tale is not Diderot's most powerful evocation of "life" in Falconet's work. This evocation the *philosophe* reserves for Pygmalion's expression: "O Falconet! how have you put in a piece of white stone surprise, joy, and love blended together? Emulator of the gods, if they have animated the statue you have renewed the miracle by enlivening sculpture."[20] Thus Diderot's comments, too, are a discourse on enthusiasm, the force that brings art to life.

That the Pygmalion story remained closely tied to concepts of enthusiasm is also evident in a short *scène lyrique* written by Jean-Jacques Rousseau in 1762. Indeed, when performed in 1775, the play was taken as a contemporary meditation on problems of artistic inspiration. The critic Friedrich-Melchior Grimm, for example, wrote that what he saw in Rousseau's "sublime and orig-

19. The similarities between these two works were noted by George Levetine in *The Sculpture of Falconet* (Greenwich, Conn., 1972), 34–35.
20. Denis Diderot, "Salon of 1763" in *Salons*, ed. J. Seznec and J. Adhémar, 4 vols. (Oxford, 1963), 245.

inal piece" was a "tableau of emotions, of enthusiasm, of transport, that can move the spectators to a true love of beauty and the arts."[21] In his *Pygmalion,* Rousseau makes certain assumptions about the relationship between the aesthetic and erotic impulses, implying an easy correspondence between male arousal and enthusiasm when he renders Pygmalion enflamed at the same moment with the fires of love and genius.[22]

The play begins with the artist confronting his works, strewn about him in the studio. Pygmalion, paralyzed by his own creations, mourns his loss of enthusiasm: "There is no soul, no life at all. . . . It is nothing but stone. . . . Where is my inspiration? What has become of my talent? My fire is extinguished. My imagination has turned to ice" (2:1224). In an effort to rekindle his fervor, Pygmalion approaches his statue of Galatea, which stands veiled in a corner of the studio. Lifting the veil, Pygmalion falls prostrate, paying homage to his "most beautiful creation": "Oh Galatea, receive my homage. Yes! I was deceived, I intended to make you a nymph and I made you a goddess" (2:1226). Amid his contemplation of such perfection, however, Pygmalion notices what cannot be tolerated—he sees a flaw. His materialized statue-woman does not adequately match his interior ideal. He has not cut away enough of her drapery, he cannot see enough of her body. He "sees" the body in the stone as an imagined ideal, but he sees it as if a body actually existed under the sculpted marble veil.[23] The concept is reminiscent of Michelangelo's Neoplatonic idea of sculpture as the art of releasing the ideal form from base matter. Thus Pygmalion must gouge into the very substance of his Galatea to remove the stone garment that cloaks his vision.[24]

To correct the flaw, Pygmalion takes up hammer and chisel, intent on sculpting Galatea to greater advantage. Only by revisualizing his ideal vision, only when his vision returns to him, can Pygmalion be inspired to work again. Only then can Galatea come to life. He returns to his creation, and he is amply

21. Friedrich-Melchior Grimm, et al., *Correspondance Littéraire, Philosophique et Critique par Grimm, Diderot, Raynal, Meister, etc.,* ed. Maurice Tourneux, 16 vols. (Paris, 1877–82).

22. J.-J. Rousseau, *Pygmalion,* in *Oeuvres complètes,* ed. Bernard Gagnebin and Marcel Raymond, 4 vols. (Paris, 1959–69): 2:1225; quotations cited henceforward in the text. For important interpretations of the piece, see Paul de Man, *Allegories of Reading* (New Haven, Conn., 1979), 160–87; Jean Starobinski, *Jean-Jacques Rousseau: Transparency and Obstruction,* trans. Arthur Goldhammer (Chicago, 1988), 65–80; and Louis Marin, "Le moi et les pouvoirs de l'image: Glose sur *Pygmalion,* scène lyrique (1772) de J.-J. Rousseau," *Modern Language Notes* 107 (September 1992): 659–72.

23. Marin, "Le moi et les pouvoirs de l'image," 666–67.

24. Ibid. For a discussion of Pygmalion's "attack" on Galatea in an image by Francisco Goya, see the excellent article by John Ciafalo, "Unveiling Goya's *Rape of Galatea,*" *Art History* 18 (December 1995): 477–98. See also de Man, *Allegories of Reading,* 180–81.

rewarded. He lifts his tools, he strikes, and after his blow he imagines he feels her flesh tremble. In Rousseau's version of Ovid there is no need for Venus; it is Pygmalion's touch, violent though it might be, that brings the statue to life. Amazed and entranced, Pygmalion watches as the statue moves, as his nude descends the staircase. She comes down from the pedestal; she touches herself and utters her first word, "moi." Her second word comes when she touches a marble block, "pas moi." And her final word escapes when she touches Pygmalion, "encore moi" (1230–31).[25]

Enthusiasm: A Life-Giving Force

Especially because Rousseau's narrative ends with Galatea proclaiming her sameness with Pygmalion, it is not clear whether Pygmalion felt Galatea's trembling or his own response after striking the marble/flesh. Contemporaneous definitions of enthusiasm, such as that posited by Diderot in the *Second Entretien sur le fils naturel*, suggest the latter: "The poet senses the moment of enthusiasm. . . . It begins as a trembling in his chest and passes in a wonderful and rapid way to the extremities of his body. Not only a trembling but a strong permanent heat which embraces him, excites him, kills him, but gives spirit and life to all that he touches."[26]

In defining enthusiasm, Diderot characterizes it as a life-giving force expressed by the artist's touch. The passage is often read, as well, for its implied association with sexual excitement, even orgasm, which produces a trembling, a heat, and here confers life on the artist's creation. Yet if sexuality is invoked, it is that of the male poet, since the discourses on artistic inspiration linked enthusiasm with male fecundity in one way or another. We see this association most directly when semen is held to be the "life-giving" force, and the Pygmalion story read into discussions of human reproduction. In Dubuisson's *Tableau de l'amour conjugal* (1812), for example, semen's role in producing a child is likened to the sculptor's work in shaping his marble: "The semen is to generation what the sculptor is to marble; the male semen is the sculptor who gives shape, the female liquor is the marble or matter, and the sculpture is the fetus or the product of generation." Dubuisson here follows an earlier tradition; in *Les principes de la nature, ou*

---

25. De Man in particular considers the meaning of this dialogue and the dialectic of self and other (*Allegories of Reading*), esp. 185ff.
26. Denis Diderot, *Second Entretien sur le fils naturel* in *Oeuvres complètes de Diderot*, ed. J. Assézat, 29 vols. (Paris, 1876), 7:103.

de la génération des choses (1731), for example, François-Marie-Pompée Colonna had used an artistic metaphor, this time making semen the instrument of reproduction: "It is true that the semen is the visible agent, but we can also say that like the Painter, the Sculptor, and other Artisans who use certain instruments to fashion their materials into desired shape, similarly an invisible workman uses the male's seminal matter as the instrument that leads the female to generate an animal."[27] This likening of artistic creativity to biological paternity has a long history in France. Montaigne, in his essay "De l'affection des peres aux enfans," compares two kinds of fatherhood—the one that produces a child of the body and the other a child of the brain: "And I do not know whether I would not like much better to have produced one perfectly formed child by intercourse with the Muses than by intercourse with my wife."[28] It is not coincidental that Montaigne concludes his essay by quoting from Ovid's Pygmalion: "Its hardness gone, the ivory softens, yields / Beneath his fingers."

Intercourse with the Muses, however, results in a peculiar sort of insemination, a self-insemination in which the Muses play no part. Concerning children of the mind, Montaigne says to those with paternal claim: "We are father and mother both in this generation."[29] In claiming the maternal role, Montaigne continues an earlier tradition of enthusiasm that transferred "natural" maternal powers of reproduction to the male cultural producer, thereby leaving the nymph sterile and the artist fecund. This transformation was already effected in Platonic dialogues about cultural production, including the classical "source" on enthusiasm, or divine madness, the *Phaedrus*.[30]

By the eighteenth century, male pregnancy, which brought forth cultural production, was deemed superior and more difficult than a woman's natural

27. Both quotations given in Marie-Hélène Huet, *Monstrous Imagination* (Cambridge, Mass., 1993), 7.

28. Montaigne, "Of the Affection of Fathers for Their Children," in *The Complete Essays of Montaigne,* trans. Donald M. Frame (Stanford, Calif., 1958), 293. For a discussion of this text and its relation to themes in Pygmalion, see Patrick Henry, "Montaigne and Pygmalion," and Jerome Schwartz, "Narcisse et Pygmalion— deux moments dans la mythologie personnelle de Montaigne," both essays in Daniel Martin, ed., *Montaigne and the Gods* (Amherst, Mass., 1993).

29. Montaigne, "Of the Affection of Fathers," 291.

30. Page duBois has shown how this text represents Plato's appropriation of maternity to the male philosopher; "reproduction" is ascribed exclusively to men, who inseminate each other with philosophy in a sexual act that gives women no place; see *Sowing the Body: Psychoanalysis and Ancient Representations of Women* (Chicago, 1991), 169–83. For a similar reading, see David Halperin, "Why is Diotima a Woman?" in *One Hundred Years of Homosexuality and Other Essays on Greek Love* (New York and London, 1990), 113–53. DuBois reads the dialogue as a text of homoerotic seduction, which establishes a "new portrait of philosopher as lover, inseminator, and fertile field," thus combining metaphors that classical culture used to represent the male (lover, inseminator) with those used to signify the female (fertile field).

reproduction. Consider Voltaire's well-known story of Madame du Châtelet's giving birth, various versions of which he recounted in 1749.[31] In writing to the Comte d'Argental, he used Madame du Châtelet's maternity as an introduction to his own creativity, concluding, "I will deliver my *Catelina* with much more difficulty" (95:151). To the Abbé de Voisenon he noted, "I give birth in eight days to *Catelina*," and then pointed out that although he did not know if Madame du Châtelet would be pregnant again, he was already carrying his *Electre* (95:155). To the Marquis d'Argenson he embellished a bit more. Whereas Madame du Châtelet has given birth to an infant who cannot speak, he has found it necessary to make his characters articulate their thoughts, and "it is more difficult to make those characters speak than to make babies" (95:151).[32]

While some discourses of male creativity appropriated the maternal, more commonly enthusiasm—in its positive sense as creative force—also aligned itself with an active, desiring sexuality that from Aristotle to Rousseau to Freud and beyond theorists granted only to the male. Such sexuality was encoded in myths of the artist whose desire motivated or expressed itself in his art. The best known prototype was, of course, Pygmalion, but the idea was also captured in stories like Zeuxis choosing his models and Apelles painting Campaspe. Throughout the eighteenth century artists identified themselves with these predecessors as well. Women who claimed a desiring sexuality risked public chastisement, for constructions of modesty as woman's virtue urged them to stifle their passions. Woman's active desire led not to cultural production but to convulsions, nymphomania, religious hysteria, trangressive sexuality, and social disorder. As Tissot was to remind his contemporaries, despite social rules, women are more easily inflamed than men.[33]

By and large, the medical profession found that in comparison to the equilibrium that marked man's body, woman's organs (both the sense and sex organs) received livelier impressions and were more easily stimulated.[34] Lively

---

31. Here is what he wrote to Marguerite Jeanne Delaunay, baronne de Staal: "She was at her desk at two o'clock in the morning, according to her admirable custom. She said in scribbling from Newton: '*But I sense (feel) something!* This something was a baby daughter who came into the world much more easily than a problem. She was received in a briefcase (*serviette*); placed on a folio volume, and the mother put herself to bed out of respect for convention"; *Les Oeuvres complètes de Voltaire*, ed. Theodore Besterman et. al., 135 vols. (Geneva, 1970), 95:154; quotations cited henceforward in the text.
32. In *Monstrous Imagination*, Huet has shown that male maternity, which she examines in terms of "monstrosity," was a central trope for Romantic writers.
33. Samuel-Auguste-David Tissot, *L'Onanisme: Dissertation sur les maladies produites par la masturbation*, 10th ed., "*considérablement augmentée*" (Toulouse, 1775), 46–47.
34. Sheriff, *The Exceptional Woman*, 20–25.

sense impressions, moreover, meant that woman's imagination was readily "fired" by lascivious thoughts. Fire, traditionally associated with the passions, was the trope Bienville used in his 1778 treatise on nymphomania to describe that disease's causes and effects.[35] Referring to those struck with nymphomania he calls it a "fire that devours them" (pp. 14, 16), "a fire that could suddenly ignite itself with greater force" (p. 55). He speaks of the inflamed atmosphere that surrounds them (p. 18), describes "the burning heat" (p. 65) that they experience. When the young Julie, suffering from nymphomania, casts her look on a young man, her eyes are "full of fire" (p. 77), and miming this young girl's imaginings he writes: "My soul is devoured by a thousand desires that nothing can moderate. I burn with a fire a thousand times more violent than the most terrible fever" (p. 75).

I stress metaphors of fire because by the seventeenth century, French art theory presented enthusiasm as fire. Often, texts related it to the heavenly fire stolen by Prometheus, who later used it to animate the clay figures he fashioned.[36] Sometimes artworks imaged Pygmalion's love and enthusiasm as fire, for example, Lagrenée's 1777 version of the theme (Museum of Foreign Art Sinebrychoff, Helsinki; figure 3), in which Galatea is ignited by the flame from the torch an amorino bears. Since the meaning of "inflamed" so readily slipped from divine inspiration to intellectual passion to creative fervor to sexual desire, women could not without risk present *themselves* as inflamed, even though men repeatedly figured them in that language. Although "fire" might characterize woman's true nature, it was neither proper nor modest for her to be burning. It was primarily immodest women in erotic representations who were thus shown or signified. The fireplace is a pun on the woman's sexual organs in François Boucher's *The Woman Tying Her Garter* (1742; Thyssen-Bornemisza Foundation, Lugano). In that work, the artist rhymes visually the woman's splayed legs and the widely set jambs of the fireplace in which we see flames sparking. In *The Private Academy* (Bibliothèque Nationale), Gabriel de Saint-Aubin asks us to look there, between the jambs of the fireplace, and he casts the woman's body as fireplace by associating the cartouche at the center of the mantle with the model's pubic triangle.

The general conception of the woman "inflamed," however, is perhaps most clearly displayed in Jean-Honoré Fragonard's *Le Feu aux poudres* (before 1778; Musée du Louvre, Paris; figure 4). In this work a putto holds a lighted torch between a young woman's legs, seeming to ignite her genitals. With her

35. D. T. de Bienville, *La Nymphomanie ou Traité de la fureur utérine* (Amsterdam, 1778).
36. Sheriff, *Fragonard*, 138–39.

Figure 3. Jean-Louis François Lagrenée, *Pygmalion* (1777); Museum of Foreign Art Sinebrychoff, Helsinki.

Figure 4. Jean-Honoré Fragonard, *Le Feu aux poudres* (before 1778); Musée du Louvre.

drapery gathered up at her waist and down at her bosom, she lolls back seductively, deep in her dreams or reveries, which we must presume to be erotic. A smile plays on her lips, and she seems pleased by the attention of this putto and his companions. Like (but also unlike) Galatea, she is enlivened by the cupid's torch and aroused by the touch of her creator. Considering Fragonard's work in terms of the implied artist, it is clear that this image trades on the doubled meaning of enthusiasm as male sexual desire and creative energy.

Because enthusiasm was the emotion that motivated the artist to execute a work of art, for the painter enthusiasm left its traces in the action, the play, the physical touch of the brush. When touch was considered a true index of the artist's mental state, the touching most apt to signify enthusiasm was that associated with the sketch. The sketchlike technique was widely perceived to be close to the "hot" stages of inspiration, as Diderot was to remark in his

Salon of 1765: "A sketch ordinarily has a fire that a painting does not. It is the heated moment for the artist, the purest verve."[37] If the sketchlike technique indicated the "fire" of enthusiasm as creative energy, when it was used to represent an erotic scene of a woman sexually aroused, it additionally both suggested her ardor and expressed the passion of the male artist. As the academic theorist Claude-Henri Watelet made clear, the artist's touch was at once an imitative sign tied to the object represented and an expressive sign, linked to how the artist saw and felt in making the representation. Thus the touch was to resemble or be appropriate for the object represented, and in this case the "fire" of the sketchlike technique depicts female ardor. But if the touch also "expressed" how the artist "felt," it suggests that like Pygmalion, this artist was inflamed with the fires of genius and love.[38]

FUROR POÉTIQUE/FUROR UTÉRINE

Figured in artful poses and mirroring male desire, Fragonard's female bodies support the subjectivity of the enthused artist; they are on fire, because he has ignited himself. But if they were to turn to their own internal mirrors, set themselves ablaze, and project their own desires, these women would instead enter the realm of nymphomania. Although female erotic activity can be staged for the patriarchal gaze, if woman imaginatively speculates on her own desires, she takes her place as the abjected underside of the enthused artist. Male creativity depends on monopolizing desire, a monopoly consolidated through repressing the potential nymphomaniac. A return to Ovid will make it clear how this dynamic structured the Pygmalion story right from the start.

Recall the beginning of the tale, recall the women who disgusted Pygmalion. Horrified by the lewd behavior of real women, Pygmalion created Galatea as a substitute for the creatures he could not abide. The women in question were the Propoetides, punished by Venus for not believing in her divinity. Their fate was to be ruled by venereal pleasures. The goddess of love made them the first women to prostitute their bodies, and struck them, it seems, with a kind of nymphomania, an insatiable desire for sexual pleasure. The Propoetides eventually turn to stone, their faces hardened when shame or modesty leaves them. Their fate is thus opposed (and compared) to that of the other woman, the one brought to life by the sculptor's touch. The Propoetides,

---

37. Diderot, "Salon of 1765," in *Salons*, 2:153–54.
38. Sheriff, *Fragonard*, 137–48.

on the other hand, are women "with all the countless vices Nature gives to Womankind," as Ovid tells us. Woman was at base a creature driven by her desires, and as eighteenth-century medical authorities knew, she had the physical capacity to act on her desires repeatedly. Tissot noted that because women did not lose fluid in the sex act, each had the potential to be a Messalina.

As a woman out of control, the Roman Messalina, with Semiramis and Coelia, became a negative ancient example invoked in cautionary tales. These women brought together nymphomania and prostitution, for their excesses were understood as a prostitution by compulsion, a disease and not a profession. They are linked with nymphomania, or *furor utérine*, in the *Encyclopédie*'s entry on that malady: "It was undoubtedly from the effects of this sort of delirium carried to excess that Messalina was tired, exhausted, even satiated by the crudest pleasures to which she prostituted herself without limit and with the most infamous bestiality. It is also perhaps as true that because of this disease Semiramis, queen of the Assyrians, . . . fell into the most shameful and excessive dissolution, to the point of giving herself to a great number of soldiers. . . . Martial mentions Coelia's enormous debauchery, which by all appearances could only be the effect of a *furor utérine*, since she was not a prostitute by profession. Otherwise there would have been nothing remarkable in her excesses" (7:380). These historical examples fit the paradigm of the disease proposed by Tissot, who defined it as a libidinous rage; a continual and insatiable desire for copulation.[39]

Although the clinical definitions of nymphomania varied, experts agreed that the disease could strike any woman. Figuring nymphomania in the familiar metaphors of heat and fire (which also conveniently recalled the punishments of hell), Bienville wrote in his treatise that every woman was susceptible at one time or another to an obsession with those things that carried "the infernal flame of lubricity" (p. 13). Women with a naturally ardent temperament were especially at risk, but nymphomania could strike young girls who had never known love, *filles débauchées*, married women, and young widows. As Bienville put it, "In a word, all of them" (p. 14).

Any woman *could* be struck by nymphomania, but it was not obvious from looking just which women had been! The difficulty in recognizing the nymphomaniac and distinguishing her from the normal woman made the disease particularly threatening and, conveniently, necessitated the surveillance and control of all women. Woman's very nature, moreover, exacerbated the problem of detection. Moralists had long characterized woman as given to deception and artifice, and thus nymphomania was a disease that mirrored the

39. Tissot, *L'Onanisme*, 88.

wiles of its female host. Warning of its dangers, Bienville wrote: "it nearly always hides itself under a deceptive exterior of apparent calm, and often it is already dangerous even if its beginnings, let alone its main progress, has not yet been perceived. Sometimes the sick woman struck with nymphomania has a foot on the precipice without being aware of the danger; [nymphomania] is like a serpent that glides imperceptibly into her heart" (p. 12). Bienville continually stresses not only the deceptiveness of the disease but also the deceptiveness of the sufferer. Although there are moments when women may wish to reform, more often they are preoccupied with the means of hiding their state from everyone else. He mentions treating women who for a long time hid the disease even from their doctors. Of one he recalls: "As she had succeeded in fooling them, she flattered herself that she would do the same with me, and told me in advance that I would not succeed better than my predecessors in giving her relief" (pp. 60–61). Patients feign, deceive, dissimulate, and in a sense his entire discussion praises women's artistry. Yet woman is a perverse artist whose performance is designed to sustain an abominable disease that could lead to delirium, melancholy, mania, and even death. As the disease progressed the woman's dissimulation was less effective, and there were times when "the sick woman shows herself as she really is."

In the later stages of the disease a nymphomaniac might even attack men, but her advances were usually resisted. In Bienville's treatise especially, men shrink from the nymphomaniac's touch. But no nymphomaniac was cured by a lack of sexual partners, and no woman escaped the disease because she could not find a willing accomplice. Despite the associations between nymphomania and prostitution, frequent sexual intercourse was not the defining feature or symptom of nymphomania. Rather, the illness was one of insatiable desire. A nymphomaniac, the *Encyclopédie* tells us, could not be cured, but only worsened, by the "ordinary remedy of love, which is orgasm" (7:380) Sexual pleasure only fueled her desire, which the woman inevitably tried to satisfy for herself with imagined partners and masturbatory practices. And although masturbation did not quell her lust, it did turn her further and further from real men, as Tissot was to point out in his treatise on this vice.[40]

This turning from men could also be a turning toward other women. Bienville tells us how women, usually servants, but sometimes companions or governesses, introduced other women into the practices of masturbation (p. 89). Although throughout Bienville's treatise the nymphomaniac is presented as having a primary heterosexual desire, sexual encounters with other

---

40. Tissot, *L'Onanisme,* 49. Here one might also point out that a slang term for the clitoris was the "mépris des hommes."

women could function as an alternative method of gratification, akin to or associated with masturbation. Even more directly than Bienville, Tissot linked tribadism, as love between women was called, to masturbation and through masturbation to nymphomania. Arguing that masturbation led to nymphomania, Tissot added to manual sullying another sort he called "clitoridienne," whose origin he traced back to Sappho and to the Roman women condemned by Juvenal. With other doctors, Tissot believed these women used a "monstrous clitoris" to mimic the virile function in sexual relations. He noted that although this form of self-pollution had not received a lot of attention, it was "frequent" in contemporary society.[41]

Masturbation of one sort or another was central to nymphomania, for it is the regular practice of *all* nymphomaniacs, not just those without other means of seeking gratification. Moreover, masturbation was connected to imagination, which stood as nymphomania's ultimate cause. Tissot stressed that masturbators were not led by need or nature, but by imagination and habit. Often they focused their attention exclusively on their disgusting desires to the point of obsession. Indeed, this obsession increased with the progress of nymphomania; the imagination was exhausted by lascivious representations and finally so saturated with them that the sick woman dreaded any return to normalcy. To emphasize the important role imagination played in nymphomania, Bienville devoted his concluding chapter to the relation between them. There he showed that imagination brought on nymphomania because it demanded masturbatory practices, which aided the disease's progress by further inflaming imagination and binding women to forbidden pleasures. In this section he cites the sad case of Julie, who dissimulates her "funeste manie de la masturbation dont l'imagination est artisanne" (p. 144).

Although Cahusac worked hard to define enthusiasm as reason's masterpiece, no one doubted that nymphomania was crafted by the female imagination. That kind of imagination was not simply a screen for reason's projections but also a mirror of sensation, and an unreliable one at that. Imagination, according to Bienville, can take an active part in remaking what it reflects; it sometimes renders objects as they are but at other times enlarges, diminishes, or multiplies them. The senses transmit information simply and naturally, but the imagination refines and augments them (pp. 133–34). In other words, imagination makes nature artful. Although Bienville does not overtly limit this sort of imagination to women, he does gender it feminine. Imagination is the "mother" of passions and excesses (p. 134) as well as the overseer of *l'amour propre*. It caters to the individual's temperament; knowing her inclinations, it

41. Ibid., 51–52.

works to exaggerate them and to favor them. Implicitly comparing insatiable sexual desire to the glutton's appetite, Bienville sees that "it is the imagination that paints for the glutton the pleasure of the table, the savoriness of such and such a meat. . . . It augments his desire to enjoy and makes him sacrifice all for it." And, he continues: "it is she [imagination] which procures for them this anticipated delight and pleasure, which in rendering what is real exaggerates it and makes it more tangible" (p. 134). Thus the imagination is the source of desire, which I take to be implied in "volupté et jouissance anticipée." Desire is a perpetual anticipation, the experience of lacking some imaginary pleasure that, because it is imaginary, cannot be satisfied by anything real. According to Bienville, imagination has great force in love, and those with lively imaginations are more susceptible to nymphomania.

I have suggested throughout this essay that Cahusac's attempts to move enthusiasm and artistic creativity from the realm of imagination (where it was traditionally located) to the realm of reason was an attempt to shift enthusiasm to the "masculine"—even when that process appropriated female reproductive powers. This attempt was ultimately to fail not only because the traditions tying enthusiasm to imagination, desire, and madness were impossible to efface, but also because discourses on woman's imagination often invoked to different ends terms current in discussions of art and inspiration. Like the nymphomaniac, the enthused artist was inflamed by what he saw painted on his imagination/screen. And like her, he suffered from a compulsion, an obsession; he was ruled by a single idea from which nothing could distract him. Moreover, both shared an idealizing function alternately given to reason (Cahusac) or imagination (Bienville).

In the discourse on nymphomania, the female imagination of the woman struck with *furor utérine* transforms the object that obsesses her—an ordinary young man—into an "Adonis" (p. 18). These are Bienville's terms, and in mentioning Adonis he is, of course, invoking an idealized construction of myth and art. In his description, the woman's imagination is stimulated to propose an ideal based on an object or objects of sensation. Thus Bienville does not attempt to separate mental activity from the physical or material sensation that generates it. Here the construction is immediately comparable not to Pygmalion's imagining of Galatea but to the invention of that other ancient creator of feminine beauty, Zeuxis. This Greek painter was not neglected by art theorists; indeed, Batteux made him the model of the enthused artist. Batteux depicts the painter as aroused by contemplating his newly created object, a woman whose ideal beauty comes from giving over to imagination the perception of real women. Zeuxis "forgets himself" and his spirit passes into what he makes.[42] Batteux's selection of Zeuxis as his model suggests that it was not so simple to write objects of sensation out of enthusiasm's picture, especially given a discourse that ultimately grounded all ideas in sensations. Cahusac's discussion of enthusiasm, as well as some versions of the Pygmalion story, represses the role of sensation; but like anything repressed, sensation makes its return.

If Cahusac separated the imagined tableau that reason presented to the genius from the painted image seen by the spectator, in using an *analogy* to distinguish one type from the other he already admits a filiation between them. And although he privileges the imagined tableau, he also has to allow for a kind of enthusiasm that is solely spectatorial, and tied to sensation. This enthusiasm is experienced by spectators who are not creators, and in describing this sort of enthusiasm Cahusac writes: "In a less lively way, to be sure, enthusiasm affects all those who experience the fine arts" (5:721). There is, he contends, an enthusiasm that produces and an enthusiasm that admires, and one gives onto the other. But these enthusiasms had long been viewed not as two unequal versions of the same phenomenon but as part of the same experience. As such, enthusiasm could operate not just by passing in a diluted form from creator to spectator through the art work but also by circulating full force from creator to creator. The tradition of enthusiasm that stemmed from Roger de Piles stressed how creative enthusiasm could be inflamed by seeing masterpieces or by looking at its own work. And this is the case in representations of Pygmalion.

In the Pygmalion story, the sculptor/king forms his ideal apart from real women. Yet what ultimately fires, and in Rousseau's text rekindles, Pygmalion's imagination is a work of art, a materialization of his own desire into an object of sensation. The work was only animated, only brought to life, through Pygmalion's sustained involvement with an art object. It is through contemplating, loving, and touching Galatea that Pygmalion can bring his ideal to life. Pygmalion was taken to represent the artist endowed with a *furor poétique;* but he was in this madness not so far from the woman stricken with *furor utérine.* In the end, his story cannot separate imagination from sensation.

Ovid tells us that Pygmalion's masterpiece fires him with love. He imagines it returning his kisses, yielding to him, speaking to him. He imagines that it responds to him, just as a nymphomaniac imagines that her Adonis returns her desire. Moreover, what gives both artist and nymphomaniac ideas is artworks— visual images or other sorts of representations. Bienville cites erotic images as among the props the nymphomaniac uses to stimulate her imagination:

---

42. Abbé Charles Batteux, *Les beaux-arts réduit à un même principe* (Paris, 1746), 33.

women, in fact, exacerbated their propensity to nymphomania by looking at lascivious pictures.[43] And no wonder; woman's imagination, it was well known, confused reality and fantasy. Is Pygmalion so different in this regard? Pygmalion's confusion, however, has a different outcome. His is not the story of insatiable desire but the fantasy of desire *fulfilled*. And in getting the woman he made for himself, Pygmalion also fulfills the desires of the Tissots and the Bienvilles to control women by compelling them to control themselves, by compelling them to restrict the workings of their imaginations.

Pygmalion's Galatea seems to have no imagination of her own. She is the mirror of Pygmalion's desire.[44] Like Narcissus (another type for the artist), Pygmalion falls in love with himself—with *his* image. Rousseau's libretto brings out this narcissism, perhaps more clearly than other versions of the story, when Pygmalion confesses: "I cannot permit myself to admire my own work . . . I am intoxicated with self love" (2:1226). And he seeks to make Galatea his double or, as he puts it, to "give her my life," to "animate her with my own soul" (2:1228). Pygmalion's love for Galatea is a love of his own imaginings, a love not unlike that of the nymphomaniac. Enthusiasm in Rousseau's hands has erotic and even autoerotic dimensions that are at once denied by and latent in Cahusac's evocation of the Pygmalion myth. But even in Rousseau's story, the self-touching is left to Galatea, or rather displaced onto her. She is the one who touches herself and makes her sameness with Pygmalion evident by declaring them both "moi." She is made to embody and enact the self-love, the enthusiasm, that drives Pygmalion.

Not every version of the Pygmalion story, however, can sustain these myths effectively—especially if one reads along with it the entangled discourses of inspiration, desire, and madness. Keeping these associations at the fore can produce an unfaithful reading, one that illuminates from another direction the sorts of interactions I have been discussing. Consider, for example, an engraving by Moreau le jeune, made to illustrate Rousseau's tale and published in the collected edition of Rousseau's works issued in Brussels between 1774 and 1783 (figure 5). The engraver's depiction of Pygmalion and Galatea is quite singular and deviates from all earlier French versions of the story. The Galatea

43. They could also make themselves more prone to the disease by upsetting their nervous equilibrium through drinking coffee and wine, eating chocolate, and generally living a life of luxury and pleasure.

44. Many interpreters—for example, Leonard Barkan in his perceptive analysis of Ovid's *Metamorphosis* and more recently J. Hillis Miller in his consideration of Pygmalion-like stories—have noticed that there are echoes of Narcissus in Pygmalion's passionate devotion; see Barkan, *The Gods Made Flesh: Metamorphosis and the Pursuit of Paganism* (New Haven, Conn., 1986); and Hillis Miller, *Versions of Pygmalion* (Cambridge, Mass., 1989). Narcissus, by the way, also eschewed real women, but he didn't have the good sense to make one of his own, to freeze his ideal into a work of art.

Figure 5. Engraving by Nicholas Le Mire after Moreau le jeune, "Pygmalion," from J. J. Rousseau, *Oeuvres* (London [Brussels], 1774–83), 7:45.

Moreau le jeune shows is scarcely the timorous, trembling creature Rousseau desires. Having stepped off her pedestal, this Galatea turns her back on Pygmalion. His gesture more or less adheres to the codes that signal surprise, but it could easily be interpreted as a plea because the outstretched hands and upturned palms slip into that sign. Is Pygmalion surprised because Galatea has come to life or because she has turned her back on him? Does he plead with her to look at him or to get back on that pedestal?

Once Galatea has stepped off her pedestal, she strides toward a sculpture of a nude man, another major deviation from Rousseau's text. The stony sculpture is also shown with equivocal gesture. On the one hand he seems about to lurch forward, but he could also be read as fending off Galatea's presumptuous advance. Is she trying to repeat Pygmalion's life-giving touch on a figure she finds more pleasing than he? Most obvious in this version of the story is that Pygmalion no longer seems to control Galatea. This Galatea striding so confidently, almost enthusiastically, toward the marble sculpture: it is difficult to imagine her turning in the next moment to melt into Pygmalion's arms, saying "moi, encore." Rousseau's Pygmalion may have thought he sculpted a goddess, but in Moreau le jeune's version he gets a nymph. Or maybe even a nymphomaniac. As soon as Galatea moves from art to nature, from sculpture to woman, as soon as she steps off her pedestal she is at risk. No real woman was immune to nymphomania. And in Ovid's tale nymphomania strikes again; not at Galatea but at her great-granddaughter, Myrrah, who develops an insatiable and incestuous desire for her father. It is from the union of Myrrah and her father that Adonis, the ideal lover conjured by Bienville's nymphomaniac, is born.

If no woman was immune to nymphomania, the disease posed the threat of becoming a contagion, especially if women introduced one another to the pleasures of Venus, as Bienville suggested they did. Indeed, Bienville hints that the disease could reach epidemic proportions. "The disease I treat," he wrote, "is not a chimera, it is not only currently existing in the sex (women), it is every day making a very rapid progress" (p. xvi). Here Bienville interacts with traditions that view female mania as spreading like wildfire. Hecquet, for example, feared the destructive power of convulsionism, and in *Le naturalisme des convulsions dans les maladies de l'épidémie convulsionnaire* cast the phenomenon as a contagion not of physical organisms but of imagination.[45]

---

45. Wilson, *Women and Medicine*, 27. Kreiser likewise points to repeated use of the image of contagion, (Miracles, *Convulsions*), 278–83. A similar vocabulary described the spread of Mesmerism, perceived to be dangerously erotic, among women. Wilson quotes a commissioner's report to the king, which warned: "Nothing prevents the convulsions from becoming habitual and from spreading in the cities into epidemics extending to future generations" (p. 110).

Given the intersection between discourses of female mania and enthusiasm, it will come as no surprise that enthusiasm was also believed contagious. Cahusac, for example, wrote: "It is in the nature of enthusiasm to communicate itself and to reproduce itself; it is a lively flame that spreads from one to the other, that nourishes itself from its own fire, and that far from weakening itself in spreading, takes on new force to the extent that it spreads itself and communicates itself" (5:721). Here he figures enthusiasm as a dissemination, but one that intensifies rather than dissipates its vital force. Moreover, the contagion of creative enthusiasm is not an evil for society.[46] Far from spreading disease to the next generation, it will transmit to them their national "gloire." Cahusac notes that "the names of the Corneilles, the Molières, the Quinaults, the Lullys, the Lebruns, the Bossuets, the Perraults, the Le Notres go from mouth to mouth, and all of Europe repeats them and admires them; they are henceforth the immutable monuments to the glory of the nation and humanity" (5:721). Enthusiasm is predictably cast as enthusiasm for the timeless achievements of great men, the national *patrimoine*.

Galatea Embodied: Enthusiasm and the Creative Woman

Despite Cahusac's limiting enthusiasm to the male artist, it was in fact often creative women who provoked a contagious response from the public. Consider the actress Raucourt, who in 1772 appeared in the role of Dido. The *Correspondance Litteraire*, a mainstream literary journal, wrote of her performance that it elicited cries of admiration and acclaim, and continued, "after the play, this same enthusiasm spread in the private residences. Those who had seen *Dido* dispersed themselves to different quarters, arriving like madmen speaking with transport of the debut, communicating their enthusiasm to those who had not seen her." Later, the same publication reported on the staying power of the enthusiasm Raucourt provoked. Engaging the familiar metaphors of fire and disease, Grimm described the way all of Paris responded: "For nearly a month these transports have continued in all their fire; it is one of the strongest and above all one of the longest relapses into enthusiasm that I have seen in Paris."

But this actress did not have access to the sort of fame that would contribute to the immortal and immutable monuments that spoke the national

---

46. In fact, in the *Phaedrus* Plato gives true poetry a philosophical function that also opens onto social utility: "A third kind of possession or madness comes from the Muses. It takes hold upon a gentle virginal soul, awakens and inspires it to song and poetry and so, glorifying the innumerable deeds of our forefathers, educates posterity" (p. 26).

glory. On the contrary, her fame attracted the sort of negative publicity given to many successful women artists, and especially actresses, who performed in public. By the late 1770s, Mlle. Raucourt was characterized in the *Mémoires secrets* as a tribade, and called "the whore of Babylon who throws a lascivious eye on all those of her sex." And on 31 December 1779 that journal announced a "competition" staged by the Royal Society of Medicine, which proposed a gold medal for the best paper on a "germ" called *furor amoris, antiphisia,* with which Raucourt (and other actresses) had "infected the capital." Women like Raucourt were attacked as sexually promiscuous, as suffering from a *furor utérine* or as given to one of the forbidden practices that caused nymphomania. The responses to Raucourt are not surprising, especially in view of the general public perception of actresses. This negative publicity, however, points to the public utility not of enthusiasm but of the link between enthusiasm and transgressive female sexuality. That link was useful for putting women in their place.[47]

Prior to the slander against her person, Raucourt's acting had taken Paris by storm. At the apex of her career, she played the chaste Galatea when the Comédie Française performed Rousseau's lyric in 1775. By enacting the role designed by Rousseau, in animating *his* Galatea, Raucourt becomes woman as male creators—Ovid, Rousseau, Falconet, Bienville, to name only a few—wanted her to be. Yet Raucourt's enthused performance that brought Galatea to life and moved the passions and emotions of her audience could only make the slander against her real person seem all the more believable. As the play's author wrote in his diatribe against actresses, "Is there even need to dispute about the moral differences between the sexes to feel how unlikely it is that she who sets herself up for sale in performance would not soon do the same in person and never let herself be tempted to satisfy desires that she takes so much effort to excite?"[48] Rousseau not only casts the actress as a prostitute, he also presents her as confusing her stage role with her real person. In this his actress resembles the many other women—novel readers, masturbators, nymphomaniacs—who confused fantasy with real life and gave themselves over to their passion. Through her art the actress arouses the desires and enthusiasm of her audience, which she satisfies in "real life" when she steps off the stage. Every actress who played Galatea would thus be other to the modest ivory virgin beloved by Pygmalion; stepping off the pedestal/stage she would give herself to any taker.

47. My discussion of Raucourt is indebted to the commentary and documents reprinted in Marie-Jo Bonnet, *Un choix sans équivoque* (Paris, 1981), 107–65. The material on Raucourt is quoted on pages 135–42.

48. Jean-Jacques Rousseau, *Letter to M. D'Alembert on the Theater,* trans. Allan Bloom (Ithaca, N.Y., 1960), 90.

Women, it should be noted, did contest their exclusion from the position of artist. Some even pointed out the contradictions in the discourse, wondering, for example, why heightened sensibility should render them incapable of making art and deem men expert at the same activity. These protests, however, did not change the prejudices and restrictions that faced each woman, although they occasionally worked to the advantage of specific individuals who were taken as "exceptions." What is most remarkable is that some women did become celebrated artists in spite of theoretical exclusions that perversely positioned *them* as aping the masculine, when male creativity had appropriated aspects of femininity for itself. These celebrated women, however, could not escape the slander that in eighteenth-century France inevitably followed a woman's success and even dogged her posthumous reputation.[49]

The binding together of nymphomania and enthusiasm made creative women of all sorts easy targets for malicious quills and tongues, and the charge of sexual immorality was not one easily disproven, especially since any woman could at any moment find the serpent of lubricity gliding imperceptibly into her heart. Although a woman artist's work might show enthusiasm—as did that of the actress Raucourt—she had no way to put her modesty on display. Not only was it suspect to offer herself or her work for public consumption, but also, since women were so adept at dissimulating their desires, no one could be certain what lurked below a chaste appearance. Emanating from the female imagination, the invisible specter of nymphomania hovered around every woman but especially attacked those given to their own fantasies. What would Galatea imagine if she were the artist? If Pygmalion did not control her desires? And what would happen if Galatea, in stepping off her pedestal, eluded Pygmalion's embrace?

University of North Carolina at Chapel Hill

---

49. How women talked back to the discourse is my subject in *The Exceptional Woman*.

The Philosopher and the *Schwärmer:*
On the Career of a German
Epithet from Luther to Kant

Anthony J. La Vopa

W hat a *Schwärmer* is, and whether this person or that one deserves the name, can be disputed forever."[1] With this nod to mounting confusion, Christian Garve began one of his several efforts to tidy the German language in the early 1790s. Over the previous quarter century, Garve's essays and translations of English and Scottish authors had made him one of the most respected voices in the German Late Enlightenment. He was a *Popularphilosoph,* a veteran of the Enlightenment's campaign to bring philosophy out of its academic ghettos and into the homes of the educated *Publikum.* His efforts had made him aware of "the poverty of language" in the face of the "many gradations" of real life, but he remained convinced that the road to truth lay through verbal precision.

Schwärmerei was a case in point. No definition, Garve acknowledged, could do justice to the gradations within this "lower order of madness." And yet the "philosopher" could perform a "distinctive" and "useful" service by roping off *Schwärmerei* conceptually, on one side from normal degrees of understanding and on the other from more severe mental disorders. He could uncover "general rules" to explain how the apparently normal became the obviously *schwärmerisch,* and how people with "various shadings" of the disease affected others.[2]

Degrees and shadings notwithstanding, Garve posited an "essential difference" between *Schwärmerei*—as self-delusion, the mistaking of "fictions" for

---

1. Christian Garve, "Ueber die Schwärmerey," in *Gesammelte Werke, 1 Abteilung: Die Aufsautzsammlungen,* vol. 3 (Hildesheim, 1985), 337. See also Garve's "Ueber die öffentliche Meinung," in *Popularphilosophiche Schriften über literarische, ästhetische und gesellschaftliche Gegenstände,* vol. 2, reprint ed. (Stuttgart, 1974): 1263–1306; and his "Von der Popularität des Vortrages," in *Werke,* 1039–66. On Garve's thought, see esp. Claus Altmayer, *Auf-klärung als Popularphilosophie: Bürgerliches Individuum und Öffentlichkeit bei Christian Garve* (St. Ingbert, 1992).
2. Garve, "Ueber die Schwärmerey," esp. 338–48.

"real knowledge"—and *Enthusiasmus* (the creative inspiration that "exalts desires, raises hopes, and beautifies what is really there"). He broke down *Schwärmerei* into the "speculative" and the "practical" (including the "fanatical"); into separatists and the "persecuting orthodox"; into politically agitating "*Religion-Schwärmer*" and the "political *Schwärmer*" of the French Revolution. Garve conceded that the ultimate organic source of the disease was probably beyond our ken, but had no doubt that certain physical states—weak nerves, the pressure of hot blood on the head, a repressed sex drive—gave rise to it. And there were ways of spotting potential *Schwärmer:* the skeptic's need for religious consolation, the isolation of the self-absorbed personality, all "eccentricity" in "dress, posture, way of life, or tone of voice."[3]

The discourse of *Schwärmerei* was not an invention of German philosophy, but, as Garve's essay suggests, *Schwärmerei* became a handy foil in philosophy's efforts to establish itself as the public voice of reason. And yet, well before the 1790s, philosophical thought had become vulnerable to the charge that it too was dangerously *schwärmerisch.* How did this curious relationship between the philosopher and the *Schwärmer* come into being, and what does it signify?

Our story rests on dichotomies (and affinities) between feeling and thought, image and abstraction, that may be inherent in the human experience. My concern, however, is with the forms these dichotomies assumed within a particular Protestant culture. The approach is contextual, and the purpose is to enhance our understanding of how German philosophical thought, in its efforts to assert a distinct and authoritative voice in modern public culture, perceived its possibilities, its constraints, and its dilemmas. The subject requires both a look back over the *longue durée* and a close-up view. We will trace continuities and changes in the career of an epithet from the early days of the Lutheran Reformation through the last quarter of the eighteenth century.

∾

Garve's essay "Ueber die Schwärmerey" can be read as a belated response to the challenge Christoph Martin Wieland had issued in his *Teutscher Merkur* in 1775. Wieland had called on the literary public to rescue the term *Schwärmerei,* along with the term *Enthusiasmus,* from the slippery terrain of "curse words" and give it a "fixed meaning."[4] In the intervening two decades a host of authors—among them Lessing, Herder, and Kant—responded to the call.

3.   Ibid., 367–406.
4.   "Schwärmerei und Enthusiasmus," *Wieland's Werke,* pt. 22 (Berlin, 1879), 369–71.

Wieland and Garve worried that the abuse of the epithet was creating dangerous confusion. While they asked their readers to confront a semantic crisis, however, they also voiced something like a consensus in the rationalist discourse of the German Late Enlightenment. *Schwärmerei* was, in Wieland's phrase, a "disease of the soul," an "actual soul fever."[5] The disease afflicted isolated individuals, but it might also become contagious and indeed reach epidemic proportions. The task of philosophy was to identify this mental disorder by its symptoms, if not by its causes; and perhaps prevent its spread, if not cure its victims.

Aside from providing an inoculation against the actual disease, philosophical clarity would prevent semantic contamination. Such clarity was needed to rescue *Enthusiasmus* from its defining association with *Schwärmerei*. So long as *Schwärmerei* and *Enthusiasmus* continued to be used synonymously, reason itself would be so narrowly defined as to exclude the creative inspiration essential to producing great literature and art, and perhaps even great philosophy. The epithet, by its very capaciousness, threatened to deprive the language of any conceptual space for "enthuasiasm" in this positive sense.

Wieland and Garve might have been expected to regard the epithet as merely a troublesome curiosity from the arsenals of confessional and sectarian warfare. It was Luther, after all, who created the discourse of *Schwärmerei* in the 1520s. He had stigmatized as *Schwärmer* a wide array of opponents, from "radicals" like Andreas Carlstadt and Thomas Muentzer to more moderate figures like Ulrich Zwingli.[6] Rather than calling for the excision of such a loaded term from public discourse, however, *Aufklärer* hoped that, by giving it a new precision, they would also grant it a new lease on life. Their attachment to the discourse of *Schwärmerei* is in itself a measure of the fact that the German Enlightenment was a profoundly Protestant phenomenon, resting on a bedrock of Lutheran values and drawing on a rich fund of Lutheran images and metaphors, even as it dissented from confessional orthodoxy.

5. Ibid., 370.
6. There is a considerable German Lutheran literature on this subject, but until recently most of it has been more or less polemical. Most useful for my purposes were Karl Thieme, "Verzückung, Enthusiasmus, Schwärmerei," in *Realencyklopädie für protestantische Theologie und Kirche*, 3d ed. (Leipzig, 1908): 586–93; Wilhelm Maurer, "Luther und die Schwärmer," in *Schriften des Theologischen Konvents Augsburgischen Bekenntnisses,* Heft 6 (Berlin-Spandau, 1952), 7–37; and Karl G. Steck, "Luther und die Schwärmer," *Theologische Studien* 44 (Zollikon-Zürich, 1955). More detached are John S. Oyer, *Lutheran Reformers against Anabaptists: Luther, Melanchthon and the Anabaptists of Central Germany* (The Hague, 1964); and Mark U. Edwards, *Luther and the False Brethren* (Stanford, Calif., 1975). On the differences in meaning between *Enthusiasmus* and *Schwärmerei*, see esp. Peter Fenves, *Raising the Tone of Philosophy: Late Essays by Immanuel Kant, Transformative Critique by Jacques Derrida* (Baltimore and London, 1993). Fenves refers to the "highly amorphous and irreducibly figural shape" of *Schwärmerei*, and aptly renders Kant's use of the term as "exaltation" rather than "fanaticism."

The point is not simply that the word was as indigenous as Lutheranism itself; Luther's invective had given it an evocative power and scope that no alternative could offer. Like *Enthusiasmus, Schwärmerei* denoted self-delusion, a mistaken conviction that one had become a receptacle of a divine inspiration or an immediate revelation. But "enthusiasm" had entered modern vernaculars as an abstract term. Rooted in the Greek word for divine possession (literally *en theos,* or "the god inside"), it did not by itself evoke the images of contagion and mass frenzy that became attached to it in Protestant polemics. *Schwärmerei,* on the other hand, drew on the sights and sounds of agricultural life, and these made it resonant with images that gave contagion and mass violence a palpable presence.

When Luther wanted to castigate the mobs that followed self-appointed field preachers or rampaged through churches, smashing the statues, the verb *schwärmen* was ready to hand. It evoked bees swarming around the hive; a flock of birds zigzagging across a field; a pack of hounds straying off the scent. One could hear an ominous buzzing and flapping (or murmuring) and imagine the erratic movement of an aggregate, a kind of perverse order in frenzied disorder. The epithet derived much of its force from this cluster of metaphors, evoking all sorts of implications about deviance and conformity, selfhood and collectivity, private fantasy and public authority. It retained that force in the passage from religious polemics to a secular language of medical science.[7]

Only by making the passage, however, did *Schwärmerei* become serviceable to eighteenth-century philosophical discourse. Luther had not hesitated to tar a wide variety of opponents with the brush of *Schwärmerei* because he saw them all as the Devil's instruments. Under Satan's manipulations, *Schwärmer* mistook the seductions of the Flesh for the inner "voice" or "light" of the Holy Spirit. By the early eighteenth century, in German-speaking Europe as in England, this supernatural explanation had largely acceded to psycho-physiological diagnoses. Ultimately, *Schwärmerei* was to be explained in Galenic terms, as an overheating of the imagination caused by excessive bile; or in mechanistic terms as an "overstraining" of the mind and the emotions. Now the *Schwärmer* was in

7. See the entries on "Schwarm" and related terms in Jacob Grimm and Wilhelm Grimm, *Deutsches Wörterbuch,* vol. 9 (Leipzig, 1899), 2283–95. Also informative are the entries in Johann Christian Adelung, *Grammatische-kritische Wörterbuch der Hochdeutschen Mundart,* pt. 3 (Leipzig, 1798), 1716–18; and J. H. Campe, *Wörterbuch der deutschen Sprache,* vol. 4 (1810; reprint, Hildesheim, 1969), 321. On the evolution of "enthusiasm," see esp. Michael Heyd, *"Be Sober and Reasonable": The Critique of Enthusiasm in the Seventeenth and Early Eighteenth Centuries* (Leiden, 1995); Susie I. Tucker, *Enthusiasm: A Study in Semantic Change* (Cambridge, 1972); and Hans-Jürgen Weckermann, *Die Figur des Enthusiasten in der amerikanischen Erzählliteratur* (Berlin, 1988).

the grip of his own fantasies, and emanations of vaporous humors or mechanical "effluvia" made the disease literally contagious.[8]

The philosophical discussion of *Schwärmerei* in the German Late Enlightenment borrowed freely and eclectically from this medical language. When the
borrowing took the form of a literal application, philosophy partook of the
authority of medicine. More striking, though, was that in the face of *Schwärmerei*, philosophy gave itself an authoritative voice *by analogy with* medicine.
The philosopher was to the social and moral health of society what the physician was to the health of the body. The philosopher, too, brought to his work
a clinical gaze that was at once penetrating and modestly aware of its limits,
severely detached and empathetic.[9]

To assume the persona of the philosopher-physician was a highly effective
rhetorical strategy, a way of pressing philosophy's claims to be the moral arbiter
of public issues facing the society and the polity. There was the illusion of
detachment and objectivity; the clinician gazed down with serene lucidity on
centuries of sectarian warfare and on the emerging clash of modern political
ideologies. In the face of the *Schwärmer's* claims to absolute truth, the clinical
gaze commanded authority by virtue of its epistemological modesty; the ultimate organic cause of *Schwärmerei* would probably always remain hidden. On
another level, however, the clinician posited a psycho-physiological essentialism. As different as they might at first seem, sixteenth-century Anabaptists and
the Parisian mobs of the early 1790s—or the Neoplatonists of the ancient
world and Mesmerists of the 1780s—were manifestations of the same elemen-
tary force. Each new outbreak of the disease confirmed that human nature had
its ineradicable dark side, its irrational urge to pervert a natural synergy of cognitive and affective energies. From this point of view, there was no need to sort
out essential differences among the phenomena lumped together under
Schwärmerei, or to ask whether those differences ought to be explained by reference to specific historical contexts. The clinician uncovered linear continuities

8.   See Michael Heyd, "The Reactions to Enthusiasm in the Seventeenth Century: Towards an Integrative
     Approach," *Journal of Modern History* 53 (1981): 266–71; Hillel Schwartz, *Knaves, Fools, Madmen, and
     that Subtile Effluvium: A Study of the Opposition to the French Prophets in England, 1706–1710* (Gaines-
     ville, Fla., 1978); and Hans-Jürgen Schings, *Melancholie und Aufklärung: Melancholiker und ihre Kritiker
     in der Erfahrungsseelenkunde des 18. Jahrhunderts* (Stuttgart, 1977). On the political significance of "con-
     tagion" as an eighteenth-century moral and social concept, see Jan Goldstein, "'Moral Contagion': A Pro-
     fessional Ideology of Medicine in Eighteenth- and Nineteenth-Century France," in Gerald L. Geison, ed.,
     Professions and the French State, 1700–1900 (Philadelphia, 1984), 185–205.
9.   There are numerous examples in Schings, *Melancholie und Aufklärung*. See also Doris Kaufmann, *Auf-
     klärung, bürgerliche Selbsterfahrung und die "Erfindung" der Psychiatrie in Deutschland, 1770–1850* (Göt-
     tingen, 1995), 55–78.

across huge expanses of time and space; his discourse swept aside the question whether in any given historical context, including his own, the rational and the natural were socially constructed.

This essentialism, however, did not prevent Garve and others from regarding *Schwärmerei* as a matter of degree and locating it on a psycho-physiological continuum. And this, too, had its rhetorical advantages. Where Luther had consigned *Schwärmer* to one side of the battle between the Word and the Devil, rationalism brought them back into the ranks of merely weak and foolish humanity. "Being a *Schwärmer*," Wieland observed, "is no more disgraceful than having a high fever."[10] The implication was that the *Schwärmer* was a helpless victim, not a culprit. Though his fellow human beings could not approve of his behavior, they owed him their sympathy; to one degree or another they too, after all, were vulnerable. This was an inclusion that excluded, a tolerance that stigmatized. Even as the clinical gaze excused the victim, it exempted the clinician from any obligation to take the victim's thoughts and his language seriously; arguing with a *Schwärmer*, it was generally agreed, was futile—he would not, and indeed could not, listen to reason. The diagnosis in itself imposed a necessary intellectual and moral quarantine; the mission of the philosopher-physician was not to heal the sick, but to prevent them from infecting others.

Ultimately, the point of the rhetorical strategy was to fix the boundaries of legitimate public discourse—to police the border between those who qualified at least minimally to take part in the rational dialogue of the public sphere and the others, the ranters and ravers, those too self-deluded to listen. But in the final quarter of the eighteenth century this strategy was breaking down; and that in turn was symptomatic of a larger crisis in the rhetoric of rationalism, and above all in the efforts of "philosophy" to reserve a rhetorical mission for itself.

The signs of breakdown were unmistakable. In the 1780s and 1790s *Schwärmerei* defied repeated efforts to give it the semantic precision Wieland had called for. As Wieland had urged, *Enthusiasmus* (in the positive sense) was separated out; but that left all the more room for a host of exhibits, past and present, of the genuine article. The religious varieties of *Schwärmerei* included—to name but a few—the Hussites, the Anabaptists, the Quakers, the Camisards, German Pietists, French Catholic mystics, the Methodists. Its philosophical cast of characters stretched from Plato to Swedenborg and Rousseau. In the 1780s and 1790s, several developments—among them the popularity of Mesmerism, the exposure of the secret Order of Illuminati, the

10. Wieland, "Schwärmerei und Enthusiasmus," 371.

vogue of sentimental novels, the radical politics of the French Revolution, and the rise of Kant's Critical Philosophy and its Idealist offshoots—seemed to confirm that a century or more of Enlightenment had not eradicated the disease and might even have generated new strains of it.[11]

The irony of Garve's contribution is that his taxonomy—the profusion of categories with which he aspired to restore order—only confirmed that confusion reigned. An epithet had become an all-purpose smear word. As the range of targets widened, Enlightenment rationalism seemed to be shrinking its own purview, atrophying into the intolerance it opposed in principle. On one level, shrinkage was the price paid for semantic sprawl. Precisely because the confluences of sacred and secular meanings had made the term so capacious—because so many aspersions could be cast on so many targets—rationalism opened itself to the charge of arbitrarily walling itself in.

And yet there was also a certain historical logic to the sprawl. The accelerating commercialization of the literary market seemed to give print a new significance both in containing and in spreading the disease. Like "enthusiasm" in the English-speaking world, *Schwärmerei* assumed new (though still familiar) shapes in the ideological arena created by the French Revolution. And then, in the 1780s and 1790s, Kant sought to fix the boundaries between philosophy and *Schwärmerei* once and for all—and found the going very treacherous indeed. Kant's Critical Philosophy offered the discourse of *Schwärmerei* a new kind of clinical precision; but it also confirmed a growing suspicion that philosophical antidotes were really new forms of the disease.

⌘ ⌘

The question Wieland posed to his readers in 1776 was whether "cold-blooded philosophers" do more harm than good in their efforts against *Enthusiasmus* and *Schwärmerei*. Herder's response, in the same year, may have surprised him. Where Wieland assumed philosophy and *Schwärmerei* to be natural enemies, Herder thought of them as "brothers and sisters in spirit [*Geistesgeschwistern*]" who "hate each other because they recognize in each other the same nature [*einerlei Natur*]." "Extremes of the human spirit," they generated each other, like the caterpillar and the butterfly. Whether the leaf was devoured by the caterpiller or disgorged by the butterfly, it became "barren."[12]

11. See esp. Schings, *Melancholie und Aufklärung*. On Rousseau as a *Schwärmer*, see Claus Süssenberger, *Rousseau im Urteil der deutschen Publizistik bis zum Ende der Französischen Revolution* (Berlin, 1974), 184.
12. Johann Gottfried Herder, "Philosophei und Schwärmerei, zwo Schwestern" (1776), in *Herders Sämmtliche Werke*, vol. 9, ed. Bernhard Suphan (Berlin, 18x77), 497–98.

Herder's essay scanned the barren fields of eighteenth-century philosophy, from the "empty" theorems of Christian Wolff to the British "philosophy of healthy human understanding":

> And where does this general healthy human reason, the true phi-losophy of a correct eye, correct images, impressions, etc., live in person? Precisely where Dulcinea of Toboso lived. . . . If it was a philosopher who named our century the age of philosophy, per-haps he understood thereby the century of cold *Schwärmerei* and *schwärmender* coldness. . . . The *Schwärmer* wants to be the great-est philosopher, and the greatest philosopher is the greatest *Schwärmer*. . . . *Schwärmerei* in abstractions of the head fights the abstractions of sensibility (*Empfindung*). . . . A human being who wants to be only head is a monster, as is one who wants to be only heart.[13]

The eighteenth-century discourse of *Schwärmerei* teemed with binary oppositions: heart and head, heat and cold, darkness and light, images and abstractions. In the rationalist version, chimeras rose, vapor-like, from the dark heat of the animal passions; and, by training the cold light of reason on them, the philosopher-clinician recognized them for what they were. Herder might be said to have radically inverted this medical language. In the very ascendancy of the clinical gaze—in the eighteenth-century penchant for cold "abstractions of the head"—he saw the disease assuming new forms.

Herder was not implying that the heat of passion was the source of mental health. Echoing an ideal as old as Protestantism itself, he sought to fix on a pre-carious middle ground, a space where head and heart, so easily given to "extremes," at once infused and restrained each other. Luther had begun to stake out just such a middle ground in the 1520s, when he found himself bat-tling on several fronts. His image of the *Schwärmer* was shaped above all by Thomas Muentzer, the preacher-agitator who joined the Peasants' Rebellion in 1525 and was executed after the battle of Frankenhausen. The "living Word" of the Holy Spirit, Muentzer contended, was "spoken nakedly" in "the abyss of the heart." One heard it only by emulating Christ's suffering in a conversion experience and thereby emptying oneself of the "lower passions." Until con-version pried open the emotional core of the personality, the Bible was a "closed" book of "dead" promises; and simple folk who received God's Word in visions or dreams could dispense with the book entirely. Muentzer accused Luther of becoming one of the "scribes" who sought to entrench their power

---

13. Ibid., 500–502.

and privileges by monopolizing the reading of Scripture. Presuming to "a rational understanding of the Word," the scribes excluded from their pulpits those who had the true calling to preach.[14]

Muentzer's elect would throw off the yoke of "external" authority, whether it lay in the written Word or in ecclesiastical hierarchy. In reaction, Luther insisted that a calling to preach had to be legitimated by an appointment to "office" (*Amt*). His pairing of calling and office was meant to contain emotional subjectivism in two ways: by insisting on the mediating role of human authority (especially the institutional authority to appoint); and by grounding the authority of the preacher in the intellectual discipline of scholarship.

Where "radicals" such as Muentzer felt a divine light (or heard a divine voice) emanating from the abyss of the heart, Luther recoiled from what he viewed as a bottomless pit of subjectivism. Against this danger, he posed the authority of the rationally disciplined mind. And yet Luther was also acutely aware that the disciplinary authority of reason could inflate itself into another kind of subjectivism, no less self-deluding and no less tyrannical. The Lord held his servant fast through the "stirrings" of the heart, not through the consent of the head. Here was the crux of the mystery of Christian freedom in slavery; only in the warmth of emotion could the grip of faith be experienced as a "living knowledge," an immediate, self-generated response. To be "persuaded" by logic and the evidence of the senses was to remain trapped within the corruption of the Flesh. Where there should be "inner" spontaneity, there was an intrusion of "external" power. This kind of coercion found expression in legalism, a rule-bound, literal-minded observance of the Law that deadened the Spirit. Jewish legalism, canon law, scholasticism: these might seem to have little in common, but each in its way represented the arrogant self-delusion of reason. No less arrogant was the reduction of the Word to a rigid set of strictures in Anabaptist sectarianism.[15]

At the close of the eighteenth century, the rhetoric of the philosopher-physician still resonated with Luther's war against solipsistic emotionalism. Diagnoses of the *Schwärmer*'s "sick" imagination fused two layers of metaphorical language about heat and cold, the one medical and particularly Galenic, and the other Lutheran. Luther's targets had taken their place in a parade of *Schwärmer* that extended all the way from the ancient world to the present. Whatever the immediate context, an "overheating," a volcanic eruption of passion, produced self-delusion.

14. Muentzer quoted in Abraham Friesen, *Thomas Muentzer, a Destroyer of the Godless: The Making of a Sixteenth-Century Revolutionary* (Berkeley and Los Angeles, 1990), 125–27, 144–48.
15. See esp. Maurer, "Luther und die Schwärmer"; and Heyd, *Critique of Enthusiasm,* esp. 22–27.

At the center of this diagnosis was the power of the emotion-saturated image. In its overheated state, the imagination—the image-producing faculty—ran riot. The result was an inversion of hierarchy in the economy of cognitive and affective energies, "a kind of conspiracy of the lower powers of the soul against the higher," with "vividness and strong images decid[ing] about reality, possibility, and probability."[16] The affinity between erotic desire and terror—between the *furor poeticus* of the lovesick poet and the rantings of the fire-and-brimstone preacher—lay in the tyranny of such images. The only remedy was a strong dose of conceptual ordering and logical consistency.

It was Luther's campaign on the other front, against the tyranny of reason, however, that echoed through Herder's attack on "cold" *Schwärmerei*. Here again Wieland may have been puzzled by Herder's response. Proceeding from another typically rationalist assumption, Wieland had characterized "cold-blooded philosophers" as "Antiplatonists"—thus assigning them the task of combatting the recurrent impulse to feverish mysticism that was commonly traced back to Plato. Herder chose to ignore Plato and instead attacked modern philosophy. His reference to Wolff's "theorems" that "contain everything and nothing" recalled the seventeenth-century system-builders, with their vast structures of logical demonstration and deduction from supposedly unassailable first principles.[17]

Herder's view of modern philosophy had been deeply influenced by his friend and mentor J. G. Hamann, who described philosophical reason to him in 1780 as "Moses incarnate" (*der leibhafte Moses*).[18] Hamann's phrase is striking; it points to the direct line of descent, and to the tenacious affinities, between the Lutheran image of Judaism as a pseudo-religion of coercive, deadening law and a distinctly German reaction to the oppressive power of modern philosophical "systems." At the "cold" and "abstract" end of the spectrum of *Schwärmerei*, the philosopher's system was one more variation on Jewish legalism. This equation of system-building with *Schwärmerei* gained a whole

16. Daniel Jenisch, "Ueber die Schwärmerey und ihre Quellen in unsern Zeiten," *Magazin zur Erfahrungs-seelenkunde* 5, no. 2 (1787): 31. See also Solomon Maimon, "Ueber die Schwärmerei," *Magazin zur Erfahrungsseelenkunde* 10, no. 2 (1793): 43–48.

17. Herder, "Philosophei und Schwärmerei," 500. This theme dates back at least to criticism of Descartes, who was perceived as advocating a "philosophical" enthusiasm that combined subjective "individualism" and "authoritarianism"; see Heyd, *Critique of Enthusiasm,* 124–39.

18. See esp. Oswald Bayer, "Die Geschichten der Vernunft sind die Kritik ihrer Reinheit: Hamanns Weg zur Metakritik Kants," in Bernhard Gajek, ed., *Hamann-Kant-Herder: Acta des vierten Internationalen Hamann-Kolloquiums im Herder-Institut zu Marburg/Lahn 1985* (Frankfurt am Main, 1987), 19–22. On Hamann's hatred of system, and on its Lutheran roots, see also Isaiah Berlin, *The Magus of the North: J. G. Hamann and the Origins of Modern Irrationalism,* ed. Henry Hardy (New York, 1993), esp. 14, 42–45.

new lease on life with the appearance of Kant's *Critique of Pure Reason* in 1781, but by then it also applied to philosophies that were, by seventeenth-century standards (or indeed by Kantian standards), emphatically antisystematic. In this direction, too, the epithet had become a smear word, as facile in conflating different positions on epistemological issues as the confessional use of the term had been in throwing all sorts of religiosity into one pot.

Again Herder's choice of targets was revealing. French philosophy, like its British counterpart, was a "system of abstraction."[19] Herder ignored the fact that French materialist psychology and British common-sense philosophy, though both indebted to Locke, offered quite different alternatives to the obsessive system-building of the previous century. To him they both exemplified the brutal power of "mechanistic" rationalism. As empirical as they claimed to be, in Herder's view they abstracted a single model of cognition from the intellectual and emotional complexity of the human personality, a universal concept of human nature from the density of particular contexts.

To characterize abstraction as *Schwärmerei* was not simply to attack the excesses of the speculative mind. It was also a way of questioning one of the cognitive procedures on which philosophy grounded its claim to assert a unique public voice. The mission of philosophy, after all, was to make a society and polity self-critical. It did so by abstracting from the particular; by hovering above contextually formed prejudices; by leaping over the constraints of context to project alternative possibilities. But where was the line between the indispensable construction of normative ideals and a visionary "project-making" that was no less self-deluding, and indeed no less the product of imaginative excess, than the unrestrained production of images? And when did the liberating thrust of criticism become the imposition of new forms of despotism?

Herder was suggesting that, like the Law, the abstract universals of modern philosophy substituted formalistic principles for the inner, self-generated freedom of the heart. In his imagery, the cold and the hot—the apparent extremes—actually formed a symbiosis. In another response to Wieland's query, probably written in late 1776, Lessing, drawing on the indigenous resonances of *Schwärmerei,* likewise suggested deep affinities between the extremes—and he did so with an eye to distinctly social and political implications. Lessing's essay proceeds from a familiar polarity: at one end, the contagious heat emanating from the religious *Schwärmer,* whose purpose is to "make a swarm";[20] and, at the other, the cold detachment of the philosopher, who

---

19. Herder, "Philosophei und Schwärmerei," 498–500.
20. "Ueber eine zeitige Aufgabe," in *Gotthold Ephraim Lessings sämtliche Schriften,* ed. Karl Lachmann (1880–1924; reprint, Berlin, 1968), 299. This essay was not published until 1795.

"never has the intention to make a swarm himself and does not easily attach himself to a swarm." It is the difference between the rabble-rouser and the speculative loner. But in "more philosophical times," Lessing suggests, the poles may converge. Hiding behind "a more philosophical mask," the "most dangerous class of *Schwärmer*" now seek to hold a "blind following" by condemning "cold investigation" as "inapplicable to certain things." The true philosopher can respond only by clarifying the concepts in question. And yet even he is tempted to abandon his splendid isolation: "among the *Schwärmer* the philosopher sees so many a brave man who *schwärmt* for the rights of mankind, and with whom, if time and circumstances required him, he would just as soon *schwärmen* as analyze ideas between his four walls."[21]

Lessing's point was that philosophy must remain self-critical, aware of its own will to power. If it did not, the philosopher's cold detachment might transmute itself into the heated frenzy of the mob. It was a prescient view—one that many German observers would see confirmed in the volatile bonding of philosophy and popular politics in the French Revolution.

❧   ❧

From its origins in Luther's invective, the discourse of *Schwärmerei* was about the efficacy and the abuse of language, both written and spoken.

Thomas Muentzer railed at the "scribes" for reducing faith to "an external matter, an intellectual assent to words." Luther in turn found that Muentzer's inflammatory preaching used "an absurd jargon and words not found in the holy Scripture, so that one might believe him to be either drunk or mad."[22] At issue was the relationship between the Word and the Flesh, between subjectivity and externality. If externality in all its forms partook of the corruption of the Flesh, as Muentzer believed, there could be no visual or vocal mediation between the Holy Spirit and the human soul. In the trauma of conversion, the Holy Spirit became an immediate, indwelling presence, an "inner light." This was the "living Word"; without it, even the words of Scripture—whether they were the visible signs on the printed page or the sounds uttered from a pulpit—represented fleshly corruption and spiritual death.

In his efforts to counteract this impulse to radical subjectivism, Luther insisted on the mediating authority of the external. The Flesh was corrupt, but only through its objects and representations did the Lord reveal his mys-

21. Ibid., 299–300.
22. Quoted in Friesen, *Thomas Muentzer,* 125, 144.

teries. The printed and the spoken word were the media for the invisible, the transcendent; for like the sacraments, they perpetuated the miracle of the Incarnation.[23]

In the Lutheran Church, mediation was the responsibility of the educated preacher, properly installed in office. When he interpreted Scripture before the assembled community, he was not simply enforcing a public orthodoxy; the interpretation exhibited a public language, the only system of visible and spoken signs through which the Word became Flesh and sanctified the Flesh. The ignorant artisan who "made a swarm"—who acted on his "call" to preach and attracted crowds in the fields—threw into question the authoritative status of public communication. He sought to arrogate "public" status for a "private" revelation—one that had not been effected by the Word as shared text, and that could not be communicated through the language of that text.

In the "enlightened" Protestant cultures of the late eighteenth century, the expectations invested in print still echoed with Luther's reverence for the Word made Flesh, although the mediating authority of print had been desacralized. As a vehicle of public exchange, print served not to convey a transcendent authority but to generate an authoritative consensus. It generated that consensus by enforcing the principle of "publicity," which tested the truth value of ideas by opening them to public scrutiny and contestation.[24] "The surest test of the truth," Garve observed, "is the clear communication through words"; and hence "everything inexpressible is more or less *schwärmerisch*." Kant made much the same point; the imagination *schwärmt* when its "illuminations . . . do not wish to be seen in the light and to allow themselves to be tested."[25]

To pass the test of public scrutiny was to acquire an authoritative status, to enter the public realm of rationally demonstrated knowledge. Print, in other words, still countered the solipsistic impulse with externality; it pulled subjectivity out of itself, into properly structured intersubjectivity. If the *Schwärmer* was no longer the Devil's mouthpiece, he was still a babbler, presuming to communicate private whims and fantasies to others and turning a deaf ear to public criticism. The obscurantist impulse might result in the harmless passivity of the

23. On subjectivism and externality, see esp. Maurer, "Luther und die Schwärmer"; Heyd, *Critique of Enthusiasm,* 22–27; and George Huntston Williams, "Sanctification in the Testimony of Several So-Called *Schwärmer*," in Ivar Asheim, ed., *Kirche, Mystik, Heiligung und das Natürliche bei Luther* (Göttingen, 1967), 194–211.

24. There is an insightful statement of the Enlightenment's ideal of print communication in Roger Chartier, *The Cultural Origins of the French Revolution,* trans. Lydia G. Cochrane (Durham, N.C., 1991), 20–37. See also Anthony J. La Vopa, "Conceiving a Public: Ideas and Society in Eighteenth-Century Europe," *Journal of Modern History* 64 (1992): 98–112.

25. Garve, "Ueber die Schwärmerey," 396; and Norbert Hinske, "Zur Verwendung der Wörter 'schwärmen,' 'Schwärmerei,' 'schwärmerisch,' im Kontext von Kants Anthropologiekolleg," *Aufklärung* 3, no. 1 (1988): 77.

quietist sect; but, when it built walls of secrecy, as in occult varieties of free-masonry or in the Order of Illuminati, it posed the danger of conspiracy. And, if the "nonsense" of *Schwärmerei* sometimes turned in on itself, it also revealed an alarming capacity to invade public space, both physical and discursive. The history of Christianity offered abundant examples, and in the early 1790s the mob violence of the French Revolution was adding to them.

In such cases *Schwärmerei* became "fanaticism," the mob spellbound by the language of fantasy. When the *Schwärmer* plunged into self-absorption—when the images that promised privileged insight trapped him in self-referentiality—subjectivity devoured itself; when he was absorbed into the mob, his subjectivity was blotted out. Did one form of self-extinction lead to the other? In an essay on Methodism as a kind of enthusiasm, Herder suggested that there was a perverse dialectic between unrestrained subjectivism and collective frenzy—or, perhaps better, between the implosion of the individual self and the explosion of the collective self. "Enthusiasm," Herder noted, has been attributed to "the inclination of the human being to flee himself":

> The human being is bound to the world with a thousand ties; restricted to himself, he finds himself in the narrowest prison. Whoever loosens him from himself, whoever creates a free, lively game for his energies, is his God, his Awakener. And he plays on him as on an instrument; if the flute tones, if his inner string sounds, he feels good; he lets it play. Hence the pleasure of the people to be put into enthusiasm; hence the drive and the joy of enthusiastic spirits to fill others with enthusiasm, to inspire them.[26]

This dialectic, Herder went on to observe, explained "the evil psychology" of hyper-Pietism (*Pietisterei*): "confused" and "weak," the isolated, self-absorbed personality follows an inspired "leader" who "forces him back into himself or forcefully turns the inwardness outward."[27]

It was rhetoric or, more precisely, the abuse of rhetoric that "forcefully turn[ed] the inwardness outward." The image of the power-hungry, manipulative orator—the virtuoso playing on the strings of a crowd—haunts the philosophical diagnosis of *Schwärmerei*. It marks a suspicion of oral performance that had its roots in ancient Greek philosophy and that found confirmation

---

26. J. G. Herder, "Enthusiasmus: Methodisten" (1802–3), in *Herders Sämmtliche Werke,* vol. 24, ed. Bernhard Suphan (Berlin, 1886), 149.
27. Ibid., 152.

again and again in the social volatility of radical Protestantism in the sixteenth and seventeenth centuries. The lesson to be drawn from the success of the "enthusiastic" preacher—whether his appeal was to the elect or to the people—was that the devices of rhetoric were perverted all too easily into coercive power. One form of rhetorical coercion was illusory logic, or sophistry; but a much more common one was figural language—a language of compelling images and metaphors—that ignited the imagination and unleashed the passions. In the physical community formed by the orator and his audience, words conducted heat. "Extravagant" language, packed with volatile images, had its visual counterpart in the ecstatic visage, the spasmodic movement. Sight and sound reinforced each other to produce a frenzied conformity, wild in its obliviousness to rational argument, and yet abjectly subservient to the "leader." Herder described "a usurped rule over the temperaments and passions of other, weaker people," with "ecstasy flying from face to face . . . on voices, on words and gestures."[28]

↩ ↪

With this spectre always looming before it in one form or another, the Enlightenment shaped its ideal of the modern public as a communion of autonomous readers. The enlightened reader avoided the *Schwärmer*'s extremes of isolation and total immersion, introversion and total conformity. Print allowed him to engage ideas in socially connected solitude. Whereas the *Schwärmer* was sucked into the crowd, the reader withdrew to the silent privacy of his study, where he could exercise his autonomous judgment. The very impersonality of print and the print market insulated the reader from the "seductive" pull of the orator's voice and the contagious swarming of the crowd. The text was a commodity he could use or put aside at will. Rather than being deafened by sounds and blinded by gestures, he scanned, at his own pace, and with a certain impersonal distance, the mute, fixed signs on the page. And yet there was also something personal, or at least something sociable, about this impersonality. It was a truism that reading was, or ought to be, a conversation between friends. The wonderful thing about friendship was that it bonded two selves as moral and intellectual equals, each respecting the integrity of the other, each drawing the

28. Ibid., 156–57. On the German view of rhetoric as an abuse of power, see Anthony J. La Vopa, "Herder's *Publikum:* Language, Print, and Sociability in Eighteenth-Century Germany," *Eighteenth-Century Studies* 29 (1995): 18–20. For parallel views in the Anglo-American world, see Heyd, "The Reactions to Enthusiasm," 265–66; Weckermann, *Die Figur des Enthusiasten,* passim; and George Williamson, "The Restoration Revolt against Enthusiasm," in *Seventeenth-Century Contexts* (London, 1960), 202–39.

other out into the give-and-take of criticism. In the *Schwärmer*'s abuse of rhetoric, sound was a supple instrument of subjection, shaped to the social particularity and tuned to the emotional resonances of an actual context. In the ideal relationship between reader and author, sound, as conversation, was the imagined social context for egalitarian communion.

In the last quarter of the century, however, the discourse of *Schwärmerei* came to reflect a certain disillusionment with print culture. There was a new surge in the production of print, marked above all by the proliferation of newspapers, periodicals, and "sentimental" novels. Hopes that this commercial expansion would make possible a truly "popular" enlightenment were accompanied by laments that the printed page was being trivialized as a mere commodity and reading was becoming a mindless act of material consumption.[29]

In the early 1790s, the sense of alarm about a spreading "reading addiction" was heightened by the radical political journalism of the French Revolution. As Edmund Burke reminded readers of his *Reflections* in 1790, revolutionary ideology infected the Parisian populace not only through "sermons delivered in all the streets and places of public resort" but also through "a multitude of writings, dispersed with incredible assiduity and expense."[30] In a sense, though, this nightmare only confirmed forebodings that were suggested in the literary realm well before 1789. The immediate occasion for Wieland's effort to disentangle *Enthusiasmus* and *Schwärmerei* in 1775 had been a literary storm, not a political upheaval. In the previous year Goethe's *The Sorrows of Young Werther* had appeared. The novel's success in winning devotees among educated young men—the cult of alienated "genius" it occasioned—jolted rationalists as well as orthodox clergymen. Garve's criticism of the novel is a case in point, though it was more measured than most. He admired Goethe's capacity to empathize with his acutely sensitive character, but could not forgive his use of "all the strength of [his] eloquence" to conceal the "false concepts" that had led Werther into "isolation" and "merely unsociable meditation."[31]

It was a measure of Werther's addiction that he became "sick of books," even as his reading drew him down the path to feverish introversion and thence

29. See esp. Helmuth Kiesel and Paul Munch, *Gesellschaft und Literatur im 18. Jahrhundert: Voraussetzungen und Entstehung der literarischen Markt in Deutschland* (Munich, 1977); Albert Ward, *Book Production, Fiction, and the German Reading Public, 1740–1800* (Oxford, 1974), 114–62; and Jochen Schulte-Sasse, *Die Kritik an der Trivialliteratur seit der Aufklärung* (Munich, 1971).
30. Edmund Burke, *Reflections on the Revolution in France,* ed. Conor Cruise O'Brien (New York, 1986), 262.
31. Christian Garve, "Aus einem Briefe," in *Popularphilosophische Schriften*, vol. 1, reprint ed. (Stuttgart, 1974), 27–32. On the controversy provoked by *Werther,* see Klaus R. Scherpe, *Werther und Wertherwirkung: Zum Syndrom bürgerlicher Gesellschaftsordnung im 18. Jahrhundert* (Bad Homberg, 1970).

to suicide. For the most part he read on isolated walks in the countryside; the immersion in the text and the withdrawal into nature reinforced each other. Here the power of print lay not in effecting a mediation between the self and society, but in nourishing a subjectivism that proved self-destructive.

Ironically, Goethe was more clinical, if not more willing to pass moral judgment, than Garve recognized. He was chagrined that readers of his own generation revered Werther as an inspiring hero. Werther, he informed a correspondent, is "gifted with a deep pure sensitivity [*Empfindsamkeit*] and true penetration," but "loses himself in *schwärmende* dreams."[32] It is precisely this awareness of the short step from emotional depth to an abyss of introversion—from the vaulting insight of the genius to *Schwärmerei*—that makes it so difficult to fix the relationship between Goethe as authorial persona and Werther as his fictive alter-ego. Confronting the world through Werther's eyes, the reader sees the shallowness and the intolerance of rationalist clinicians; and yet Werther is also the object of a diagnostic judgment, confirming their diagnosis of *Schwärmerei* as a corruption of natural energies.

By the 1790s it was conventional wisdom in rationalist discourse that modern print culture, and particularly fiction, was producing secular mutations of *Schwärmerei*. In the proposal he issued in 1783 for a magazine on "experimental psychology," Karl Philipp Moritz, a young protegé of the Berlin Enlightenment, had blamed novels for hermetically sealing their readers in a world of "ideals."[33] Moritz demonstrated the point in *Anton Reiser*, a "psychological novel" published in four parts from 1785 to 1790. His novel is in fact autobiographical, but he divides his autobiographical self into a third-person character (Anton) and a detached narrator who at once empathizes with the character and analyzes the causes and effects of his pathological insecurity. Hence the clinical gaze is built into the very narrative structure of the text. And that in turn allows Moritz to trace his alienated withdrawal back to his initiation under his father's tutelage to the "dry, metaphysical *Schwärmerei*" of the French mystic Madame Guyon. Through Guyon's writings, the child Anton enters an existential void by striving to achieve a state of "nothingness," to "exit from oneself." His reading of fiction (including *Werther*) and poetry as a schoolboy—far from pulling him out—fills the void with paralyzing fantasies.[34]

32. Goethe to G. F. E. Schönborn (1774); quoted in Schings, *Melancholie und Aufklärung*, 274.
33. Karl Philipp Moritz, "Vorschlag zu einem *Magazin einer Erfahrungs-Seelenkunde*," *Magazin zur Erfahrungsseelenkunde* 1 (1783): no page (originally published in *Deutsches Museum* 1 [1782]: 485–503).
34. Karl Philipp Moritz, *Anton Reiser: Ein Psychologischer Roman* (Frankfurt am Main, 1980), esp. 11–15, 252–59. On Moritz and his "novel," see also Mark Boulby, *Karl Philipp Moritz: At the Fringe of Genius* (Toronto, 1979), 3–50; and Anthony J. La Vopa, *Grace, Talent, and Merit: Poor Students, Clerical Careers, and Professional Ideology in Eighteenth-Century Germany* (Cambridge, 1988), 97–110.

To the elders of the *Aufklärung*, looking back from the 1790s, *Werther* had marked the beginning of an avalanche of "sentimental" and "trivial" novels. In language reminiscent of Luther's insistence on the externality of the Word, Garve observed that reading had to be undertaken as a physical act, an engagement with an external thing. Like seeing and hearing, reading ought to prevent the self from taking "refuge" in the "empty imaginings" of the *Schwärmer*.[35] But novels had failed to provide this engagement and instead seemed to have become vehicles of escapism. If the print market could effect a new kind of communion, it also made for new variations on the *Schwärmer*'s paradox of ordered disorder and on the underlying dialectic between isolated introversion and mass conformity. Self-indulgent subjectivity replaced the rigorous self-examination that reading ought to effect. Pulled outward into the aimless flux of consumption, the self was distended to the point of extinction.

This perception marks the sense of disappointment, even bitterness, with which an academic and literary intelligentsia, aspiring to be the authoritative voice of a new public culture, saw itself increasingly undercut by the expansion of the print market. At stake was philosophical and scientific rigor as well as aesthetic standards. In 1790, in a letter to his friend Ernst Borowski, Kant assumed the voice of the philosopher-clinician to vent his frustration about the popularity of the Mesmerist Cagliostro. In this charlatan and his following, Kant saw a new epidemic of *Schwärmerei*. He blamed it on "the universally disseminated *mania for reading*," which was not only "the guiding instrument (vehicle) in the spread of this disease," but also "the poison (miasma) that engenders it." In a sense, Mesmerism was an unusual case; particularly at risk were not the popular classes, but the "well-to-do," whose consumption of print was lazy and superficial. But "from there," Kant warned, "the mania spreads out also into the community."[36]

---

35. Garve, "Ueber die Schwärmerey," 404.
36. Immanuel Kant, "On Exaltation and the Remedy for It" (1790), in Fenves, ed., *Raising the Tone*, 107–8. The letter was published as the introduction to Borowski's pamphlet on Cagliostro. On Kant's view of the print market, see also his "Über die Buchmacherei: Zwei Briefe an Herrn Friedrich Nicolai," in *Kants gesammelte Schriften*, ed. Königlich Preussichen Akademie der Wissenschaften, vol. 8, pt. 1 (Berlin and Leipzig, 1912), 431–38.

✎ ✎

In December 1790, Friedrich Gentz spoke for many German observers when he hailed the French Revolution as "the first practical triumph of philosophy, the first example in the history of the world of the construction of government upon the principles of an orderly, rational system."[37] Over the next several years, this vision of a brave new world acceded to a politically charged perception that the Revolution had unleashed *Schwärmerei* with a vengeance. It became a commonplace of German antirevolutionary discourse that philosophical *Schwärmerei* was assuming especially virulent forms in the rhetoric of radical intellectuals and in the frenzy of violent mobs.

That perception was shaped in part, of course, by Burke's *Reflections,* which appeared in Germany in Gentz's translation in 1793. In Burke's rhetoric, a subtle process of adaptation—the recasting of a weapon of Protestant polemic to meet the needs of an emerging arena of modern ideological contestation—was completed. Burke's indictment of what he called the "philosophic revolution" rested on two linked paradoxes: that revolutionary ideology, for all its anti-Christian animus, was directly descended from the "enthusiastic" excesses of Christianity; and that its appeal to universal principles, with all they implied about the illegitimacy of particular interests, camouflaged the combined power of a "monied interest" and "the political Men of Letters." In a sense, Burke's Men of Letters were the successors to generations of field preachers; both operated beyond the disciplining hand of patronage. But there was a critical difference. The field preachers had gathered crowds on the fringes of public space; the *gens de lettre* controlled the public circulation of "opinion."[38]

It was the coldness of it all that Burke hated—the "mechanical" and ultimately brutalizing coldness of universal abstractions, oblivious to the affections and loyalties that human beings develop naturally, within the warm embrace of particular, inherited contexts. The coercive power long attributed to philosophy's "systematic reasoning" had revealed itself as ideological brutality. If revolutionary ideology was "the offspring of cold hearts," however, it was also "enthusiasm" in "full blaze."[39] Burke's rhetoric, like Herder's and Lessing's,

---

37. Quoted in Klaus Epstein, *The Genesis of German Conservatism* (Princeton, N.J., 1966), 436.
38. Burke, *Reflections,* esp. 211–14. My analysis of the *Reflections* is indebted to J. G. A. Pocock, "The Political Economy of Burke's Analysis of the French Revolution," in *Virtue, Commerce, and History: Essays on Political Thought and History, Chiefly in the Eighteenth Century* (Cambridge, 1985), 193–212; and Pocock, "Edmund Burke and the Redefinition of Enthusiasm," in François Furet and Mona Ozouf, eds., *The Transformation of Political Culture, 1789–1848,* vol. 3, *The French Revolution and the Creation of Modern Political Culture* (Oxford, 1989), 19–43. Particularly important for my purposes is Pocock's contrast of "enthusiasm" and "contextuality."
39. Burke, *Reflections,* 165–72.

transformed the conventional polarity of heat and cold into a metaphorical blending. In the mob, the brutality of system became a collective heat, a frenzy feeding on its own violence. The Münster Anabaptists, with their "system of leveling," had anticipated the "spirit of atheistic fanaticism" that "filled the populace [of Paris] with a black and savage atrocity of mind, which supersedes in them the common feelings of nature, as well as all sentiments of morality and religion."[40]

German critics of the Revolution found inspiration in Burke, but they were not simply echoing him. Their own misgivings about philosophical *Schwärmerei*, deeply rooted in the Lutheran tradition, already pointed them in the same direction. Two images—the one of systematic reasoning as a dehumanizing form of power, and the other of mass politics as religious fanaticism in a new guise—fused into the trope of popular revolution as an outbreak of *Schwärmerei*. In the fusion, what might have seemed blatantly contradictory—could a revolution really be at once "metaphysical" and "democratic"?—became an instructive paradox. Garve observed that the human being "distances himself" from "the actual visible world" when he distills "abstract concepts" from "sense impressions," just as when he "depicts unreal [*sich abwesende*] scenes in the imagination." Ascending "to an order of things that exists nowhere, and of which there is not even a definite concept," the new political *Schwärmer* produced "the same derangement as the *Religionsschwärmerey* of earlier times."[41]

Cries of alarm about *Schwärmerei* always had implicit political agendas, but now the politicization of the epithet was evident, and the accusations assumed recognizably modern forms. The discourse had produced a kind of secular demonology. Stigmatizing popular revolution as *Schwärmerei* in effect dismissed the possibility that the Revolution was giving expression to legitimate popular grievances. In the grip of ideology—so this ideological twist in the discourse would have it—individuals surrendered the intellectual and moral autonomy on which any rational formation of "opinion" would have to be grounded. Mass grievances had produced something unnatural and monstrous. There could no greater contrast to the "natural" (that is, gradual and orderly) process of enlightenment from above that Wieland and other *Aufklärer* had long envisioned as the alternative to revolution. As revolutionary politics became more democratic, Wieland concluded that the French had not been morally prepared to "know how to be free"; they had made "a leap that

40. Ibid., 172, 262.
41. Garve, "Ueber die Schwärmerey," 340, 373.

Nature never makes."[42] Figured as "the contagion of *Schwärmerey*," popular mobilization was the collective analogue to individual pathology, the violent spasm of a diseased (or corrupted) body.

❧ ❧

We have seen the discourse of *Schwärmerei* increasingly secularized in several ways in the last quarter of the eighteenth century. All brought new complexities to the relationship between the philosopher and the *Schwärmer*. The philosopher-clinician still had abundant evidence that "the age of Enlightenment" was not immune to new epidemics of religious *Schwärmerei*; but to Garve, as to many others, a number of phenomena—the addiction to novel-reading, the cult of genius, the appeal of Mesmerism—were alarming reminders that secular forms of print communication were another source of hyper-emotional subjectivism. But there were senses in which the extremes of head and heart—the hyper-rationality of system-building and the hyper-emotionalism of individual and collective fantasy—were mirror images. They seemed to have an alarming tendency to converge, particularly in mass politics. In the emotionalism of revolutionary politics, as in religious fervor, individual introversion and collective frenzy entered a frightening dialectic. Philosophical *Schwärmer* abused reason's claim to public authority, thus giving false legitimacy to a congeries of private subjectivisms, each in its way imposing "system" as an arbitrary regime.

Within this dense semantic field, where binary opposites so easily became points of convergence, Kant made his contribution to the discourse of *Schwärmerei*. In the preparatory notes for his lectures on philosophical anthropology, delivered from 1772 to 1798, we find Kant clarifying the term *Schwärmerei* repeatedly. Though he distinguished *Schwärmerei* carefully from the true *Enthusiasmus* of the original genius, he otherwise used it as a kind a diagnostic catch-all, with ample room for madness, melancholy, mysticism, biblical literalism, excessive introspection, traditional metaphysics, and "lazy free-thinking."[43]

---

42. Quoted in Bernd Weyergraf, *Der skeptische Bürger: Wielands Schriften zur französischen Revolution* (Stuttgart, 1972), 30–40. Perhaps the clearest echo of Burke's indictment of French radicalism as metaphysical "enthusiasm" is August Wilhelm Rehberg, *Untersuchungen über die französische Revolution,* 2 vols. (Hanover, 1793). Rehberg also prefers "Schwärmer" to "Enthusiast."

43. The comments on *Schwärmerei* from the lecture notes and from *Anthropologie in pragmatischer Hinsicht* (1798) have been reprinted in Hinske, "Zur Verwendung der Wörter," 373–81.

This definitional sweep notwithstanding, Kant had reason to claim that he was subjecting *Schwärmerei* to new order of public clarity, at least within the dualistic terms of his own system. There were two antidotes to *Schwärmerei*: reason's capacity to critique itself, and the unrestricted openness of "public" communication. Truth claims proved their objectivity by passing the test of relentless public scrutiny, in an arena where the only legitimate power was the cogency of ideas. Such a process was now possible because reason, by critiquing itself, had made it clear that the a priori categories of theoretical understanding—the categories with which the mind ordered raw sense experience—could not be applied to the supersensible. The *Schwärmer's* inner voices and emotionally charged visions were mere chimeras, emblems of reason's failure to police itself. By refusing to violate the limits imposed by its own cognitive structure, reason legitimized its right to judge in its proper jurisdictions. Above all, reason opened itself to the certainty of practical (or moral) truths. God's attributes or the nature of the afterlife are unknowable, but it was a necessary corollary of the Moral Law that God existed and that the soul was immortal.

In addition to his *Critiques,* Kant published a series of more or less polemical essays from the mid-1780s to the late 1790s. He could not engage in polemics without folding his technical terminology into the more resonant but less controllable discourse of *Schwärmerei.* And that meant that he had entered a minefield. Even as he hurled the epithet at opponents on all sides, he had to dodge it. Why was his own "system" not one more example of the arbitrary power of philosophical abstractions? If he tried to provide a counterpoint in "feeling" to the rational dictates of the Moral Law, was he not inevitably entering a path to hyper-subjectivity? And, if he entered that path, was he not claiming "public" status for what was merely private experience? Was he not indulging in the same abuse of figurative language and the same cult of secrecy that he castigated in others? As we watch Kant negotiating these issues, we come to appreciate why, in his efforts to avoid dangers on all sides, he pursued strategies that now seem excessively intricate, if not convoluted.[44]

The first of these polemical essays is "What Does It Mean to Orient Oneself in Thought?" Published in the *Berlinische Monatsschrift* in 1786, it was Kant's long expected contribution to the Spinoza controversy. Over the previous three years the stakes in the controversy had risen dramatically: having originally been asked simply to decide whether Lessing had in fact been a secret

---

44. The most recent and successful attempt to place Kant's essays within the larger constellation of ideological forces in late-eighteenth-century Germany is Steven K. Lestition, "Kant and the End of the Enlightenment in Prussia," *Journal of Modern History* 65 (1993): 57–112. On Kant's polemical tactics see Hans Saner, *Kant's Political Thought, Its Origin and Development,* trans. E. B. Ashton (Chicago, 1973).

Spinozist (as Friedrich Jacobi claimed), the educated public was now faced with a fundamental choice between faith and reason. As Jacobi's unorthodox but still deeply Lutheran fideism confronted the rationalist metaphysics of Moses Mendelssohn, the polar meanings of *Schwärmerei* collided. Jacobi and his young protegé, Thomas Wizenmann, argued that, if philosophical rationality was consequential, it led inexorably to determinism and atheism. Atheism, in other words, became the logical consequence of *Schwärmerei* as system, the confirmation that the despotism of systematic abstraction snuffed out spontaneous belief. To Mendelssohn and other *Aufklärer* in Berlin, Jacobi's alternative—the immediate intuition of God in a *salto mortale*—substituted emotional self-delusion for rational demonstration.[45]

What finally pulled Kant into the controversy was a letter from Friedrich Biester, the coeditor of the *Berlinische Monatsschrift*, urging him to intervene on behalf of Mendelssohn and his allies. If Kant did not end the "disorder," Biester warned, his silence would be taken as agreement with Jacobi that "philosophy" inevitably ended in atheism, the most alarming species of philosophical *Schwärmerei*.[46] Kant's essay left no doubt that he intended to preclude that misperception. His stated purpose was to support Mendelssohn's contention that we know that God exists, and that the soul is immortal, through "actual pure human reason," and not through "a pretended secret sense of truth." As the latter phrase implied, Jacobi's and Wizenmann's intuitionism threatened to license still another descent into the cultish subjectivism of *Schwärmerei*. They were indulging in "flights of genius," and thereby initiating a process in which blind submission to "guardians" and "formulas of belief" would replace the freedom to think and to communicate publicly.[47]

Kant ended the essay with a warning to "the genius" that "delights itself with its daring flights, having cast aside the thread with which reason formerly guided it." He sketched out "the rough course of things" that would ensue from such recklessness:

45. Immanuel Kant, "Was Heisst: Sich im Denken Orientieren." The translation of this essay in *Kant: Political Writings*, ed. Hans Reiss, 2d ed., enlarged (Cambridge, 1991), 237–49, uses "zealotry" (rather than "enthusiasm" or "fanaticism") for *Schwärmerei*, noting that it "is perhaps the least unsatisfactory term in the present context" (p. 284). There is an insightful discussion of the essay in Lestition, "Kant and the End of the Enlightenment," 75–86. On the Spinoza (or "Pantheism") Controversy and Kant's intervention, see esp. Frederick C. Beiser, *The Fate of Reason: German Philosophy from Kant to Fichte* (Cambridge, Mass., 1987), 44–126.
46. Biester to Kant, 6 March 1786 and 11 June 1786, in *Kant's gesammelte Schriften,* ed. Königlich Preussischen Akademie der Wissenschaften, vol. 10, 2d Abteilung (Briefwechsel), vol. 1 (1747–88) (Berlin, 1900), 410, 429–34.
47. Kant, "Was Heisst: Sich im Denken Orientieren," 267–68, 278–82.

[The genius] soon entrances others through claims to power and great expectations, and appears from now on to have set itself up on a throne which slow and cumbersome Reason had so poorly adorned; and yet it still applies to itself the language of Reason. The accepted maxim—that the supreme legislation of reason is invalid—we ordinary people call *Schwärmerei;* these favorites of a benevolent Nature call it *illumination.* A chaos of language must soon spring up among these, since Reason alone can command validly for each person, but now each follows his own inspiration. Thus in the end, through witnesses, externally guaranteed facts must arise from inner inspiration, traditions that were originally freely chosen eventually become binding documents, in a word, the complete subjection of Reason to facts—i.e., superstition— must ensue, because this can at least be reduced to a legal form and thus peace can be restored.[48]

Echoing the familiar trope of contagion, Kant describes how the inner self-delusion of the *Schwärmer* externalizes itself and overpowers an audience. In his variation, however, the result is not the frenzy of the mob but the coercive power of system, in the form of authoritarian legalism. A chaotic proliferation of private inspirations—a proliferation in which language ceases to effect public exchanges—inevitably accedes to institutionally enforced dogma.

Kant's point was that, if reason was to retain its objective authority, it had to avoid abusing its freedom. And yet Kant was also acutely aware that the Moral Law itself would be held responsible for precluding freedom—it would, in fact, represent a new tyranny of system, imposing abstraction from without—if it were not in some sense subjective, and indeed if it did not somehow endow reason with an affective impulse. A morality deprived of "all power of springs to the heart [*Triebfedern auf das Herz*]" would eventually lose "all authority."[49] He needed an epistemologically legitimate analogue to the inner spontaneity of the Lutheran believer—an irreducible feeling within reason itself, and hence not vulnerable to corruption into *Schwärmerei.*

The pivotal move was to shift from "theoretical" understanding of the sense world, where Mendelssohn had pursued his speculations, to "practical" (that is, moral) knowledge. The concept of God as "the highest independent good," Kant argued, was a "belief of reason" (*Vernunftglaube*). Kant had introduced a richly paradoxical term, making belief in God a "subjective" maxim of practical

48. Ibid., 280–82.
49. Ibid., 282.

reason, and not, as Mendelssohn would have it, an "objective principle" of theoretical reason. Aware that he might seem to be opening the door to fideism and
thence to *Schwärmerei*, Kant took great pains to keep the door shut tight. What
he had in mind was not the irrational subjectivity in which Jacobi took refuge;
Vernunftglaube did not imply a blind "leap of faith." Rather, the assumption
that God exists was a "postulate," produced by a felt "need" of practical reason,
and grounded only in the "data" of "pure reason." Unlike theoretical knowledge
of the natural world, a "belief of reason" could not be demonstrated; even so, it
was different in kind from such knowledge, not inferior to it in degree.[50]

Hence Kant tried to suffuse the Moral Law with a subjective certainty—a
felt need that was entirely different from the religious *Schwärmer*'s self-deluding
emotionalism, and yet, unlike the philosophical *Schwärmer*'s relentless abstractions, secured an inner space for spontaneity. To his critics, particularly among
the younger generation, his project remained suspect at both ends. Wizenmann's response to Kant's essay attacked it at its most vulnerable point—and
paid him back in kind. Kant's concept of a *Vernunftglaube* moved from the felt
presence of a need to the existence of an object that would satisfy it. Was that
not the essence of the self-delusion called *Schwärmerei*?[51] Ironically, others—
most notably Wilhelm von Humboldt and Georg Forster—found no space for
feeling in the abstract formalism of Kant's ethics. Conceiving of the
"personality" as an *Individualität,* a unique symbiosis of thought and feeling,
spirit and sensuality, they complained that the Kantian obsession with abstract
universals would produce a "systematic tyranny of the soul," a "slavish, petty
uniformity in heads." Again the polar opposites were turning out to be mirror
images. In religious *Schwärmerei*, "the most secret interior of the capacity for
feeling" had yielded "absolute truth"; its modern counterpart was a philosophy
that aimed to "banish human beings to a magic circle of system."[52]

With the concept of a "belief of reason," Kant sought to counter the charge
that his system was dehumanizing. What he could not do was abandon his
insistence that philosophy produce abstract universals systematically. However
much system might seem to threaten the self-cultivation of the individual, it
was essential to philosophy's mission as the public conscience, the source of the
regulative ideas needed to critique the status quo and guide reform. Kant had
defended this mission in his introduction to the concept of "transcendental

---

50. Ibid., 274–78.
51. Beiser, *The Fate of Reason,* 119–20.
52. Georg Forster, "Über lokale und allgemeine Bildung" (1791); and "Über den gelehrten Zunftzwang: Vorrede
    zu Volneys Ruinen," in Foster, *Werke in vier Bänden,* ed. Gerhard Steiner, vol. 3 (1967), 279–84 and
    372–73.

ideas" in the *Critique of Pure Reason*. Framed as a corrective to the conventional stereotype of Plato as the "*Ur-Schwärmer*" in philosophy, the defense was calculated to provoke. Kant acknowledged that Plato's thought was a kind of "mysticism," full of "extravagances"; but, detached from his mysticism, Plato's concept of pure "ideas" was by no means chimerical. Such ideas included—in addition to the a priori categories of the understanding—normative archetypes of virtue and legal order. The *Republic*, so often dismissed as an "idle" pursuit of "visionary perfection," merited "respect and imitation" for laying out the ideal of human freedom with which law and government ought to be "brought into harmony." Only by "following out" this "spiritual flight" to an "architectonic ordering . . . according to ends" did philosophy acquire "its peculiar dignity."[53]

Sometime in the mid-1790s, in an essay on moral progress, Kant returned to this theme, once again pointing to Plato's *Republic* as the source of "the eternal norm for all civil constitutions whatsoever."[54] By then, opponents of the Revolution (including Burke and Garve) were contrasting philosophical and political *Schwärmerei* with true political wisdom, which was the product of the statesman's "practice" and "experience," not the philosopher's abstract "theory." Fearing that this logic would justify immobilism—that it would preclude reform as well as revolution—Kant came to the defense of theory. In an unpublished early draft of the essay on moral progress, he issued an explicit challenge to the recent politicization of the discourse of *Schwärmerei*. Now it was not simply apocalyptic prophecies and millenarian visions of total rebirth that were being branded as *Schwärmerei*. "Well-intentioned pure moral philosophers" were applying the epithet to those who believed that the "human species" would experience "continual progress toward the better."[55]

The draft registers Kant's awareness that a priori theory, by itself, would not suffice to counter this appeal to experience in defense of the status quo; ideals had to have their own experiential grounding, or at least their own historical moment of awareness for "people in the mass." What was needed to confirm the belief in moral progress, Kant argued, was a historically contingent but "undeniably public" experience—an experience in which "moral capacities

53. Immanuel Kant, *Critique of Pure Reason,* trans. Norman Kemp Smith (New York, 1965), 309–13. Kant's most ambitious defenses of theory against "experience" and pragmatism are "On the Common Saying: 'This may be true in theory, but it does not apply in practice'" (1793), and "Perpetual Peace: A Philosophical Sketch" (1795), in *Kant: Political Writings,* 61–130.
54. "Ob das menschliche Geschlecht im beständigen Fortschreiten zum Besseren sei," in *Immanuel Kant. Politische Schriften,* ed. Otto Heinrich von der Gablentz (Cologne and Opladen, 1965), 162–63. The essay was published in *Der Streit der Fakultäten, zweiter Abschnitt: Der Streit der philosophischen Fakultät mit der juristischen* (1798). It is also available in *Kant: Political Writings,* 177–90.
55. "Krakauer Fragment zum 'Streit der Fakultäten,'" in *Immanuel Kant: Politische Schriften,* 167–68.

for ideas that lie hidden in people can be awakened to activity," so that the result would be a collective *Enthusiasmus* not of "a wild crowd," but of "an enlightened people." In the draft he located that experience in the modern era's increasingly oppressive burden of wars, which would provoke collective efforts to introduce "freedom and equality."[56]

In the published version of the essay, Kant omitted any explicit censure of the equation of moral optimism with *Schwärmerei.* That was probably because he had given his argument a more radical application—one that made him more vulnerable to the charge that he too had become a revolutionary *Schwärmer,* and hence also made him reluctant to put the epithet on the table. Now the needed historical experience was not war, but the Revolution itself. Kant's delicate task was to deny that there could be a right to revolution (as he had already done in earlier essays), but at the same time to defend the French Revolution as a source of moral inspiration. The Revolution became a "historical sign," a "drama of great political changes" suggesting that man can be "the *author* of his own improvement."[57] However misguided and excessive the revolutionaries themselves had become, there was a sense in which "the public observing from outside sympathized with [their] exaltation [*Exaltation*] without the slightest intention of collaborating." Thus the event allowed "participation in the good with *Affekt,* with *Enthusiasm.*" Kant was careful to note that this was an exceptional case of "true *Enthusiasm,*" aimed only at the "purely moral." It did not negate the fact that "all *Affekt* as such deserves censure and is not to be entirely approved."[58]

The essay implicitly recalls Wieland's effort two decades earlier to distinguish *Schwärmerei* from the true *Enthusiasmus* of artistic creativity. Now Kant sought to introduce a parallel distinction in politics. He knew he was walking a conceptual and rhetorical tightrope. Where his argument required the most daring—and hence where it became most acrobatic—was in legitimating the moral exaltation of the audience, even as he withheld moral approval from the exaltation of the political actors. The Revolution was a historically particular source of emotion-laden images; but, far from being merely private for that reason, it was a spectacularly visible public sign. Its effect was "public," not only in the sense that the "sympathy" for it was "openly" expressed, but also in the sense that the moral capacities it activated were potentially universal. With this line of argument, painfully cautious in execution but still a bold move in the context of the mid-1790s, Kant appropriated the Revolution as a mediating symbol for

---

56. Ibid., 168–71.
57. Kant, "Ob das menschliche Geschlecht im beständigen Fortschreiten zum Besseren sei," 156–57.
58. Ibid., 158.

philosophical criticism. He had not, of course, collapsed the distinction between rational moral norms and the imagination's emotionally grounded illusions; but he had claimed to find an empirical locus for rational norms, and indeed an imagistic source of moral inspiration, in the emotive politics of revolution. It was a paradoxical claim, designed to introduce a kind of collective moral passion into public life without licensing a *Schwärmerei* of popular politics.

❧ · ❧

Could philosophy be an authoritative public voice without becoming complicit in the exercise of power? The question had an ancient lineage, but by the 1790s it had acquired a new urgency and a new complexity in German-speaking Europe. *Schwärmerei* was a looming presence, both in framing the question and in narrowing the parameters for answering it. *Schwärmerei* was not simply the endemic disease that philosophy was uniquely qualified to diagnose and to quarantine. Nor was it simply the binary opposite in philosophy's efforts to define itself and its public mission. It was also the temptation—the invitation to complicity—that philosophy had to shun.

Several features of this philosophical self-scrutiny merit more attention than this essay can devote to them. It is striking, for example, that, to thinkers as different as Garve and Kant, the only sure way to dispel the temptation of *Schwärmerei* was to embrace hard work. In a sense, there was nothing new about this theme. From its origins, *Schwärmerei* had been conceived as a kind of emotional and ultimately sensual self-indulgence, a failure of moral as well as cognitive self-discipline. Some notorious examples—men like Jakob Boehme and George Fox—had not only shunned rigorous study, they had also abandoned their occupations.

What *is* new in the 1790s is the application of a distinctly modern discourse of labor and consumption to the received contrast between self-discipline and self-indulgence. The spectre of *Schwärmerei* came to reflect a larger eighteenth-century fear that the ethic of productive work would be sapped by the very leisure-time consumption it made possible. In the expanding world of print, reading would mediate effectively between subjectivity and collectivity only if it was drawn out of the self-indulgent culture of an emerging consumer economy. For this mediation to be achieved, reading had to be more than a simulated conversation with a friend. Author and reader had to be socially connected through the modern division of labor, which would link their silent solitudes through the reciprocal duties of their callings. If most readers were now passive, "lazy," and fickle consumers, the new reader would actively appropriate the text, as nature was appropriated in other forms of labor, and indeed would, in Kant's sober phrase, "exert effort on the thorny path of thorough learning."

The philosopher would join the reader in a new community of work discipline. This was the implication Kant spelled out in 1796, in a biting essay linking the recent revival of Christian Neoplatonism to the cults of monastic asceticism, alchemy, and freemasonry. Kant attributed to the modern Neoplatonic *Schwärmer* the same disdain for work that characterized the privileged man of leisure living off inherited wealth. Claiming ineffable insights from "the oracle within," he "flies above all labor" and does not feel "bound to speak with anyone." He hides his laziness under the veil of secrecy. Philosophy, on the other hand, was laborious system-building, "the systematic arrangement of concepts." If the building itself required strenuous effort, so did the communication of the results. Where the philosophical *Schwärmer* resorted to an obscurantist "figural" language, the genuine philosopher had to labor to communicate to a potentially universal audience, as one "work[s] to acquire a possession." Only in that way could philosophy legitimate a claim to *"public validity."*[59]

There was a certain tension in Kant's vision. In a sense, philosophy had to enforce a clean distinction between hardworking insiders and dilettantish consumers. Philosophizing was an earned professional right, limited to those who accepted the rigors of an academic discipline. And yet that disciplinary community, as circumscribed as it was, had to engage in genuinely public communication. Even as it bounded itself as a "community of the competent," it had to address a potentially universal audience.

To resolve this tension, philosophy needed its own rhetoric *in print*—a way of constituting a kind of rhetorical community beyond its academic walls, but without endowing print with oratory's power to "make a swarm." What would such a print rhetoric look like? Garve, the tireless practitioner of *Popularphilosophie,* approached this question with the same sober confidence and precision that he brought to the semantic sprawl of *Schwärmerei.* To claim public authority, philosophy had to pass the test of objectivity; and that in turn required that it be accessible to the educated public and, eventually, to the broad masses as well. Kantian *Systematiker* notwithstanding, a simple language could make thought transparent without sacrificing philosophical integrity.

---

59. Immanuel Kant, "On a Newly Arisen Superior Tone in Philosophy" (1796), in Fenves, ed., *Raising the Tone,* 51–72. See also Garve, "Ueber die Schwärmerey," 398–99. On the background to Kant's essay, see, in addition to Fenves's notes, Ingegrete Kreienbrink, "Johann Georg Schlossers Streit mit Kant," in *Festschrift für Detlev W. Schumann zum 70. Geburtstag,* ed. Albert R. Schmitt (Munich, 1970), 246–55.

What was needed was a prose with an "easy flow of concepts" and with images that brought the imagination to the aid of the understanding.[60]

To the younger generation of German intellectuals in the 1790s, Garve was something of a fossil. It was one thing to call for a philosophical rhetoric that effectively braided abstraction with imagery, but quite another to achieve it. The problem was not simply that such a rhetoric was elusive; the very search for it registered an awareness that each of its elements, by itself, threatened to make philosophy an instrument of coercive power. Surely the philosopher's only point of entry into the dense contextuality of a particular culture was an imagistic rhetoric (the kind that Burke had used to such effect). This appeal to the visual imagination would not simply empower philosophy to speak through a fund of shared representations; it would also ground public reception of philosophical guidance in the moral passion that Kant called "sympathy" and "enthusiasm." If images were the emblems of "inner" freedom, however, they were also the socially volatile medium of contagion; having plunged the reader into the abyss of self, they might pull him out to enlarge the mob. Abstractions posed their own bind. They promised to remove the blinders imposed by context, and hence to make criticism possible. But they also erased individuality; the reader effaced himself before a relentless cognitive regime.[61]

The spectres of *Schwärmerei* pointed German philosophy to a unique mission in modern public culture, but they also severely circumscribed its options. Emblematic in this regard was the prickly exchange between Friedrich Schiller and Johann Gottlieb Fichte in 1795. By then Schiller had spent several years trying to aestheticize, and thereby to humanize, Kant's forbidding moral rigorism. Schiller sought a rhetoric in which concepts would "develop according to the laws of necessity," but would "migrate into the power of the imagination according to the law of freedom."[62] When he accused Fichte of using imagery to

60. Garve, "Von der Popularität des Vortrages," 338–40. See also Garve's complaint to Kant in 1783 about the impenetrability of the *Critique of Pure Reason,* in Kant, *Briefwechsel,* ed. Königlich Preussischen Akademie der Wissenschaften, vol. 10, pt. 2 (Berlin and Leipzig, 1922), 328–33. On Garve's view of prose and rhetoric, see Altmayer, *Aufklärung als Popularphilosophie,* esp. 640–61; Monika Ammermann, *Gemeines Leben: Gewandelter Naturbegriff und literarische Spätaufklärung. Lichtenberg, Wezel, Garve* (Bonn, 1978). On the larger context of *Popularphilosophie* and its rhetorical strategy, see also Gert Ueding, "Rhetorik und Popularphilosophie," in *Rhetorik: Ein internationales Jahrbuch* 1 (1980): 122–34.
61. For a different but related analysis of "rhetoric" as "power," see Jill Anne Kowalik, "Kleist's Essay on Rhetoric," *Monatshefte* 81, no. 4 (1989): 434–46.
62. "Ueber die nothwendigen Grenzen beim Gebrauch schönen Formen," in *Schillers Werke: Nationalausgabe,* vol. 21, pt. 2 (Weimar, 1963), 13–15. On Schiller's efforts to develop a new rhetoric for philosophy, see esp. Todd Curtis Kontje, *Constructing Reality: A Rhetorical Analysis of Friedrich Schiller's "Letters*

camouflage a bludgeoning logic, the philosopher countered that in Schiller's prose an "immeasurable stock" of images "chained" the imagination.

Schiller and Fichte stopped short of calling each other *Schwärmer*.[63] They preferred to keep the epithet implicit, lurking behind the perceptions of danger it had bequeathed to German literary and philosophical culture.

North Carolina State University, Raleigh

---

on the Aesthetic Education of Man " (New York and Berne, 1987). On his view of the reading public, see Klaus L. Berghahn, "Volkstümlichkeit ohne Volk? Kritische Überlegungen zu einem Kulturkonzept Schillers," in *Popularität und Trivialität,* ed. Reinhold Grimm and Jost Hermand (Frankfurt am Main, 1974), 51–75.

63. The exchange was over an essay Fichte had submitted to Schiller's new journal *Die Horen.* See Johann Gottlieb Fichte, *Gesamtausgabe der Bayerischen Akademie der Wissenschaften* (1970) 3:333–40. Looking back in 1801, Schiller likened his "metaphysical critical" period to the "smallpox infection," which "sticks in us and must come out"; see Schiller's letter to Rochlitz, 16 April 1801, quoted in Friedrich Wilhelm Wentzlaff-Eggebert, *Schillers Weg zu Goethe,* 2d ed. (Berlin, 1963), 275.

The Scale of Enthusiasm

—— PETER FENVES

A SWARM OF SINGULARITIES

Ever since Plato deployed the word *entheos* in battle with the Homeric gods, it has played a decisive role in a wide variety of attempts to define the relation among thinking, knowing, and speaking. The word *enthousiasmos* is of service to philosophy whenever a discussion turns toward something that cannot be understood as a particular case of a general rule and must therefore be considered singular. The word does not so much explain the singularity under discussion as mark the place of its inexplicability: a god is said to be responsible for something, but this god does not respond to our inquiries and cannot therefore serve as the basis of an unambiguous explanation. In the case of Ion—the flighty and, one might say, "ionic" rhetor whom Socrates encounters—the word comes to mark the singularity of his excitement: Ion is thrilled *only* when Homer is the topic of conversation, and he has things to say *only* about Homer; but for this reason, nothing he says about Homer accedes to the generality of *technē* ("know-how").[1] Socrates thus proposes the term *enthousiazein* as an explanation of the singularity of this "rhetorical" enthralldom. Ion is *ekphron*, "out of his mind," whenever he comes into contact with the Homeric poems. He is not alone, however, when he is *ekphron*: just as the god communicates to the poet his ability to communicate, the poet communicates to the rhetor this ability to communicate, and the rhetor communicates to his auditors this "enthusiasm"

---

1. See Plato, *The Ion*, ed. John Burnet, vol. 3 of *Opera* (Oxford, 1987); and *Two Comic Dialogues, Ion and Hippias Major*, trans. Paul Woodruff (Indianapolis, 1983). The statement that *The Ion* contains Plato's first use of the term *entheos* is not without controversy, of course; see John Moore, "The Dating of Plato's *Ion*," *Greek, Roman and Byzantine Studies* 15 (1974): 421–39. For the purposes of this paper I have set aside the other, far greater dialogue in which the word *enthousiazein* plays a distinguished role, *The Phaedrus*. The reading of Plato's texts that I propose here is oriented toward an understanding of the transformation of Platonic thought undertaken by German philosophers and poets in the 1790s. The confines of this essay preclude any discussion of *The Phaedrus* and its reception in this period.

alone—no "know-how," no *technē*, and no further ability to communicate. Whenever Ion comes into contact with the Homeric poems, he takes part in this paradoxical community: a community of singularities whose ecstatic members are unaware of its very existence.

But *The Ion* does not conclude with Socrates' apparently "enthused" speech on enthusiasm[2]—apparently "enthused," because, as Ion concedes, Socrates' speech, like the poems about which he speaks, communicates something about which he is not in a position to speak: "somehow you touch my soul with your words" (535a). Socrates interrogates Ion a second time, and in almost the same terms, after this "touching" speech because the rhetor rejects Socrates' explanation for the singularity of his excitement: he knows himself to be entirely *emphron*—sober, collected—at the very moment he turns his audience into an ecstatic collective. As long as he maintains that he remains "in his right mind," he cannot make good on the promise with which the dialogue begins—the promise, namely, to say what he knows, what he does, what and therefore who he is. This is no small failure: the very possibility of an ordered community in which each member has a proper function rests on the ability of its members to make good on an original promise to say what they do for the community and, by so doing, define what and who they are. Ion can abrogate this promise only if he admits to being an "enthusiast." The term *entheos* in *The Ion* does not so much explain anything as *excuse* an otherwise inexcusable singularity by bringing it into line with a new multiplicity: the audience, the rhetor, the poet, and even the god are all held together in a "Heraclitean" or "magnetic" chain. Those who are able to communicate only the ability to communicate are unable to make good on their promises; but they can still belong to an ordered community. "Enthusiasm" thus becomes an ironic term of excuse—ironic at the very least because the community to which the "enthusiasts" belong is always only *momentary*, a temporary community whose origin is supposed to be divine.

Because Ion cannot find the general term under which his activity falls and because he cannot therefore say what he is, he could be anything. As Socrates says in the final words of the dialogue, Ion resembles no one so much as Pro-

---

2. Socrates' speech thus speaks of itself: it is not grounded in a recognizable *technē*, and to the extent that it does speak of itself, it could belong only to a *technē* of *technē*, which would not itself be a *technē*, but would be either philosophy or poetry. After Socrates explains for a second time that poetry consists in being "enthused," Ion is less excited, and makes the following remark: "You speak well, Socrates, but I would be amazed [*thaumazoimi*] if you could speak well enough to convince me that I am possessed and maniacal [*mainomenos*] when I praise Homer" (536d). *Thauma* is the other "explanation" (*aition*) for the scandal of singularity, but *thaumazein* explains *philosophical* speech: how someone can come to ask about *physis* as such. That Ion is not "amazed" means that he is "enthused."

teus. As long as he rejects Socrates' interpretation of his excitability, Ion is not
"being" (*on*) but is, rather, a movement (*ion*) that—before, outside, or beyond
"being" understood in terms of constancy, standing still, or permanence—represents nothing in particular, nothing in general, and therefore *anything whatsoever*. By speaking of Ion in terms of *entheos,* Socrates places him in a well-
articulated "chain," grants him a certain distinction, and thereby assigns him a
function after all: an unpromising and futile function, to be sure, but a function nevertheless. As long as Ion presents himself as one who does indeed
represent—or acts as the spokesman for[3]—the god, he no longer represents
anything whatsoever. The god gives distinction to whoever participates in the
poetic and rhetorical community; "anything whatsoever," by contrast, is a term
for complete nondistinction. The ontological—or perhaps iontological[4]—
problem of enthusiasm can thus be stated in the following terms: *entheos* is a
word by which a movement that would otherwise present the greatest possible
nondistinction is understood as an entity that represents the greatest possible
distinction—the distinction, namely, between divine and human beings.

Because Ion in the end accedes to Socrates' interpretation of his singularity
and allows himself to be designated a spokesman for the god, *The Ion* is drawn
toward an ironic solution to the question of how singularity comes to speech: it
comes to speech in the *performance* of a poem, that is, in the re-presentation of
something "made" by a god. Nothing *about* which one speaks would be singular; indeed, everything about which a poem speaks, according to the premise of
Socrates' interrogative procedure, belongs to a particular kind of general
"know-how." The question remains, however: Can singularity come to speech
outside of a poetic performance? This question is of enormous importance
when it is assumed that the unnamed god about whom Socrates remains silent
in *The Ion* does not have a Homeric provenance but is, instead, God, the
absolutely unique and incomparable One from whom everything else originates, so incomparably unique in fact that its proper name is unpronounceable.
Speaking about this One, predicating something of the unique God, and making statements concerning his nature would also bring singularity into speech,

3.　The terms "representative" and "spokesman" are used to translate the Greek word *hermeneus,* but it almost
　　goes without saying that both terms are inadequate. For an attempt to translate the "hermeneutic" character
　　of Plato's *hermeneus,* see the remarkable essay of Jean-Luc Nancy, *Le partage des voix* (Paris, 1982). For an
　　equally remarkable explication of the kind of community in which singularities alone can participate, see
　　Giorgio Agamben, *The Coming Community,* trans. Michael Hardt (Minneapolis, 1993).

4.　In Plato's most extensive investigation into language, *The Cratylus* (*Opera,* vol. 1 [Oxford, 1987]), Socrates
　　explains the iota of *ion* (infinitive, *ienai*) as an expression of "subtle elements that pass through all things.
　　This is why he [the one who has mastered the *technē* of speaking] uses the letter iota to mimic motion, *ienai,
　　iesthai*" (426d). Ion, too, passes through all *poleis*.

but those who speak about the One cannot escape the predicament in which, according to Socrates' interpretation, Ion finds himself whenever he touches on the Homeric poems: even when the Singular one is only the subject of predication, not the "maker" of the speech, the act of speaking is nonetheless singularized, for no *technē,* no body of knowledge, and no faculty of insight could offer a solid foundation upon which a true statement about the One could be made. Only the One could grant a basis on which to speak in a positive manner about the One.

Ungrounded and therefore false statements about the One, by contrast, could have a variety of sources. If singularity cannot be spoken about without the performance of this speech finding a ground in—or, as Socrates ironically proposes, a link to—the unique One about whom one speaks, whoever speaks in this way will be open to the same accusation leveled against Ion: the speaker cannot disclose the "real" basis for the speech. Once "ideality" is no longer seen as the fundamental character of "what is" and, instead, is understood in terms of "mental contents," then it is possible to draw this conclusion: speakers who cannot ground their speech in something real—whether it be the One or the multiplicity of created things—can find a foundation for their speech only in something altogether "ideal": illusions, fantasies, creatures of the imagination. Those who speak about the One on the unstable basis of the imagination can no longer be interpreted as singularities who participate in an exalted community during the time of a poetic performance; on the contrary, such speakers are singular not in the sense that they are more than a "natural" kind but in the sense that they are *less* than a kind: oddities, aberrations, or monsters.

A host of words have been used to designate what, as an indefinite multitude, is less than a natural kind. One of these words gains particular importance because it points toward the natural—and therefore nontranscendent—origin of "enthusiasm": the German word *Schwarm,* "swarm." The members of a swarm are not only impossible to distinguish from one another but are also, for this reason, not even members of the swarm: instead of belonging to a stable collective according to which they would be recognized and named, each one is a temporary participant in an act of "swarming," or *Schwärmerei.* Whereas the term enthusiasm refers without ambiguity, although not without irony, to something more than humankind, *Schwärmerei* points toward something more and less than humankind—less than human because animals, not human beings, aggregate into swarms; and more than human because the only animals whose multitudes turn into swarms are those that, like the gods, are able to take leave of the earth. A desire to depart from the earth, if only in a *Fischschwarm* ("swarm of fish"), is implied in every use of the term

Schwärmerei, just as, *ordine inverso,* the descent of a god to the earth is implicated in Socrates' use of the term *entheos.* And "swarmers" associate with one another precisely because they desire something more than terrestrial society: "*Schwärmer; Schwärmerei* comes from 'swarm,' 'to swarm,' particularly as it is used for bees. The desire to make a swarm is thus the definitive mark of the *Schwärmer.*"[5] By disassociating themselves from civil society, swarmers collect into non-civil (if not un-civil), non-social (if not anti-social), non-natural (if not un-natural), and always temporary, multiplicities.

The "swarmer" exists only in the swarm, just as the poet, the rhetor, and the audience of a poem exist only in relation to the god; but the relation of the "swarmers" to one another is not an *ordered* relation: no "chain" holds them together, and so each "swarmer" is out of order, disorderly, or, to use an already familiar word in another way, singular. *Schwärmerei* names the aporetic condition of a coordinated disorderliness. *Schwärmer* may want to distinguish themselves from everyone else—and the origin of the word *Schwärmerei* in accusations of radical sectarianism points toward this desire—but the word itself says the opposite: the swarm allows for no distinctions within its ranks. The disorder of the swarm is reflected in the disorderly vision of the *Schwärmer,* and insofar as the term "world" always indicates a certain order, the *Schwärmer* is not "otherworldly" or "spiritual," but non-worldly, or acosmic.

Schwärmerei is for this reason one of the terms by which the German *Aufklärung* sought to define itself. If those who champion *Aufklärung* speak of something singular—and in the context of the *Aufklärung,* this generally means the One God—they speak of him only as something superlative: all "perfections" can be attributed to him. But if, as the *Critique of Pure Reason*

---

5. G. E. Lessing, "Über eine zeitige Aufgabe: Wird durch die Bemühung kaltblutiger Philosophen und Lucianischer Geister gegen das, was sie Enthusiasmus und Schwärmerei nennen, mehr Böses als Gutes gestiftet. Und in welchen Schranken müssen die Antiplatoniker halten um nützlich zu sein?" (On a Timely Task: Is More Evil Than Good Established by the Effort of Cold-Blooded Philosophers and Lucianian Minds Against That Which They Call Enthusiasm and *Schwärmerei?* And Within Which Limits Must the Anti-Platonist Stop so as to be Useful?), reprinted in *Gotthold Ephraim Lessings sämtliche Werke,* ed. Karl Lachmann (Leipzig, 1853–57), 16:297. Less incisive definitions of the term *Schwärmerei* can be found in the *Deutsches Wörterbuch* begun by the Grimm brothers (Leipzig, 1954), 9:2290–93.

Luther's attacks on radical sectarians appear to have given the impetus for the widespread use of this term. See K. G. Steck, *Luther und die Schwärmer* (Zollikon-Zürich, 1955); and Eric Gritsch, "Luther und die Schwärmer: Verworfene Anfechtung?" in *Luther, Zeitschrift der Luther-Gesellschaft* 47 (1976): 105–21. *Schwärmer* are the ones who cannot belong to any stable society because they want something more than society. They therefore play a particularly important function in a large number of eighteenth-century literary texts in which the limits of civil society were, so to speak, tested for the first time; for an introductory examination of these issues, see Victor Lange, "Zur Gestalt des Schwärmers im deutschen Roman des 18. Jahrhunderts," in *Festschrift für Richard Alewyn* (Cologne, 1967), 151–64. For a fuller discussion, see Anthony La Vopa's essay in this volume.

sets out to show, this talk, too, is illegitimate; if nothing positive can be said of God, not even the statement "he exists," then it becomes impossible to avoid this question: Under what conditions am I, or is the self, in a position to speak *of* singularity, especially when the self, too, is singular insofar as it is free?

This essay concerns two responses to these questions that were given in the last years of the eighteenth century: one from the side of philosophical criticism (Friedrich Schelling), the other from the side of critical poetology (Friedrich Hölderlin). Both of these responses can be understood to develop the implications of Kant's sole definition of *Schwärmerei* within the space of a *Critique,* and each one undertakes a "critique" of critical thought that refines, redefines, and in the end finishes off Kant's definition. If the self-definition of the *Aufklärung* depends on the definition of a particularly unclear word—*Schwärmerei*—then the attempts to define this term can show the limits of the self upon which the appeal for "clearing up" finally depends. Because they leave no room for a God *about* whom one could speak, Schelling and Hölderlin together execute the Kantian legacy. Whereas Schelling seeks to save *Schwärmerei* as a term against which critical thought can define itself, Hölderlin allows for no such defensive self-definition: the principle of subjectivity—the principle upon which the critical project of a self-critique of reason rests—is shown to be nothing short of *Schwärmerei.*

"If in Its Most General Meaning 'Schwärmerei' Is . . ." (Kant)

Enthousiasmos can be translated in many ways. The multiplicity of possible translations for this word would not of itself pose a problem if one could point toward a univocal experience through which its sense and meaning could be secured once and for all. But it is the point of Kantian critique to dispute the possibility of the experience named in the word enthusiasm: something "holy," according to Kant, may make itself known to us—we will come back to this—but a god cannot be said to *appear* as long as "god" refers to something unconditioned and every appearance is necessarily conditioned. "Enthusiasm" cannot therefore mean what it says. But as long as something "holy," if not divine, makes itself know, "enthusiasm" does not have to be an entirely ironic term. From his earliest writings onward Kant is drawn into the critical project of distinguishing an empowering enthusiasm from a debilitating *Schwärmerei.* This project of definition becomes all the more important when, following the publication of the three *Critiques,* the very act of reading Kant—especially a

Kant who has assumed the divine function of "lawgiver and patron of peace"
—came to be considered a cause for enthusiasm.[6]

In an early text, "Versuch über die Krankheiten des Kopfes" (Essay on the
Sicknesses of the Head), Kant proposes to distinguish enthusiasm from
Schwärmerei on the basis of an impressive but nevertheless undefined cri-
terion—the former gives rise to great action, whereas the latter remains within the inactive sphere of imagined intimacy: "This ambiguous appearance of
phantasy [*Phantasterei*] in moral sentiments that are in themselves good is
enthusiasm [*Enthusiasmus*], and nothing great in the world has been done
without it. Things are altogether different with the fanatic (visionary,
Schwärmer). The latter is actually a lunatic with a supposed immediate inspiration and great intimacy with the powers of heaven. Human nature knows no
more dangerous delusion" (Ak., 2:267). When phantasy appears "in" moral
sentiments, these become apparent: they are converted from mere sentiments
into "great" actions "in the world." Since, however, phantasy is not itself
grounded in moral sentiments, it cannot be judged altogether good. Phantasy
makes up for a failure on the part of moral sentiments to ground worldly
action, and the phenomenon of enthusiasm is supposed to bear witness to this
phantasmatic function. "Enthusiasm" names the condition under which moral
feeling turns into effective action; but it is not a *pure* condition of conversion.

6.   This latter quotation comes from a letter Maternus Renus sent Kant in 1796: "I cannot describe to you how
      enthusiastically [*enthusiastisch*] people have taken up your principles, even those who otherwise are against
      them, and even now our ladies have taken them up since we read in a number of newspapers that you have
      been called to France to act as lawgiver and patron of peace." See Kant, *Gesammelte Schriften*, ed. Königlich
      Preußischen [later, German] Akademie der Wissenschaften (Berlin, 1900–), 12:69; hereafter, "Ak." (Since
      almost all reliable translations of Kant include the Akademie edition pagination, for the sake of economy I
      will refer only to these volumes, except in the case of the *Critique of Pure Reason*, where I refer to the first
      two editions, "A" and "B"; all translations are my own.) According to a certain Conrad Stang, men rejected
      Kantian thought, whereas women could be counted on for its dispersion: "But if the men are struggling so
      vigorously against critical philosophy, its fortunes are better among the women. You cannot believe how
      enthusiastically [*enthusiastisch*] young ladies and women are taken with your system and how eager they all
      are to learn about it. There are many women's groups here in Würzburg, where each one is eager to outdo
      the others in showing knowledge of your system: it is the favorite topic of conversation" (Ak., 12:100). The
      formation of these reading societies deserves attention in the context of any discussion of Kant and enthusi-
      asm, for it is in the solitary activity of reading that, according to Kant, the "disease" of *Schwärmerei* is spread
      in contemporary society. One of Kant's earliest attempts to connect certain mental aberrations, especially
      "melancholic vapor," with too much reading can be found in the "Essay on the Sicknesses of the Head"
      (Ak., 2:266). One of his last attempts in this direction can be found in the concluding chapter of the *Streit
      der Fakultäten*, "On the Power of the Mind to Master its Mordant Feeling by Intention Alone." Of particu-
      lar importance is Kant's open letter to Ernst Borowski, which was later printed as an appendix to his book
      on Cagliostro (1790): "As I see it, the universally disseminated *mania for reading* [*Lesesucht*] not only is the
      guiding instrument (vehicle) in the spread of this disease but also is the poison (miasma) that engenders it"
      (Ak., 11:107).

The "Essay on the Sicknesses of the Head" seeks empirically recognizable causes not only for the sicknesses it identifies but also for the ambiguous state of health in which great things are done in the world. Enthusiasm must therefore have an empirical cause, and Kant has no better name for this cause than the rather phantastic term *Phantasterei.*

The term *Phantasterei* is a monument to one of Kant's earliest attempts to address an imposing problem: Under what condition does the possibility of morality give way to moral action? Ultimately, its solution discloses the pillar on which Kant's critical metaphysics will rest; here, in the "Essay on the Sicknesses of the Head," the possibility of morality is understood in terms of "moral sentiment," moral action in terms of those accomplishments that are "great in the world," and the ambiguous condition of conversion from possibility into actuality in terms of an "enthusiasm" that stands opposed to *Schwärmerei.* By the time Kant comes to write his ground-breaking exploration of the principle of morality in *Laying the Ground for the Metaphysics of Morals* (1785), each of the terms of this schema changes, but a radicalized version of the same schema still structures his thought: no empirical cause serves as a condition under which the possibility of morality is translated into moral action; the possibility of morality, being able to be moral, is itself the condition for moral conduct *under the ambiguous condition* that the agent regard itself as altogether free. Unconditional freedom thus takes over the function of enthusiasm: "nothing great in the world has been done without it" (Ak., 2:267).[7] And the entire project of laying the ground not only for the metaphysics of morals but also for metaphysics as such rests on the principle that our actions can be and therefore must be regarded from a certain perspective as free. Because this freedom is unconditional, however, it is impossible to construct a general rule under which a particular case of free action could be recognized. No one who is free, in turn, can be treated as a particular case that falls under a general rule, and so everyone must be regarded from the same perspective as singular. As long as the singularity implied in the claim to freedom finds its correlate in the universality of the law under which those who claim to be free must act, it remains an *ordered* singularity, and those free beings who submit themselves to the order of an absolutely universal law do not so much

7. Kant's earliest use of the term enthusiasm draws it into an even closer relation to freedom or, more precisely, the "love of freedom": "*Enthusiasmus* inspired [*begeistert*] ancient peoples toward great things," and this enthusiasm may be connected to the warming of the earth's surface; see "The Question Whether the Earth Aged, Considered Physically" (1754), Ak, 1:212. For a brief description of Kant's use of the term *Enthusiasmus* and his attempt to distinguish it from *Schwärmerei,* see Peter Fenves, *A Peculiar Fate* (Ithaca, N.Y., 1991), 241–43.

constitute a *Schwarm* as its exact inversion: an active order of singularities, a nonnatural, immediate, and thus magical chain of moral enthusiasts—or, to use the critical vocabulary developed in the *Critique of Pure Reason,* a *"corpus mysticum* of rational beings in the [sensible world]" (A 808; B 836).

From *Laying the Groundwork for the Metaphysics of Morals* to the *Critique of Practical Reason, Religion within the Limits of Reason Alone,* and the *Metaphysics of Morals,* Kant laid out the same fundamental and irresolvable circle: the condition under which we can respond to categorical, apodictic, unconditional— which is to say, moral—commands *as* commands addressed to us is unconditional freedom; but according to Kant, only in the experience of being commanded to act without regard for empirical conditions can one recognize oneself as free, and this latter "experience" is so unlike any other that it threatens to undo the unity of experience. Saying "we are free" does not amount to *Schwärmerei* only if this statement is understood to mean: we recognize "in ourselves" unconditional commands. But, once again, this is the recognition of something singular—a unique "fact of pure reason." To the extent that this fact is singular, it cannot be said simply to fall under the concept "fact" but must, instead, present itself as a "fact, as it were" (*gleichsam ein Faktum*),[8] and the recognition of this fact can itself be understood only as a recognition "as it were." Thus, the supreme point of Kantian criticism, *das Faktum der reinen Vernunft,* cannot escape an association with the operation by which the "Essay on the Sicknesses of the Head" describes the generation of *Schwärmerei:* moral commands may do without "inner vision," but the *exposition* of the basic principle on which all of the *Critiques* will come to rest—the principle of autonomy—cannot do without certain *Gleichnisse* ("likenesses," "images"). Saying "we are free" cannot be justified unless the statement includes at least one "as it were."

Yet there is an even more compelling reason to associate the supreme point of Kantian criticism with enthusiasm: the very fact that moral commands are unconditional brings them into the vicinity of *Schwärmerei.* The definition Kant proposes for this term in the section of the *Critique of Practical Reason* (1788) devoted to the "driving springs [*Triebfedern*] of pure practical reason" is therefore of no small significance for the entire critical project. It is not only the *sole* definition of *Schwärmerei* within any of the *Critiques,* it is also a definition about which Kant seems to hold certain reservations, for he proposes it in the

---

8. See Kant, *Critique of Practical Reason,* Ak., 5:47; for a standard commentary on, and a useful guide to, the difficulties of this peculiar phrase, see Lewis White Beck, *A Commentary on Kant's "Critique of Practical Reason"* (Chicago, 1960), 166–70. Kant sometimes speaks of the "sole fact [*Faktum*] of pure reason" (e.g., Ak., 5:31), sometimes of the "fact, as it were, of pure reason" (e.g., Ak., 5:47), sometimes of "practical data of reason" (e.g., *Critique of Pure Reason,* B xxii and xviii).

form of a conditional judgment: "If in its most general meaning [*in der allerge-meinsten Bedeutung*] *Schwärmerei* is a transgression of the limits of human reason undertaken according to principles . . ." (Ak., 5:85). This definition of *Schwärmerei* is conditional for at least one reason: it does not correspond to the general tendency of Kant's other definitions of this word. The last word one would expect Kant to associate with *Schwärmerei* in his many anthropological reflections on "sicknesses of the head" is "principles" (*Grundsätze*). In these writings, as in most contemporaneous attempts on the part of those engaged in the project of *Aufklärung* to explain the irrational character of *Schwärmerei,* the word is defined in terms of vision, fantasy, imagination, figurality, or "symbols."⁹ The remarkable character of the definition Kant proposes in the *Critique of Practical Reason* can perhaps be judged by citing Lewis White Beck's otherwise meticulous translation: "If fanaticism in its most general sense is a deliberate overstepping of the limits of human reason . . ."¹⁰ "Principles" drops out. If *Schwärmerei* is "principled," it cannot be entirely irrational, and if its principle is freedom—from limits, conditions, natural causes—it gestures toward the very doctrine Kant is in the process of defining. Defining this doctrine against *Schwärmerei* demands that the latter be *defined* in the first place; that is, it must have limits, even if it consists in taking a basic stand against limits. The conditionality of Kant's definition, for this reason, deserves more attention. The limit on the use of the term *Schwärmerei,* its "definition," is predicated on the definition of another even more problematic term: *moralische Schwärmerei.* The fate of enthusiasm within the context of Kantian thought is inscribed within these paragraphs of the *Critique of Practical Reason.*

There are at least two further reasons for the conditional character of Kant's only definition of *Schwärmerei* within the space of the *Critiques.* Explicating the reasons for Kant's hesitation on this point allows one to understand certain developments of Kant's thought as genuine developments of—and not simply expressions of enthusiasm for—the enterprise Kant undertook under the rubric of "critique."

---

9.   See the useful concordance assembled by Norbert Hinske, "Zur Verwendung der Wörter 'schwärmen' 'Schwärmer,' 'Schwärmerei,' 'schwärmerisch' im Kontext von Kants Anthropologiekolleg" in N. Hinske, ed., *Die Aufklärung und die Schwärmer* (Hamburg, 1988), 73–81; see also Hinske's introductory essay, "Die Aufklärung und die Schwärmer—Sinn und Funktion einer Kampfidee." Within the context of the anthropological writings, *Schwärmerei* generally includes a moment of unbound imagination: "The originality (not imitated production) of imagination [*Einbildungskraft*], if it harmonizes with concepts, is called 'genius'; if it does not harmonize, *Schwärmerei*" (Ak., 7:172). It is not only in the anthropological writings, however, that Kant refrains from explicating *Schwärmerei* in terms of principles. In the second edition of the *Critique of Pure Reason* Kant accuses Locke of having "opened the door" to *Schwärmerei* by "sensualizing" concepts (see B 127–28).
10. Kant, *Critique of Practical Reason,* trans. L. W. Beck (Indianapolis, 1956), 88.

First, the problem of defining *moralische Schwärmerei*: Kant may have proposed the definition of *Schwärmerei* in conditional terms because the definition on which it is predicated—that of *moralische Schwärmerei*—is genuinely problematic. The moral law, by definition, commands unconditionally; and, as Kant explains in the very first words of the second *Critique,* he has therefore chosen not to write a *Critique of Pure Practical Reason* but, rather, a *Critique of Practical Reason:* pure practical reason requires no critique—on the contrary, it is precisely what ought to be *promoted,* for it is morality itself (Ak., 5:3). One can, of course, transgress the limits of pure practical reason—this would be the most general definition of immorality—but it appears entirely problematic, if not impossible, to transgress these limits in the direction of being "too moral" or "too virtuous." Kant's renunciation of the classical ethics of the "just mean" supplies sufficient proof of this: "For really to be too virtuous—that is, to be too attached to one's duty—would be almost equivalent to making a circle round or a straight line too straight" (*Metaphysics of Morals,* Ak., 7:434). In the *Religion within the Limits of Reason Alone,* Kant defends his "rigorism" against Schiller's polemical remarks in "On Grace and Dignity" (Ak., 6:23), and it is this defense of rigorism, perhaps more than anything else, that imparts to Kant the image of a "moral *Schwärmer*" in the eyes of certain of his readers—in those of Johann Schlosser, for example,[11] who, by attacking Kant throughout the 1790s, brought about one of the last wide-scale debates around the concept of *Schwärmerei* in the eighteenth century. Schlosser not only takes offense at Kant's unorthodox conception of religion but also attacks the "inhuman" doctrine of moral conduct upon which this conception is founded.[12] Because critical philosophy does not recognize "human" limitations, Schlosser presents it as a version of moral *Schwärmerei,* and Kant responds in kind by accusing Schlosser—and an unnamed nobleman who had recently translated Plato's

---

11. But Schlosser is only one example—and by no means the most interesting or important one. He is, however, the only one to whom Kant makes an explicit and well-articulated response. It is a common project among a wide variety of Kant's critics in the 1790s to insist not so much that his moral doctrine be made to fit the limits of humanity as that it be revised from the perspective of those demands that cannot be formulated according to a categorical command precisely because they do not admit of formally defined limits—demands like "grace" (Schiller), "life" (Hölderlin), or "love" (Hegel).

12. See Johann Georg Schlosser, "Plato's Briefe über die Syrakusianische Staats-Revolution aus dem griechischen übersetzt" (Plato's Letters on the Revolution in Syracuse, Translated from the Greek). Schlosser's translation with commentary was first published in a journal in 1793, then republished as a book in 1795. For a description of the struggle between Schlosser and Kant, see P. Fenves, ed., *Raising the Tone of Philosophy* (Baltimore, 1993), esp. 72–76; cf. Rüdiger Bubner, "Platon—der Vater aller Schwärmerei: Zu Kants Aufsatz 'Von einem neuerdings erhobenen vornehmen Ton in der Philosophie,'" in *Antike Themen und ihre moderne Verwandlung* (Frankfurt am Main, 1992), 80, 93.

Ion[13]—of theoretical *Schwärmerei*. Only a univocal definition of *Schwärmerei* can bring these reciprocal accusations to an end; but the definition of this term presupposes a definition of human limits as such, and this, in turn, demands an answer to the question to which, according to Kant, all questions of philosophy "in its cosmopolitan sense" ultimately refer: *was ist der Mensch?*[14]

Kant's definition of moral *Schwärmerei* is meant to forestall the accusation that his moral rigorism amounts to an excessive and, at least to this extent, *schwärmische* morality. And this accusation is not altogether unjustified, since moral demands, according to Kant, are by definition demands to exceed earthly conditions: when one experiences the singular feeling of *Achtung* ("respect," "attention"), and thus attends to one's duty, one must no longer pay any attention to natural limitations. Making oneself too virtuous should therefore be considered exactly equivalent to making a circle round, which is to say, doing what is demanded if there is to be a circle—or virtue—in the first place. Moral *Schwärmerei* must therefore be defined in such a way as to disregard the concept of virtue: a moral *Schwärmer*, according to Kant's initial treatment of the term in the *Critique of Practical Reason*, does not seek exceptional virtue but, rather, claims to "possess" an inviolable "purity." Instead of attending to "holy prescriptions" from which everyone remains at a certain remove, moral *Schwärmer* regard *themselves* as holy and therefore deceive themselves into thinking that moral action can be done out of their successfully secured holiness. All action that is not grounded on moral commands alone is, according to Kant, based on certain pathological inclinations, and so moral *Schwärmer* are those who have worked themselves into a position where they confuse their pathos with holiness. But Kant does not conclude his discussion of moral *Schwärmerei* with a diagnosis of this confusion of feeling. Instead, he undertakes a definition of the term, and in the course of defining it, he does not so much erase the distinction between the clarity of his doctrine and the confusion of the moral *Schwärmer* as inscribe the "holy prescriptions" to which his doctrine appeals within another, this time "critical" enthusiasm: an enthusiasm in which nothing is communicated—no philosophical knowledge, no technical "know-how"—but the ability of the law to communicate itself. The law occupies the place Socrates assigned to the god in his interpretation of the singularity of Ion's excitability:

13. Count Friedrich Leopold zu Stolberg, *Auserlesene Gespräche des Platon* (Königsberg, 1796). For more on Stolberg, see note 38 below.
14. See Kant, *Logic*, Ak., 9:25.

If in its most general meaning *Schwärmerei* is a transgression of
the limits of human reason undertaken according to principles,
then moral *Schwärmerei* is this transgression of the limits that
pure practical reason poses to humanity through which it forbids
us to place the subjective determining ground of dutiful actions,
i.e., their dutiful driving spring, anywhere else than in the law
itself, and to posit the disposition [*Gesinnung*] which is thereby
brought into the maxims elsewhere than in the respect for this
law [*Achtung für das Gesetz*]; it commands that we make the
thought of duty, which strikes down all arrogance as well as idle
philautia, the supreme life-principle [*Lebensprinzip*] of all morality in man. (Ak., 5:85–86)

This definition of moral *Schwärmerei* would follow directly from the conditional definition of *Schwärmerei* if it were not for one unresolved problem:
pure practical reason poses limits on human *action*—*not* on "humanity"
(*Menschheit*) itself. The latter is doubtless "limited" (finite), but no human
being *ought* to respect any natural (pathological) limitations in determining a
course of action. Kant's definition thus takes a curious direction: whereas it is
supposed to draw a boundary between his own doctrine and *Schwärmerei,* it
concludes by speaking of morality taking up residence "in man." And since the
moral law, as Kant emphasizes again and again, not only is "holy" but is also
our only access to an acceptable concept of God and is therefore in its own way
"divine,"[15] its ability to inhabit, if not possess, "man" gives rise to something
like a critical *enthousiasmos.* In order to defend his doctrine from the accusation of enthusiasm, Kant gestures toward a distinction for which he has no
clearly defined terms, an otherwise impossible distinction between a criminal
transgression and a noncriminal, if not altogether innocent, overstepping of
the limits imposed on humanity.

The first term by which he wishes to install this distinction is "novel-
writing" (*Romanschreibung*). Writing novels runs counter to critical reflection
when it fails to recognize any limit to the possibility of actualizing moral perfection. But novelists are not alone in this regard: they are the representatives
of this failure. Anyone who entertains the idea of moral perfection as something other than a *sheer* possibility—a possibility without the possibility of
actualization—engages in a version of novel-writing. Failure to recognize the

---

15. For a striking example of Kant's use of the word "holy" (*heilig*) to describe the moral law, see the *Critique of
Practical Reason*, Ak., 5:77; for his use of the term "divine" (*göttlich*) in connection with the law, see *Religion
within the Limits of Reason Alone*, Ak., 6:113.

necessity of this sheer possibility gives rise to the fictional discourses of novelists, educators, and Stoic moral philosophers. The massive discourse of "aesthetic education" unleashed by Schiller's *Letters* and a less conspicuous but still
significant burst of novels inspired by Kant's *Critiques*[16] take their point of
departure from here: the association of novelists with educators in the context
of a rigorous doctrine of moral practice. Another "if" seals the definition of
"moral *Schwärmerei*" and begins the next paragraph: "If this is so, then not
only novelists [*Romanschreiber*], or sentimental educators (even though they
may be zealously opposed to sentimentalism [*Empfindelei*]) but also philosophers and indeed the most rigorous of them, the Stoics, have introduced moral
Schwärmerei instead of a sober [*nüchtern*] but wise moral discipline, although
the *Schwärmerei* of the latter was more heroic, while that of the former is a
more shallow and pliable nature" (Ak., 5:86).

"Sober *but* wise": the definition of *Schwärmerei* comes down to this
phrase, for it captures the distinction by which Kant distinguishes his own discourse from that of novelists. Sobriety by itself is not wisdom, as the "but"
indicates; and wisdom, as the Stoics demonstrate, is not always sober. "Sobriety" does not simply mean being aware, staying awake, opening one's eyes, or
even waking up from "dogmatic slumbers";[17] it means acknowledging the possibility of a sheer possibility, a possibility—and indeed the most necessary of
all possibilities, moral perfection—that nevertheless cannot be fulfilled: "the
sage (of the Stoics)," according to the *Critique of Pure Reason*, "is an ideal, that
is, someone who exists merely in thought" (A 569; B 597). As long as the aim
of novel-writing is to make pure possibilities—"ideals," fictional beings—seem
real, anyone who claims to be able to actualize the possibility of wisdom takes
part in a "novelistic" failure: each one converts a sheer possibility into an
apparently real one. Sobriety, by contrast, consists in nonconversion: one rec-
ognizes the command to become wise but acknowledges at the same time that

16. The first of these novels is Wilhelm Karol von Wobester's *Elisa, oder das Weib, wie es seyn sollte* (Elisa, or
     How A Woman Should be) (Leipzig, 1796). This novel was reprinted at least seven times before the
     turn of the century, and it was translated into French, English, Dutch, and Danish. It gave rise to a
     swarm of imitators, including a series of counterparts to Elisa's story of "how a woman should be," the
     first of which was *Robert, oder der Mann, wie er seyn sollte* (Robert, or How a Man Should Be). A novel
     depicting how an officer "should be" soon followed, and so did a parody of the newly invented genre in
     which a family is shown how it "ought to be." Elise is closer to a Stoic than to the one who acts accord-
     ing to Kantian moral doctrine, and indeed she conforms to the image of moral *Schwärmerei* that Kant
     rejects in the *Critical of Practical Reason*. These novels deserve more attention than they have received,
     since they point toward the way Kant's work was interpreted when it first appeared in German-speaking
     countries. For a brief description of *Elise* and a list of the novels to which it gave rise, see Erich Adickes,
     German Kantian Bibliography (1893–96, reprint, New York, 1970), 234–36.
17. For an analysis of Kant's discourse of sleeping, dreaming, and awakening, see Fenves, *Peculiar Fate*,
     69–80.

wisdom is nothing more than a possibility and that the sage is nothing more than a pure fiction. Any claim to have actualized this fiction, even if this actualization takes place in the fictional form of the novel, does violence to its purity. The *Critique of Practical Reason* could therefore be called the *Critique of Impure Fiction.*

Kant's *Critique of Practical Reason* is nonetheless dedicated to the demonstration that pure reason *can* be practical. But this "can" must be kept "sober." No one can secure the condition under which the ability to be moral turns into the actuality of moral conduct—or, to use the terms introduced in the "Essay on the Sicknesses of the Head," something great in the world. It is therefore no small matter to understand what Kant means by "sobriety": it names the affective condition for the possibility of the effectiveness of pure reason. The term "sobriety" thus replaces the one Kant everywhere else favors, namely "critique." The *Critique of Practical Reason* could be given a more active and thus more accurate title: *Sobering Wisdom.* And yet nowhere does Kant appear less sober than in the subsequent paragraph, for he interrupts the exposition of his argument that pure reason can be practical with the naming of the singular being in whose favor the discourse of argumentation is undertaken in the first and last place:

> *Duty!* You sublime great name that embraces nothing charming
> or insinuating but requires submission and yet seeks not to move
> the will by threatening aught that would arouse natural aversion
> or terror, but only holds forth a law which of itself finds entrance
> into the mind and yet gains reverence [*Verehrung*] against my will
> (though not always obedience) before whom all inclinations are
> silenced. . . . What origin is there worthy of you, and where to
> find the root of your noble descent, which proudly rejects all kin-
> ship with inclinations? (Ak., 5:86)

Kant does not simply address duty in this rare rhetorical performance: duty makes possible the apostrophe to duty, hence to *itself,* by silencing all other voices, including Kant's. Only when all these voices have fallen silent can Kant act as the spokesman for the duty whom he addresses. His apostrophe does not so much speak the language of duty—it is an address, not an imperative—as communicate the ability of the law of duty to communicate on its own, without any prior condition other than the a priori condition of unconditional freedom. Inasmuch as duty is here called a name, not a concept, it designates some*one*, not something. Inasmuch as it is a sublime name, it rises above every common name or noun and thus removes itself entirely from the order of generality; and inasmuch as it is a "someone" singled out in the address, it comes forth, or withdraws, as a You through which the I itself is defined: a You by virtue of which the "authentic self" (Ak., 5:118) *is* a self in the first place.[18] By interrupting the course of a philosophical "analytic," the apostrophe may not associate Kant's program with "novel-writing," but it nevertheless shows that the language by which human reason justifies its practices is itself grounded in a prior language, the language of hymnic address. Duty, converted into a heroic demi-god by virtue of antonomasia, is not only singular, it also founds the universal order of singularity Kant generally calls "the kingdom of ends." The conditional definition of *moralische Schwärmerei* thus draws Kant toward a question from which he shies away: Under what condition can one speak not of critical enthusiasm but of a *sober* one? This is the question to which Hölderlin will turn when he presents the relation between poetry, knowledge, and *Schwärmerei*.

And the second reason that Kant may have presented his definition of *Schwärmerei* "in its most general meaning" under the sign of conditionality derives from the controversy surrounding Spinoza and Spinozism. Kant had only recently published his contribution to the so-called *Pantheismusstreit,* "What Does It Mean: To Orient Oneself in Thought?" (1786), and it is in view of Spinoza—not just his exceptional thought but his exemplary life—that certain debates around the concept of enthusiasm took another and decisive turn. Unlike Swedenborg, for example, Spinoza could hardly be accused of allowing himself to be swept up in fantasy or "symbols." And yet, in a certain sense, "enthusiasm" is found in the very heart of Spinoza's speculative system: God is not "in us," of course, but we are all "in" God or nature. If Kant wants to enlist Spinoza into the ranks of *Schwärmer,* then he cannot define *Schwärmerei* in terms of imagination, fantasy, or figuration, for, as Kant knows—although he may know very little else about the legendary "atheist"—Spinoza makes no use of these in the explication of his system and indeed condemns them as sources of error. One definition of *Schwärmerei,* however, could be understood to include the author of the *Ethics,* since this book postpones talk of "human reason" until its second section: "If in its most general meaning *Schwärmerei* is a transgression of the limits of human reason undertaken according to principles. . . ." The principle on which Spinoza transgresses the limits of *human* reason is the principle of principles—the principle of reason, or, as Lessing says, *a nihilo nihil fit*—and the conflict over Spinoza did not erupt simply because Friedrich Jacobi had announced Lessing's allegiance to

---

18. For an especially rich example, see Kant's exposition of the moral law in terms a "veiled goddess" in "On a Newly Arisen Superior Tone in Philosophy" (Ak., 8:405).

Spinoza (and by so doing caused great discomfort to Moses Mendelssohn);[19] but because he presented Spinoza's thought as the outcome of all philosophical speculation: "nihilism," a term he invented,[20] which is tantamount to the denial of freedom.

However complicated the swarm of controversies unleashed by Jacobi's publication of the most famous *Aufklärer*'s allegiance to Spinoza, the question around which it turns is quite simple: Can anyone, or anything, be said to be free? Whatever is said to be free would have to be understood as singular; but all talk of singularity—regardless of whether it is the singularity of Spinoza's "substance" or the singularity of Jacobi's *salto morale*—implies a certain enthusiasm, if not *Schwärmerei*. To the extent that the term *Schwärmerei* arises out of an experience of disorderly swarming in which one loses all sense of direction, it calls for a radical reorientation; and the only point of reference for an orientation of thinking that does not depend on the dogmatic assumption of "right thinking" will be the principle upon which all thinking about movement, motives, and motivation—or, in short, practical reasoning—is based, namely, the principle of freedom. "What Does It Mean: To Orient Oneself in Thinking?" thus gravitates toward Kant's impassioned plea not for freedom *in* but for freedom *of* thought. This freedom is endangered, according to Kant, whenever self-proclaimed "geniuses" excuse themselves from the generality of the law, including the laws of thought, and proclaim their singularity. Yet the freedom of thought cannot do without a certain freedom of speech, as Kant himself insists in the closing paragraphs of "What is Enlightenment?" The paradox of transcendental freedom, the very possibility of which cannot be grasped, comes to a head whenever "free thinking" is brought into conflict with "free speech." Only a self-restrained speech—more precisely, speech that refrains from expressing "free thinking"—allows for a space in which there can be a sustained freedom of speech. Kant orients his thought toward such a space: it is the arena of "openness" or "publicity." "Spinozism" demands a renewed encounter with *Schwärmerei* precisely because Spinoza freely lets his "free thinking" come to speech. Kant must show that Spinozism can do so only

---

19. A large number of the texts involved in the debate can be found in *Die Hauptschriften zum Pantheismusstreit zwischen Jacobi und Mendelssohn,* ed. and intro. Heinrich Scholz (Berlin, 1916); cf. *The Spinoza Conversations between Lessing and Jacobi,* intro., G. Vallée; trans. G. Vallée, J. B. Lawson, and C. G. Chapple (Lanham, Md., 1988), 87. The standard work in English on this controversy is found in the chapters devoted to Jacobi and Mendelssohn in Frederick Beiser, *The Fate of Reason* (Cambridge, Mass., 1987). A useful review of the controversy, including a critique of Beiser, can be found in Allen Arkush, *Mendelssohn and the Enlightenment* (Albany, N.Y., 1994), 69–97.

20. See Friedrich Jacobi, *Werke* (Leipzig, 1812–25), 3:44.

as long as Spinozists, if not Spinoza himself, ground their thought in an unwarranted claim. Spinozism, then, functions as the exact counterpart of novel-writer. Whereas novelists present the sheer possibility of moral perfection as a fictional reality, Spinozists must ultimately base themselves on an insight they are not in a position to perceive—the insight, namely, that a perfect and absolutely independent intellect is impossible:

> The *Critique* [*of Pure Reason*] shows that, in order to assert the possibility of a being which is itself an object of thought, it is not nearly enough that its concept should be free from contradiction (although it remains permissible to assume this possibility when there arises a case of need [*nötigenfalls*]). Spinozism, however, proposes to have perceived the impossibility of a being the idea of which consists solely of pure concepts of the understanding which have only been detached from all conditions of sense-experience, and in which it is therefore impossible ever to discover a contradiction; yet it is altogether incapable of supporting this excessive demand [*Anmaßung*], which goes beyond all limits. For precisely this reason Spinozism leads directly to *Schwärmerei*. (Ak., 8:143)[21]

Spinozism and criticism agree on at least one point: the possibility of an entity completely detached from sense-experience does not go without saying. But something, according to Kant, can be said in favor of this sheer possibility: no such entity can be known, to be sure, since knowledge is grounded in the possibility of sense-experience; but whenever there is an emergency

21. Kant made notes for an essay on "Philosophical *Schwärmerei*" in which he would trace the development of this disorder from Plato to Spinoza; see *Reflexionen* 6050, Ak. 17:434–37: "Spinozism is the true conclusion to dogmatic metaphysics. Critique of propositions has no success here. For the difference between the subjective and the objective with respect to their validity cannot be recalled, because the subjective propositions that are at the same time objective have not been previously distinguished" (Ak., 17:436). Kant's conception of both Plato and Spinoza is, of course, firmly rooted in eighteenth-century commonplaces about these philosophers. Kant's anti-Platonism, which he owes in large part to the historian of philosophy whom he generally relies on (namely, J. J. Brucker; see A 316, B 372), never goes as far as his anti-Spinozism, for Plato—or at least Plato, "the academic" (Ak., 8:62)—poses a genuine philosophical problem, whereas Spinozism, according to Kant, derives from a failure to distinguish subjective and objective propositions. There is one philosopher whom Kant calls an enthusiast whose enthusiasm never gives rise to philosophical *Schwärmerei*—namely, Rousseau. As early as "On the Sicknesses of the Head," Kant calls Rousseau a "Phantast" (Ak., 2:267), but because Kant presents Rousseau's *Schwärmerei* in terms of moral—not theoretical—positions, Rousseau never enters into Kant's accounts of the genesis of contemporary philosophical enthusiasm. For an insightful presentation of Kant's relation to Rousseau, particularly in his early writings, see Richard Velkley, *Freedom and the End of Reason* (Chicago, 1989).

(*nötigenfalls*), like the strife unleashed by Jacobi's publication, this pure possibility comes to fulfill a need (*Bedürfnis*): "the need of reason" (Ak., 8:140–41). Spinozism, by contrast, leaves no room for the sheer possibility of an utterly "detached" being to whom all other beings would nevertheless be attached. According to Spinozism, a self-sufficient intellect is not simply unpresentable, it is altogether impossible. For Kant, this amounts to a denial of a God in whose existence one can have a rational faith. But the denial could also mean, on second thought—or for another Kant—that reason has no place for an *agent* who detaches *itself* from "all conditions of sense-experience" for the tautological reason that it, the agent, consists solely *in* acting. It is on the basis of the distinction between these two explications of the thought whose possibility Spinozism denies that a *radical* criticism—criticism for which any talk of "things in themselves" is itself an *Anmaßung* ("unwarranted demand")—develops. Spinozism leads toward *Schwärmerei* insofar as the being about which it speaks is so singular that everything different from this being, including the one who speaks about it, is only its modification, and in this way everything, including the self, subsists in God or nature. "There is no one more secure means of eradicating *Schwärmerei* at the root [*mit der Wurzel*]," Kant concludes, "than the determination of the limits of the pure faculty of reason" (Ak., 143). But this still leaves the question: What is the root of all possible *Schwärmerei*? Under what condition does one say "I am not free," which is to say, "I do not act" and therefore "I do not exist"? It is toward these questions that Schelling turns in his belated contribution to the same controversy, *Philosophical Letters on Dogmatism and Criticism* (1795).

"THE MIDDLE-POINT OF ALL POSSIBLE SCHWÄRMEREI" (SCHELLING)

Instead of recommending a medicine (*Mittel*) to eradicate *Schwärmerei,* Schelling seeks out its middle-point (*Mittelpunkt*), and by the time he has reached the eighth of his "philosophical letters," he finds himself in this position: "By speaking of the moral principle of dogmatism, I believe that I am at the middle-point of all possible *Schwärmerei*."[22] Once he has reached this middle-point, he can overcome the distance inscribed in the epistolary form

---

22. Friedrich Schelling, *Philosophische Briefe über den Dogmatismus und Kriticismus,* in *Historisch-kritisch Ausgabe,* ed. H. M. Baumgartner, W. G. Jacobs, H. Krings, and H. Zeltner, vol. 3, ed. H. Buchner, W. G. Jacobs, and A. Pieper (Stuttgart, 1982), 3:85; hereafter, S. (All references are to the first series of volumes.) There is an idiosyncratic translation of the *Letters* in Schelling, *The Unconditional in Human Knowledge,* ed. and trans. Fritz Marti (Lewisburg, Pa., 1980).

and join his addressee: "Here, my friend, we stand at the principle of all *Schwärmerei*" (S, 90). The multiplicity of enthusiasms converges on this "moral principle," which is, for its part, not itself a kind of *Schwärmerei*—not even of "moral *Schwärmerei*"—but the law of its generation. From this point of view Schelling's *Philosophical Letters* presents itself as a universal solution to the problem of *Schwärmerei*. Once the "friend" to whom Schelling addresses himself is able to join him at the point from which enthusiasm originates, he will have distanced himself from every kind of enthusiasm.[23] But the radicality of his analysis drives Schelling to the point where *any* self-assertion is necessarily nonenthusiastic: I cannot mean what I say when I say "I am a *Schwärmer.*" The meaning of *Schwärmerei* lies in this impossibility.

As Schelling announces in the preface, the point of the *Philosophical Letters* is to make a distinction that is not sharply enough made in the *Critique of Pure Reason:* the distinction between dogmatism and criticism. The distinction is of significance to philosophy to the extent that dogmatism and criticism do not simply hold conflicting opinions about something; rather, they name completely opposed systems about everything—or, more precisely, about the nature of the unconditioned, the absolute, or, to use a misleading term, God. Conflict cannot take place about the absolute unless one has taken a distance from the absolute. Criticism and dogmatism are, according to Schelling, the only two ways one can take a stand with respect to the absolute and, by taking a stand, found a system: "Anyone whose task consists in settling the dispute [*Streit*] of *philosophers* must proceed from precisely the point from which the dispute of *philosophy* itself, or, to say the same, the original conflict [*Widerstreit*] in the human *spirit* [*Geist*] proceeds. But this point is none other than the steeping-out from the absolute, for we would all be one about the absolute if we never left its sphere" (S, 3:60). In the simplest of terms—and Schelling promises clarity, if not simplicity, in the preface—criticism proposes to found a system in which the absolute is understood as the subject (the I, or the self), whereas dogmatism proposes to establish a system in which the absolute is understood as the object (the not-I, Spinoza's substance, or the thing-in-itself). The singularity of the absolute, its ability to escape the schemata of subsump-

---

23. In this sense Schelling's *Philosophische Briefe* belongs to at least two specific genres: epistolary philosophy, of which Schiller's *Letters on Aesthetic Education* is the most famous example, and the anti-*Schwärmerei* novel. Novels that belong to the later genre set out to describe a cycle of *Schwärmerei;* once the *Schwärmer* has passed through the entire cycle, the novel comes to an end and he is generally "cured" of his "sickness of the head." Wieland's *Geschichte des Agathon* is perhaps the best-known example of this genre, but it could also be seen to include, with certain important modifications, Hölderlin's *Hyperion;* see Walter Erhart, "'In guten Zeiten giebt es selten Schwärmer'—Wielands 'Agathon' und Hölderlins 'Hyperion,'" *Hölderlin Jahrbuch* 28 (1992–93): 173–91.

tion whereby a particularity falls under a general rule, guarantees that it—the absolute—will always be absolutely ambiguous: it can be systematized in two ways, and neither of these two systems can say precisely what it means to say; each system can only announce, in two different versions, "I demand . . ."

Although there is little doubt that *Philosophical Letters,* like Schelling's other contemporaneous writings, is meant to elucidate and thereby promote "criticism,"[24] it does not simply reject dogmatism; on the contrary, it seeks to show that the latter, like criticism, is *theoretically* irrefutable. The same cannot be said of what Schelling calls "dogmaticism," and the opening letters consist for the most part in the refutation of the apparently critical systems developed by Schelling's more orthodox teachers in the Theological Institute in Tübingen—*apparently* critical because they constantly cite Kant's *Critiques* and, in particular, make use of their gestures toward an apology "without hypocrisy" for Christianity (Ak., 5:86). But they are nevertheless uncritical for the simple reason that they rely at every point on a thing-in-itself: they still think it is possible to speak about God without having to inquire into the freedom upon which the act of speaking is itself based.[25] For Schelling, there is only one representative of genuine dogmatism, Spinoza, whose major work not only represents a thoroughgoing dogmatic system but also, by presenting this system in terms of an "ethics," points toward the *practical* resolution of the dispute within philosophy. In order for the dispute to be settled with a *theorem,* either the subject or the object would have to be shown to be absolute; but an absolute subject is no longer a subject, and an absolute object is no longer an object: "If the conflict between subject and object stops, then the subject must no longer have the need to step outside itself; both must become absolutely identical, that is, either the subject must lose itself in the object or the object must lose itself in the subject" (S, 3:64). For the subject to win the dispute, it would have

24. *Little* doubt—not *no* doubt. For in the note Schelling added to the *Letters* when he republished them in 1809, he emphasizes something else entirely: the ninth letter contains the "clearest germs of later and more positive views" (S, 3:49). The possibility that the *Letters* were not entirely devoted to the explication of "criticism" did not escape Fichte, whose "First Introduction" (to the *Wissenschaftslehre,* 1797) consists of a tacit evaluation and refutation of Schelling's exposition of the difference between dogmatism and criticism. A translation of this text, along with an exceptionally useful guide to the philosophical controversies in which it plays an important role, can be found in J. G. Fichte, *Introductions to the Wissenschaftslehre and Other Writings,* ed. and trans. D. Breazeale (Indianapolis, 1994).

25. "If the *Critique of Pure Reason* spoke against dogmatism, it spoke against dogmaticism, that is, a system of dogmatism that is erected blindly, and without a preceding investigation of the faculty of knowledge" (S, 3:69). Kant had several definitions of "dogmatic," but as Daniel Breazeale points out (*Introductions to the Wissenschaftslehre,* xxiii–xxiv), Schelling and Fichte's use of this term is determined by Solomon Maimon's clear and univocal definition. According to Maimon's *Philosophisches Wörterbuch oder Beleuchtung der wichtigsten Gegenstände der Philosophie in alphabetischer Ordnung* (1790), dogmatism is the belief that one possesses cognition of things-in-themselves.

to lose itself, and for the object to win, it would have to lose itself. No wonder *Philosophical Letters* veers toward a discussion of *Schwärmerei* and ends up with an unprecedented discussion of tragedy.

"One or the other must happen. Either no subject and an absolute object or no object and an absolute subject. How can this dispute be settled?" (S, 3:65). This dispute can be settled, according to Schelling, by converting a theoretical statement about the nature of the absolute into an ethical demand to make good on this theorem: "Here philosophy passes into the domain of *demands* [*Foderungen*], that is, into the domain of practical philosophy, and here must the principle that we established at the beginning of philosophy, and that was dispensable for theoretical philosophy if it was to constitute a separate domain, decide the victor" (S, 3:65). Every assertion about the absolute is, therefore, as Schelling remarks, "proleptic" (S, 3:80): it does not solve the unique problem of philosophy—"the riddle of the world" (S, 3:78), the enigma that there is a world of finite things after all—but, instead, anticipates a solution in lieu of its practical realization: "No philosopher will imagine having done *everything* merely by setting up the highest principles. For those principles themselves have as foundations of his system only subjective value; that is, they are valid *for him* only insofar as he has anticipated *his* practical decision" (S, 3:81). One may want to say something about the absolute—and this desire is, for Schelling, inscribed in the very name "philosophy"—but every assertion about the absolute is at bottom a self-assertion: each one says not precisely what the speaker will decide *to be* but *if* the speaker will decide to be at all: "'To be or not to be'" (S, 3:89, quoted in English) is the question every genuine system of philosophy (theoretically) answers in advance of *the* (practical) decision.

From this perspective Schelling not only comes to the resolution of a theoretically irresolvable problem, the nature of the absolute, but also approaches the root of all *Schwärmerei*. According to the "Seventh Letter," the *Critique of Pure Reason* and the Jacobi-Mendelssohn dispute result in the same demand: the two genuine philosophical systems—unlike "dogmaticism," which still speaks of a creation *ex nihilo*—join together in demanding that there be absolutely no passage from the infinite to the finite: "Philosophy cannot, to be sure, pass from the infinite to the finite, but it can, on the contrary, pass from the finite to the infinite" (S, 3:83). Both criticism and dogmatism demand or "postulate" this passage from the finite to the infinite; but they demand it in opposite ways: criticism demands that the I strive to be infinite, whereas dogmatism demands that the I strive to be identical with the infinite "and to collapse [*unterzugehen*] into the infinitude of the absolute object" (S, 3:84).

Dogmatism thus comes down to the command "annihilate yourself! [*Vernichte dich selbst*]" (S, 3:84), and it is in the command of self-annihilation that Schelling finally finds the "middle-point of all possible *Schwärmerei*" (S, 3:85). There is no limit to the number of different kinds of *Schwärmerei,* but all forms of *Schwärmerei* make the otherwise unbearable thought of non-being bearable: "The holiest thoughts of the ancients and the monstrosities of human insanity come together. 'Return to the divinity, the primal source of all existence, unification with the absolute, annihilation of oneself'—is the principle of all *schwärmerisch* philosophy, which has only been laid out, interpreted, veiled in images by different people in different ways, according to their cast of mind and thought. The principle for the history of all *Schwärmerei* is to be found here" (S, 3:85–86).

But this, the principle for the history of all *Schwärmerei,* is not yet the principle of *Schwärmerei* itself. The thought of self-annihilation can be made bearable if the self "outlives" (*überlebt;* S, 3:84) its own annihilation, and it can outlive its own annihilation while demanding the very same annihilation because of something "we" all do: we "translate" (*übertragen*) the word "being" from its literal, or "proper," sense to an improper, or metaphorical sense (S, 3:87). The origin of *Schwärmerei*—which is now tantamount to the command "annihilate yourself!"—can henceforth be sought in a fundamental failure of nonphilosophical language: we mean "appearances" or "non-being" when we say "being." This *Übertragen* of "being" from the I to the not-I makes it bearable (*erträglich*) to demand that the "passage" (*Übergang*) from the finite to the infinite result in an absolute not-I, for "being," properly understood, outlives, or "over-lives," this annihilation—and *I am being in the proper sense of the word.*

On this, Schelling has no doubts: doubts would arise only when an intuition is lacking, but it is impossible, according to Schelling, for one to lack self-intuition and still be oneself. Schelling's exposition of the principle of *Schwärmerei* depends on a self-intuition in which the self reveals itself to itself: "A secret, marvelous capacity (*Vermögen*) dwells within all of us: to withdraw ourselves from the alteration of time into our greatest inwardness, to withdraw ourselves from everything that comes from the outside, and there, under the form of immutability to intuit the eternal in us" (S, 3:87).[26] Schelling considers himself justified in using the term intuition for this revelation of the self to itself

---

26. This Gnostic and Kabbalistic motif of "withdrawal" becomes ever more important in Schelling's subsequent writings, especially those that no longer attempt to "elucidate" Fichte's *Wissenschaftslehre.* Of particular interest is his use of the term *Kontraktion* in the so-called *Stuttgarter Privatvorlesung* (1810); see *Sämmtliche Werke,* ed. M. Schröter (Munich, 1927–54), 7:429 and *passim.* The "contraction" of which he speaks in these lectures is not, of course, the withdrawal of the I into itself but the withdrawal of God into himself.

because Kant had defined "intuition" at the very opening of the first *Critique* as a singular, immediate, and hence nonderivable relation. What corresponds to this definition better than the relation of the self to itself? This relation (*Beziehung*) can then be seen to consist in a withdrawal (*Zurückziehung*) from everything outside the self, and since this withdrawal leaves no room for sensation, self-intuition must be considered "intellectual": "This intellectual intuition comes on stage when we stop being objects for ourselves, where, withdrawn into ourselves, the intuiting self is identical with the intuited" (S, 3:88).[27] Once this intuition has been secured in a moment of world-consuming withdrawal in which everything disappears into the self, Schelling can at last join the one to whom he addresses his remarks, his friend, who is himself perhaps a *Schwärmer*[28] and who, if he outlives his friend's self-intuition, does so only *in* being addressed by his friend. The friends finally meet when they are most apart: "Here, my friend, we stand at the principle of all *Schwärmerei*. It originates, when it turns into a system, through nothing other than objectivized intellectual intuition, whenever one takes an intuition of oneself for an intuition of an object outside oneself, the intuition of the inner intellectual world for the intuition of a supersensible world outside oneself" (S, 3:90).

More than anything else, the discovery of a "secret capacity" for self-intuition distances Schelling not only from his "friend" but also from Kant. For one of the decisive "facts" to which the first *Critique,* like Hume's *Treatise,* returns is a radical absence of self-intuition: I never encounter myself as such. To account for this "fact" is one of the all-important tasks of any critique of reason. To discount it, by contrast, amounts to engaging in the "dreams of spirit-seers." From the perspective of this basic doctrine of Kantian critique, Schelling would arrive at the origin of *Schwärmerei* by falling into one of its versions. But Schelling's talk of a "secret, marvelous capacity" also runs counter to everything previously argued, for criticism *does* seem to be in a position to

---

27. Much has been written about "intellectual intuition" in Kant, Fichte, Schelling, and Hölderlin. For an assessment of what is at stake in this variously spelled term, see John Neubauer, "Intellektuelle, intellektuale und ästhetische Anschauung: Zur Entstehung der romantischen Kunstauffassung," *Deutsche Vierteljahrschrift für Literaturwissenschaft und Geistesgeschichte* 46 (1972): 294–319; and Manfred Frank, "Intellektuale Anschauung': Drei Stellungnahmen zu einem Deutungsversuch von Selbstbewußtsein: Kant, Fichte, Hölderlin/Novalis," in E. Behler and J. Hörisch, eds., *Die Aktualität der Frühromantik* (Paderborn, 1987): 96–126.

28. And is also perhaps Hölderlin, who, as a young man, wrote a poem entitled "Schwärmerei" (1788), which begins with the apostrophe: "Freunde! Freunde!" More than once, Hölderlin has been suggested as the addressee of the *Philosophical Letters;* see the introduction to the Baverian academy edition by Annamarie Pieper (S, 3:29–34) and the provocative study by Margerethe Wegenast, *Hölderlins Spinoza-Rezeption* (Tübingen, 1990), 106–23. Pieper rejects the suggestion, whereas Wegenast argues strenuously for it.

offer a strictly *theoretical* refutation of dogmatism. What is more "theoretical," what is more closely connected to *theorein* ("looking"), than *Anschauung* ("looking at")? The ability to refute dogmatism in a theoretical manner lies in the "secret, marvelous capacity" itself: the secret of this "capacity" is that it *can* be actualized, and because the actualization of this capacity obeys no causal law, it is a marvel. Having arrived at "the principle of all *Schwärmerei*" by virtue of this capacity, Schelling then finds another kind of *Schwärmerei* in its very actualization. There is always one more kind, an excessive kind that escapes the "principle" by which each kind is defined as one, and Schelling comes across this other kind of *Schwärmerei* at the end of the ninth letter: it is, as one might expect, the *Schwärmerei* of criticism, a kind of swarming that exactly corresponds to what Kant called "moral *Schwärmerei*." If all objective causality is negated by my own causality, "I would be absolute.—But criticism would fall into *Schwärmerei* if it also represented this last goal only as *attainable* (not as *attained*)" (S, 3:106). The dash points toward an elision and a paradox: Schelling should have written in parenthesis "even if not yet attained," but this would make the thesis of the I, the thesis of "intellectual intuition," into . . . a paren-thesis.

Schelling could therefore only arrive at a paradox: "criticism would fall into *Schwärmerei* if it also represented this last goal only as *attainable* (not as *attained*)." What is represented as attained cannot be represented as possible "only" to attain: it is, and it is impossible. Just as Kant places his doctrine of pure practical reason under the sign of a "sobriety" in which one remains aware of the impossibility of attaining the moral perfection one must nevertheless be able to attain, Schelling thrusts any criticism that represents the goal it demands of itself into the hands of the *Schwärmer*: the possibility of the self absolving itself of all relations other than those it institutes on its own is supposed to be—this is the law—a sheer possibility, a fiction so pure that it corresponds to no representation, no image, and no idea. By doing so, Schelling is no longer in a position to claim that he has found a single "principle of all *Schwärmerei*." But this is by no means the only disadvantage of his disclosure of a critical *Schwärmerei*. Criticism can keep itself sober only under the ambiguous condition of a radical self-censorship: it cannot represent the goal of its activity, which is "itself"; and this prohibition on making an image of itself as the absolute makes it impossible for the activity of criticism to know in advance the direction of its movement. Critical activity, the act of the I as it posits itself in relation to something other than itself, cannot therefore distinguish itself from the meandering, disorderly, disoriented, aimless buzzing of the "swarmer." By defining a *Schwärmerei* of criticism, Schelling comes close to confessing that criticism, which takes the principle of subjectivity as the foundation of knowledge, action, and being, is itself *Schwärmerei*. Sobriety— or the peculiar knowledge that one cannot act as one can, should, and must act—would have to be sought in something other than this principle.[29]

Schelling can save himself from confessing that his presentation of the *Schwärmerei* in the *Philosophical Letters* is not under-critical, if not hypocritical, only on one condition: he must justify the hypercritical thesis of self-intuition. And this is precisely what he proceeds to do in the essays he published in the *Philosophisches Journal* after the completion of the *Philosophical Letters*. One of his methods for justifying himself by justifying the self as the sole ground on which philosophy can build consists in showing that although Kant may have denied the possibility of intellectual intuition, he built his edifice on the very same ground. Schelling thus quotes Kant himself to refute Kant's interpretation of his own work: he first cites the recently published polemic against Schlosser, "On a Newly Arisen Superior Tone in Philosophy," and then the well-known but, according to Schelling, little read *Critique of Pure Reason*. In the former text Kant speaks of freedom as the "Archimedean point" on which reason can move the world (Ak., 8:404), and in the latter work he describes the I as a "purely intellectual representation" (B 423) in the very section where he vigorously denies the possibility of intuiting oneself. Schelling draws the following conclusion from these two quotations: "This constant activity of self-intuition and transcendental freedom on which it maintains itself is alone what makes it such that *I myself* do not drown in the stream of representations, and it is what carries me over [*fortträgt*] from act to act, from thought to thought, from time to time (on invisible wings, as it were)" (S, 4:128–29).

The "carrying over" (*Forttragen*) by which the I maintains itself runs directly counter to the "transfer" (*Übertragen*) in which *Schwärmerei* is grounded: the "translation" of the word "being" from one sphere—that of the I—to another. But this "carrying over" on which the entire exposition of idealism rests is itself a "transfer," "translation," or "metaphor," and it is, moreover, an *Übertragen* whose every word calls out for an elucidation of the relation of figural to philosophical language: the "as" (*wie*) of the phrase "as on invisible wings" marks a

---

29. In the *Philosophical Letters* Schelling does not draw on the distinction between absolute and transcendental freedom that he had developed in the final sections of *On the I as the Principle of Philosophy*. This distinction may allow him to reformulate the idea of a "*Schwärmerei* of criticism," but Schelling has good reason to avoid it in the last sections of the *Philosophical Letters*. Transcendental freedom is absolute in the *active* sense of the term "absolute": to be free in a transcendental sense is to absolve one-self of all relations other than one's own self-relation. Any talk of absolute freedom in contrast to transcendental freedom runs the risk of making the absolute into an inert substance and therefore falling into what Schelling calls "dogmatism."

metaphorical moment; the word "invisible" (*unsichtbar*), especially within a discussion of "intuition" (*Anschauung*), inscribes this moment into one of foundational metaphorics of Kantian metaphysics; and the generally poetic term for "wings" (*Fittige*)—which is, furthermore, a term poets apply to their own activity[30]—enlists this metaphysical metaphorics in a poetic movement that makes it impossible to decide on the metaphorical character of its terms. For "wings"—especially the often invisible ones of bees—constitute the condition for the creation of a *swarm* in the original sense of the term. By disclosing "the principle of all possible *Schwärmerei*," Schelling returns to its root.[31]

The I carries itself over the stream of representations "as on invisible wings." On the basis of this statement Schelling finds himself in a position not only to define Schwärmerei but also to defend himself against the accusation that he, like the hapless Schlosser whom Kant had attacked in the essay he quotes, is a *Schwärmer*.[32] Schelling's definition of *Schwärmerei* accords with Kant's but for one telling detail: he drops the term "human" from Kant's talk of "human reason," and he therefore abandons the term by which he has hitherto explicated the critical system, namely "the I." Instead of speaking of the I, Schelling finds it necessary to determine *Schwärmerei* in relation to "the spirit" (*der Geist*): "All *Schwärmerei* transgresses the limits of reason. Spirit itself, we maintain, draws these limits, for it gives itself its sphere, intuits itself in this sphere, and out of this sphere there is nothing for it. It is ridiculous to find *Schwärmerei* in *that which* forever makes all *Schwärmerei* impossible" (S, 4:129). By drawing its own limits, "spirit" withdraws into itself. "Spirit" is not the same as the I, and yet it is no different than the I: it is the *philosophical* I, and only insofar as the I is properly philosophical can Schelling authorize his definition with a "we maintain." But even more to the point: "spirit" is the name for the I that *actualizes* the "secret, marvelous capacity" for self-intuition. Philosophers, for Schelling, cannot acknowledge the sheer possibility of self-intuition without at the same

30. See, for example, the compilation of eighteenth-century examples of *Fittich* in the Grimm brothers' *Deutsches Wörterbuch*, 3:1693–94. For an example of its contemporaneous use, see the striking lines of the first stanza of Hölderlin's "Patmos," lines that defy any translation of sense (*Sinn*) because they are concerned with the translation (and return) of "the most faithful sense": "O Fittige gib uns, treuesten Sinns / Hinüberzugehen und wiederzukehren" (lines 14–15).

31. Schelling, like Hölderlin, inspired comparison with bees. August von Platen concludes one of his odes to Schelling ("An Schelling, Bei demselben Anlasse") in the following way: "Du aber [in contrast to Platen, who compares himself to a butterfly] tauch die heil'ge Bienenschwinge / Herab vom Saum des Weltenblumenrandes / In das geheimnißvolle Wie der Dinge" (August von Platen, *Gesammelte Werke* [Stuttgart-Tübingen, 1847], 2:95). I thank Arnd Wedemeyer for drawing my attention to von Platen's poem.

32. The degree to which Schelling understood Kant's polemic attack against Schlosser and Stolberg as an attack on every use of the term "intellectual intuition," including his own, can be gauged by his review of the controversy in the *Allgemeine Literatur-Zeitung*, one of the official organs of Kantian thought; see S, 4:283–87.

time actualizing this possibility, for philosophy consists in precisely this: the actualization of "the secret, marvelous capacity."[33]

But Schelling does not present "spirit" in quite this way. Or, more precisely, the assertion that spirit is the actualization of the capacity for self-intuition goes without saying and therefore says *nothing:* spirit is not something about which philosophy, properly speaking, is able to speak because all philosophical communication presupposes a common philosophical spirit. In a footnote appended to his remarks about "invisible wings, as it were," Schelling rejects the possibility of a properly philosophical explanation of the term "spirit," and this rejection of philosophy's ability to explicate its own spirit keeps it sober: "After what Herr Professor Fichte in volume 5, no. 4 of the *Philosophical Journal* has said about this, there remains nothing more to add.[34]—The entire investigation, properly speaking [*eigentlich*], belongs in *aesthetics* (where I will also return to it). For this science first shows the entrance to all philosophy because only in aesthetics can it be explained what philosophical spirit [*philosophischer Geist*] is. Wanting to philosophize without such spirit is no better than wanting to endure outside of time or to write poetry without imagination" (S, 4:129n).

33. A more thorough investigation into Schelling's disclosure of a "secret, marvelous capacity"—which confirms Nietzsche's suspicion that the young men in the Tübingen Theological Institute (Hegel, Schelling, and Hölderlin) sought to discover new "capacities" after having read Kant's *Critiques (Beyond Good and Evil,* para. 11)—would have to consider in detail the theory of modality Schelling proposes in the then recently published *Vom Ich als Prinzip der Philosophie* (On the I as the Principle of Philosophy, 1795). According to Schelling, modal judgments (possibility, actuality, necessity) are not, as Kant argues in the "Principles of Empirical Thought," synthetic but rather "sylleptic" (a term he invents): they do not add anything to the judgments of quality, quantity, and relation; they "take up" (syllepsis) what has already been "posited together" (synthesis). Modal terms cannot therefore be applied to the absolute I, understood as an absolute act of positing; but these terms can then, in turn, serve to describe the *structure* of the I or the unconditioned. (To show how this is done, how the modal terms turn into the "powers" (or "potencies") of Schelling's later thought, is impossible within the confines of this essay.) The "secret, marvelous capacity" of the I to intuit itself must therefore be understood not as a property of the I but as a moment of its structure: in Schelling's later thought, the unconditioned to the first power (where the term *Potenz,* "power," replaces the Kantian word *Vermögen,* "faculty" or "capacity").

34. This is a reference to Fichte's "Second Introduction" (to the *Wissenschaftslehre*). But this reference points in another direction as well—toward the last widely contested battle between philosophers over the reciprocal accusations of *Schwärmerei.* For it is Fichte who accuses Schelling of *Schwärmerei* after the latter abandons his efforts to "elucidate the idealism of the *Wissenschaftslehre*" and begins to articulate his own "natural philosophy" (*Naturphilosophie*): "Contemporary *Schwärmerei,*" Fichte writes in 1806, consists in a "reaction" to the formalism and emptiness of current concepts of experience and knowledge. This reaction finds its expression in the speculative *Naturphilosophie* of Schelling and his associates (Ritter, von Baader): *Schwärmerei* "is and will necessarily be *Naturphilosophie*" ("Basic Features of the Present Age," reprinted in *Johann Gottlieb Fichtes sämmtliche Werke,* ed. I. H. Fichte [reprint, Berlin, 1971], 7:118). Schelling responds almost immediately to this accusation. *Schwärmerei,* he asserts, is rooted in the funda-

This footnote displaces Schelling's entire exposition, including his definition *Schwärmerei,* for, insofar as this exposition constitutes an introduction to the idealism of the *Wissenschaftslehre* and at this very moment directs its readers to Fichte's "Second Introduction," it ought to take place, properly speaking, within the parameters of an "aesthetics." Without "philosophical spirit" there can be no philosophy, no actualization of the capacity for self-intuition; but only a "science" that treats this actualization as a poetic act—or a pure fiction—can teach philosophy what it means to philosophize. Without this supplementary science, the capacity for self-intuition cannot be distinguished from its actualization, and philosophy, in turn, cannot keep itself from falling into *Schwärmerei.* Although aesthetics should come first, it is not even last, for Schelling never makes good on his promise to return to this topic within the context of his elucidation of critical idealism.[35]

"In Good Times There are Seldom Schwärmer" (Hölderlin)

The same cannot be said of Hölderlin. In the course of repeating Schelling's footnote, he does not so much propose "the principle of all possible *Schwärmerei*" as offer a genealogy of the *Schwärmer.* This repetition of the footnote in which Schelling proposes "aesthetics" as a solution for the otherwise intractable difficulties of "criticism" takes place in Hölderlin's sole experiment

mental insufficiency of the I as the principle of philosophy, and it is in view of the inability of the isolated subject to ground its activities on its own that "Luther and his contemporaries" invented the term: "The *Schwärmer* needs someone else in order to confirm his belief; everyone who does not clearly know what he wants swarms. . . . If an inflexible striving to drive home his subjectivity through his own subjectivity and to make it universal, to exterminate all nature wherever possible . . . is called *Schwärmen,* who in these times has in a proper sense 'swarmed' more spitefully and more loudly than Herr Fichte?" ("Laying Out the True Relation of *Naturphilosophie* to the Improved Fichtean Doctrine" [1806], in *Werke,* ed. Schröter, 7:45 and 47).

35. He does make good on this promise in the concluding section of the *System of Transcendental Idealism,* of course, but the paradoxes to which the phrase "philosophical spirit" bears witness are not henceforth resolved. In the section of the *System* devoted to aesthetics, the "postulate" of intellectual intuition is supposed to find its conclusive demonstration: it should cease to be a sheer demand made on the philosopher to actualize his potential for self-intuition and become, instead, a self-evident axiom or, to use the Aristotelian-Euclidean vocabulary to which the term "postulate" alludes, a "common notion." Artworks are therefore the organon of philosophy; but *the* artwork of which all other ones are merely parts—the artwork of artwork—is and perhaps always will be absent. The absence of this artwork is no small failure: as Schelling indicates in the first footnote to the section on "aesthetics as the organon of philosophy," artworks are by definition something present (*eine Gegenwart*), and only insofar as they are "a present" can they convert the demand for self-intuition into an axiom on which philosophy can henceforth rely; see *Werke,* ed. Schröter, 3:614. In the final pages of the *System,* which proudly display 1800 as the date of its birth, Schelling displaces these paradoxes concerning philosophical spirit onto another epoch, an epoch founded on a "new mythology" that *will be* the solution.

in writing prose-fragments, a collection of seven "maxims" to which his twentieth-century editors have attached the title "Reflections." Each of the seven fragments is concerned with the nature of *enthousiazein,* and together they constitute one of the most concentrated confrontations in modern European thought with the tradition inaugurated by Plato's *Ion.* By opening the collection with the bold statement "There is a scale of enthusiasm" (*Es giebt Grade der Begeisterung*),[36] Hölderlin associates his reflections with those of Renaissance neo-Platonism, and in some of the later fragments, particularly in the third and fourth, he takes up, takes to task, and transforms certain remarks of Pseudo-Longinus in praise of enthusiasm that had been understood throughout the eighteenth century as programmatic statements for poetic productivity.[37] Later fragments go even further and challenge the very foundation on which every critical venture—Schelling's no less than Kant's—seeks to distinguish a heroic *Enthusiasmus* from a debilitating *Schwärmerei.* The second half of the penultimate fragment pursues this challenge by repeating Schelling's statement: "The entire investigation, properly speaking, belongs in *aesthetics.*" But this repetition is only a preparation for the striking assertion that *Schwärmerei* is *good:*

> All knowledge [*alles Erkennen*] should begin with the study of the beautiful. For, the one who can understand life without mourning [*ohne zu trauern*] has gained much. Moreover, even *Schwärmerei* and passion are good, devotional prayers [*Andacht*], which life does not touch and may not know, and then despair, when life itself breaks forth from its infinity. The deep feeling of mortality, of change, of his temporal limitations enflames man so that he attempts much; [it] exercises all his powers, and does not allow him to fall into idleness, and one struggles so long with chimeras until finally something true and real [*etwas Wahres und Reelles*] is again found for knowledge and creative occupation [*Erkenntniß und Beschäfftigung*]. In good times there are seldom *Schwärmer.* Yet when man lacks great, pure objects, then he creates some phantom out of this or that, and [he] closes his eyes in order to be able to take an interest in it and live for it. (H, 4:235–36)[38]

---

36. Friedrich Hölderlin, *Sämtliche Werke,* ed. F. Beißner (Stuttgart, 1943–85), 4:233; hereafter, "H."
37. For analysis of this reception, see Martin Vöhler, "Hölderlins Longin-Rezeption," *Hölderlin-Jahrbuch* 28 (1992–93): 152–72.
38. The first sentence in this quotation is introduced by a *deswegen* ("for this reason"), which refers to an incomplete sentence the subject of which is "love." Within the context of *The Phaedrus* and *The Symposium*—the two dialogues to which Hölderlin is particularly drawn—the subject of love cannot be detached from that of "enthusiasm." But any discussion of these texts in relation to Hölderlin would go far beyond the boundaries of this essay.

Knowledge—which means, above all, the science of philosophy[39]—begins with aesthetics, or the "study of beauty," because it alone allows one to understand life without mourning. Since mourning is itself related to life as the experience of its loss, the reason Hölderlin proposes aesthetics as the foundation of knowledge can be expressed in another manner: the study of beauty allows one to understand life without experiencing the loss of the very thing to be understood, and it therefore allows one to study something without having to add "and it has been lost." Since, however, the one who studies is also alive, the "object" of study cannot be really distinguished from its "subject." Without a study of beauty neither subject nor object is itself, which is to say, "alive." All of the concepts to which Hölderlin then turns—*Schwärmerei,* passion, devotional prayer, and despair—are from this perspective specific modes of mourning: life has lost its infinitude for the one who, having succumbed to despair (*Verzweiflung*), is now two (*zwei*); life never even touches the one who is devoted to memorial prayers (*Andacht*); passion (*Leidenschaft*), as the condition of suffering (*Leiden*), is by definition removed from the pure activity of life; and finally—or, more precisely, at first—there is *Schwärmerei,* which, however, unlike the others, does let itself be so easily understood as a specific mode of mourning.

Schwärmerei distinguishes itself from the other modes of mourning to the extent that the word does not indicate a way in which life has been lost. But *Schwärmerei* is different in another manner as well: passion, devotional prayer,

---

    One representative of late-eighteenth-century Platonism whose work serves as a point of intersection for the thought of Kant, Goethe, and Hölderlin is Count Friedrich Leopold zu Stolberg. Like Kant, Goethe rejects his version of Platonism and especially his interpretation of *The Ion* (see Fenves, *Raising the Tone of Philosophy,* 74–75). Hölderlin never explicitly attacks Stolberg, and there is good reason to think that he learned something about lyric-form from his verse; nevertheless, the opening aphorisms of "Reflections" can be read as an implicit critique of Stolberg's essay "Über die Begeisterung" (1782), which is, as it were, a direct assault on the Berlin *Aufklärung.* The essay has been reprinted in Friedrich Leopold Graf zu Stolberg, *Über die Fülle des Herzens: Frühe Prosa,* ed. Jürgen Behrens (Stuttgart, 1970), 32–42. Stolberg translates Plato's *enthousiazein* by *Begeisterung* (pp. 34–35), but this translation, he concludes, cannot define the nature of *Begeisterung* itself: "Enthousiasme ist noch nicht Begeisterung. Inspiration (Eingebung) ist etwas ganz verschiedenes. Der Begeisterte elektisiert, der von Enthusiasmus Erfüllte wird elektrisiert" (p. 42; for an account of Hölderlin's debt to Stolberg, see Ulrich Gaier, *Hölderlin* [Tübingen and Basel, 1993], esp. pp. 414–16).

39. Throughout his theoretical writings Hölderlin uses the term *Erkenntnis* for philosophical knowledge; see especially the proposition he poses in the so-called "Verfahrungsweise des poetischen Geistes" (a proposition that can be read as a direct response to the section of Schelling's *System of Transcendental Idealism* on "art as the organon of philosophy"): "Just as the knowledge [i.e. philosophy] intimates the language [i.e. poetry], thus does the language remember the knowledge" (H, 4:261). One of Hölderlin's most often cited versions of the same thought can be found in the final chapter of the first book of *Hyperion:* "Poetry, I [Hyperion] said, certain of my matter at hand, is the beginning and end of this [philosophical] science" (H, 3:81). The letter in which Hyperion relates his certainty with regard to the beginning and end of philosophy is addressed to a certain Bellarmin, which is to say, "The Beautiful German" (Bell-Arminius). Schelling was known as a young man to be quite beautiful, and for this reason (among others) it is possible to read the addressee of this remark as Schelling.

and even despair can be understood as kinds of *Schwärmerei*. And all of them, Hölderlin insists, are "good." This apparent approbation of *Schwärmerei* doubtless corresponds to a certain revaluation of the term in the last decades of the eighteenth century. What better way to express a dissatisfaction with the image of reason promulgated by the *Aufklärung* than to extol its polemical opponent?[40] But Hölderlin's fragment cannot simply be understood as an "Apologie der Schwärmerei," to use Novalis's phrase.[41] For the goodness of *Schwärmerei* is not unconditional: "In good times there are seldom *Schwärmer*" —which means at the very least that the goodness of *Schwärmerei* lies in its relation to bad times. Hölderlin, furthermore, specifies the character of these times: there is nothing "true" for "knowledge" and nothing "real" for "creative occupation." *Schwärmerei* is good, in other words, as long as there is neither philosophy nor poetry; and since philosophy, or "knowledge," should begin with the study of beauty, one comes back to the formula: *Schwärmerei* is good "for the remainder" (*übrigens*)—as long as life, in other words, cannot be understood without mourning.

Every action based on mourning is thus brought into the orbit of *Schwärmerei*. Whereas Kant defined *Schwärmerei* as a "principled" overstepping of all boundaries, and Schelling sought the "principle of all possible *Schwärmerei*" in the almost unbearable demand of the self to pass into the infinitude of the nonself, Hölderlin presents it as the very experience of limitation—and, above all, the experience of a limited, defined, and thus principled life: "The deep feeling of mortality, of change, of his temporal limitations enflames man so that he attempts much; [it] exercises all his powers, and does not allow him to fall into idleness. . . . In good times there are seldom

40. Evidence for this dissatisfaction can be found in many quarters. Of particular interest is a novel by Johann Jung-Stilling, *Theobald; oder die Schwärmer, eine wahre Geschichte* (Leipzig, 1784). The editors of the *Deutsches Wörterbuch* note a "transformation of the strict meaning into a milder one during the last quarter of the eighteenth century" (*Deutsches Wörterbuch,* 2292); they cite some lines from Goethe to demonstrate this tendency, but in one of his *Venetianische Epigramme* Goethe demonstrates that he could use this term with the same degree of invective fury as Luther himself—but with the opposite effect: "Jeglichen Schwärmer schlagt mir ans Kreuz im dreifiligsten Jahre; / Kennt er nur einmal die Welt, wird der Betrogne der Schelm" [Let me have every *Schwärmer* nailed to the cross in his thirtieth year; if he ever gets familiar with the world, the deceived becomes a deceiver] (*Werke,* ed. E. Trunz [Munich, 1981], 1:179). In other words, Jesus, the arch-*Schwärmer,* should have been crucified before he took up his "enthusiastic" mission. Goethe's poem plays an important role in Hölderlin's "An den klugen Ratgeber" (On the Clever Adviser), for it allows him to respond to Schiller's "clever advice" that he limit his enthusiasm (see his letter of 24 November 1796).

41. Novalis wrote his "Apologie der Schwärmerei" (sometime between 1788 and 1790) in order to attack "apostles of enlightenment and preachers of reason" (*Schriften,* ed. Richard Samuel [Stuttgart, 1960], 2:20–22); Novalis's youthful note is directed for the most part against Wieland's essay "Enthusiasmus und Schwärmerei" (*Teutscher Merkur,* 1775).

Schwärmer. Yet when man lacks great, pure objects, then he creates some phantom out of this or that, and [he] closes his eyes in order to be able to take an interest in it and live for it."[42] *Schwärmerei* is defined by the feeling of being defined. This feeling does not express itself in the attempt to overstep all limits but, on the contrary, in ever renewed efforts at self-definition. Only in self-definition is the indeterminacy of "idleness" converted into activity. By defining *Schwärmerei* as the experience of being defined, Hölderlin is then in a position to determine its provenance: *Schwärmerei* arises whenever those "objects" that, by virtue of their purity and greatness, are "true" and "real" have been lost. But only "true" and "real" objects are objects in the first place. "Something true and real" cannot be understood as some-one-thing among other things; rather, it is thinghood—or "being"[43]—as such. No one can define this "something." It can present itself only as infinite. The name for "infinitude" in the context of this fragment—and this naming is itself a "creative occupation"—is "life." The loss of "living objects" makes *Schwärmerei* possible, and this possibility is realized whenever this loss goes unnoticed. Instead of seeing the loss as such, the *Schwärmer* "closes his eyes," and by losing sight of this loss in this tragic act of self-blinding, he creates for himself a "nothing"—which is to say, a "phantom," not "something true and real," but a phenomenon to which sensible intuition corresponds and a duty to which he can devote himself. Making for itself a phenomenal world in which it can discover occasions for devotional activity is, however, the fundamental operation Kantian critique ascribes to the I. By the time Hölderlin has completed the fragment, the word *Schwärmerei* has become exactly equivalent to the term *subjectivity:* In good times there are seldom subjects.

But *Schwärmerei*—and, one may now add, subjectivity—is nevertheless "good." When *Schwärmer* lose sight of the loss as such, they mourn for something about which they are unaware, and this very unawareness keeps the loss "pure." To this extent, *Schwärmerei* distinguishes itself from the other modes of mourning Hölderlin mentions: passion, devotion, and despair. For each of these names an experience of suffering, commemoration, and division. Not so with *Schwärmerei:* insofar as it is associated with an experience of flight, it

---

42. Hölderlin almost repeats the point on which Kant first distinguishes enthusiasm from *Schwärmerei:* "nothing great in the world has been done without it" (quoted above).

43. "Objectivity as such" cannot mean the counterpart of subjectivity. Since "pure, great objects" are defined in relation to "something true and real," and since this "something" is a singularity of which both truth and reality are its predicates, these "pure, great objects" cannot simply be objects *for* a subject; they must be objects as such, objects before the distinction between subject and object. The term Hölderlin uses for this "before"—as absolutely original a priori—is *Seyn* ("being"). See the much discussed fragment that often goes under the title "Urteil und Sein" (H, 4:216–17).

points in the opposite direction—toward *Freude* ("joy"), more precisely, toward the hyperbolic hermeneutic imperative with which the fragment begins: "It is from joy that you must understand the pure in general [*das Reine überhaupt*], human beings, and other kinds of being, grasp 'everything essential about and characteristic of' these beings, and know their relations to one another" (H, 4:235).[44] Even if passion, devotion, and despair are kinds of *Schwärmerei,* the latter term can still be understood as a specific mode of mourning: *Schwärmer* mourn in joy. They are able to mourn in joy because they do not know that they mourn. Because they are unaware of the loss that they mourn, *Schwärmer* themselves—not the "phantoms" in which they take an "interest"—*represent* this loss: they are the very "objects" with which to begin understanding life without mourning. In a letter to Immanuel Niethammer, Hölderlin wrote that he would soon write "New Letters on Aesthetic Education."[45] To this, one might add: aesthetic education begins *here*—with the study of the *Schwärmer.*

The structure of the poet corresponds to that of the *Schwärmer.* According to the opening fragment of "Reflections," the "calling and bliss of the poet" does not consist in *being* inspired, enthused, or otherwise linked to a higher being, but rather in *moving* "up and down the ladder of *Begeisterung*" (H, 4:233). The *Schwärmer* mourns in a joyful fashion—whatever "joy" and "mourning" may

44. The following would be easy to say: the "pure, great objects" and the "other kinds of being" about which Hölderlin here speaks are "the gods"; knowing the relation between gods and human beings is the basis of everything "poetic"; poetry, as a result, is "mythological," and mythology is from its inception poetic (the last terms are taken from a fragment of a philosophical treatise in epistolary form that Hölderlin probably wrote around 1797, which goes by the title "On Religion"; esp. H, 4:280–81). All of this is, as far as it goes, correct; but since each of the words in quotation marks means something very specific to Hölderlin, and all of them deviate from their colloquial usage, saying something like this would be more misleading than informative. The same can be said of another correct statement: the *Schwärmer* is the term Hölderlin uses in "Reflections" to designate what he elsewhere calls "the halfgods" (*Halbgötter*). The complicated relation between the *Schwärmer* and the *Halbgott* is directly presented at the end of the central stanza of "Der Rhein." In these lines, Hölderlin indicates why Herakles is condemned to destroy his own house: he is the one who "sein will und nicht / Ungleiches dulden, der Schwärmer" (wants to be and will not bear inequality, the *Schwärmer*) (S, 2:145). There is perhaps no more incisive "definition" of *Schwärmerei* than this: not simply wanting to be equal to absolutely pure beings—or *being* pure and simple—but at the same time wanting *to be* without the condition for the *demonstrability of being,* namely "inequality," or to use a term Hölderlin elsewhere favors, "difference."
45. "In the philosophical letters I want to find the principle which explains to me the divisions in which we think and exist, yet which is also capable of dispelling the conflict between subject and object, between our self and the world, even between reason and revelation—theoretically, in intellectual intuition, without our practical reason having to come to our aid. We need aesthetic sense for this, and I will call my philosophical letters 'New Letters on the Aesthetic Education of Man'" (H, 6:202–3). In this same letter Hölderlin indicates in very subtle terms that he finds Schelling's *Philosophical Letters* unacceptable (presumably because it seeks a ground for philosophical knowledge in practical reason).

themselves mean—whereas the poet is "enthused" (*begeistert*) in a sober manner. Aesthetics, or the study of beauty, thus gives rise to a definition not of *Geist,* as Schelling wanted, but of *Begeisterung.* This term, as the basic condition of poetry, cannot simply be translated as "inspiration." Since *Geist,* for the pietists under whom Hölderlin studied, stands for "God,"[46] *be-geistern* could serve, for him, as a literal translation of *enthousiazein.* Hölderlin, however, defines it in precisely the same way he presents *Schwärmerei*—by way of its opposite. The defining limit of *Begeisterung* is "sobriety" (*Nüchternheit*): "Wherever sobriety forsakes you, there are the limits of your *Begeisterung*" (H, 4:233). The sober enthusiasm of the poet corresponds to the mournful joy of the enthusiasts, and at the very point in which the "Reflections" turns away from its original concentration of the task, nature, and feeling of the poet, which is also the point at which the principle of "aesthetic education" is laid down—"All knowledge should begin with the study of beauty"—Hölderlin turns toward the definition, provenance, and principle of *Schwärmerei.* The two belong together, poets and *Schwärmer*— not because poets are *Schwärmer* but, on the contrary, because poets, who do not devote themselves to phantoms and are not therefore subjects, bring to speech what *Schwärmer* represent: the loss of life.

Life, for Hölderlin, is infinite, but it is not an infinite being. *Begeisterung,* in turn, cannot be understood as a relation to something infinite—a conduit to an all-encompassing God, or a link in a chain supported by an immortal God. Rather, *Begeisterung,* like life, is infinite in relation to itself; but unlike life, it is intensely infinite in a finite manner, for, as Hölderlin says, *Begeisterung* always remains limited, at the point where "sobriety forsakes you." Only one image can then capture *Begeisterung*: that of a finite scale with infinitely many degrees of intensity. As a scale, moreover, *Begeisterung* is related to something else as its measure: not, of course, to an all-encompassing God or an immortal God but, instead, to poets. The measure of the poet is not, however, the degree of *Begeisterung,* and the scale does not have the function of rating the relative value of individual poets; rather, the measure poets apply to themselves is the scale of enthusiasm *as a whole.* Poets respond to their calling whenever they correspond to the scale of enthusiasm: whenever, in other words, the intensity of their self-relation does not make them withdraw into

---

46. Since Hölderlin was rediscovered in the early part of this century, scholars have staged elaborate arguments about the function and significance of the term *Geist* ("spirit") in his work—whether it should be understood in light of Hegel's *Phenomenology of Spirit* or as another name for "the coming God" ("Brot und Wein"). For an analysis of "Reflections" from the perspective of certain theological circles in which Hölderlin was educated, see Walter Dierauer, *Hölderlin und der spekulative Pietismus Württembergs: gemeinsame Anschauungshorizonte im Werke Oetingers und Hölderlins* (Zürich, 1986), esp. 34–44.

themselves and try to create out of themselves but, on the contrary, allows them to open themselves to—and thus measure themselves against[47]—something else altogether:

> There is a scale of *Begeisterung*. From joviality, which is surely the lowest, up to the *Begeisterung* of the general who in the midst of battle maintains control of his genius through concentration [*Besonnenheit*], there is an infinite ladder. To climb up and down this ladder is the calling and bliss of the poet. (H, 4:233)

The freedom of poets consists in their ability to move up and down the ladder of enthusiasm and to free themselves, in turn, from the particular perspective opened by each of its rungs. Nowhere, however, does Hölderlin indicate that this freedom from particular perspectives gives rise to a general point of view. At the highest level of the ladder there is, to be sure, a general, but the viewpoint of the general (*Feldherr*) is still of a particular field: it opens onto the field of slaughter. From this, the highest perspective, life is seen to be lost.

At the end of *The Ion,* the "ionic" rhetor whom Socrates has relentlessly pursued finally claims a *technē* for himself: the general "know-how" of the general (*strategos*). Socrates demands that Ion make a decision: explain why the Athenians have not chosen him as a general; or enlist himself into the ranks of "enthusiasts." To this demand, Hölderlin, who, like Plato, was doing battle against the Homeric gods, responds: poets climb up to the enthusiasm of generals but distinguish themselves as poets and are distinguished in their poetry because they see and bring to speech not simply the loss of life but the fact—this fact can only be seen *in* their speech—that life is lost.

Northwestern University

---

47. The importance of the term *Maß* ("measure") to Hölderlin can be judged from the stanza of "Der Rhein" in which he defines "the highest" and "the best" with reference to the final image of Socrates in *The Symposium*—ever sober, even after a night of drinking: "Nur hat ein jeder sein Maas" (Only each one has its measure; H, 2:148). On this line, see Peter Fenves, "Measure for Measure: Hölderlin and the Place of Philosophy," *Philosophy Today* (winter 1993): 369-82.

Sociability, Solitude, and Enthusiasm

LAWRENCE E. KLEIN

Richard Baxter, the distinguished and long-lived Nonconformist divine, was hostile to the Protestant sects that multiplied in England in the unregulated religious climate of the 1640s and 1650s. While some were "tolerable," others were not: "Many of them (the Behmenists, Fifth-Monarchy men, Quakers, and some Anabaptists) are proper Fanatics, looking too much to revelations within, instead of the Holy Scriptures."[1] According to Baxter, the fanatic sought fresh revelations in place of the standard record of Revelation and expected to find them by looking inward, instead of outward at the objective record of Scripture.

A century and a half later, Samuel Taylor Coleridge corrected Baxter:

> Baxter makes the usual mistake of writing *Fanatic* when he clearly means *Enthusiast*. The Field-Methodists are fanatics, *i.e. circà fana densâ turbâ conçalefacti;* those who catch heat by crowding together round the same *Fane*. Fanaticism is the *fever* of *superstition*. Enthusiasm, on the contrary, implies an undue (or when used in a good sense, an unusual) vividness of ideas, as opposed to perceptions, or of the obscure inward feelings.[2]

Baxter had conflated religious types that Coleridge sought to keep distinct. For Coleridge, the fanatic was a social being whose identity emerged in a collective process in a specific venue whereas the enthusiast was an isolated figure whose transcendental motions were inward and unsituated. Fanatics were dangerously gregarious and extroverted, but enthusiasts were harmlessly solitary and introverted.[3]

1. Richard Baxter's *Reliquiae Baxterianae* (London, 1696), quoted in Samuel Taylor Coleridge, *Notes on English Divines*, ed. Derwent Coleridge (London, 1853), 39.
2. Coleridge, *Notes on English Divines*, 39–40.
3. In *Aids to Reflection* (1825), Coleridge linked fanaticism with the 'swarming' of *Schwärmer* in Germany. So did Thomas Carlyle. See Susie I. Tucker, *Enthusiasm: A Study in Semantic Change* (Cambridge, 1972), 47–48, 167–68, 177.

The discourse of religion in Baxter's era lacked the lexical tidiness presumed in Coleridge's criticism; "enthusiasm" and the other vocabulary by and against which it was often defined (including "fanaticism," "superstition," "zeal," "atheism," "bigotry," and "skepticism") were used in a fascinatingly disorderly fashion in the later seventeenth and eighteenth centuries. Yet Coleridge usefully pointed to a theme in the discourse of religion from the previous two centuries. In contrasting extroverted and introverted forms of religious behavior, he indicated one aspect of a larger polarity between sociability and unsociability. As the gap between Baxter's usage and Coleridge's lexical expectations indicates, labels were not assigned to these poles with any consistency. Indeed, enthusiasm could be viewed as either a social or unsociable phenomenon, and it is this variable status that I seek to trace.

The contrast between extroversion and introversion was only one aspect of the larger polarity. What were some of the other aspects? According to Benjamin Whichcote, Cambridge Platonist and contemporary of Richard Baxter, "they do not advance Religion, who Embody it (draw it down to bodily Acts) or who carry it up highest, into what is Mystical, Symbolical, Emblematical, etc."[4] This assertion rests on a distinction between the low and the high, but it is also phrased in terms of the outward and the inward. Whichcote, seeking to define a middle ground between those who over-ceremonialize and those who over-cerebrate, contrasted the external, the physically embodied, to the internal, mental, and abstract.[5] Thus Whichcote's contrast between the external and internal orientations of believers parallels Coleridge's. In Coleridge's view, external orientation took the form of social extroversion, participating in a collective endeavor. For Whichcote, external orientation took the form of ceremonial practice, making much of ritual forms. But for both writers, the contrast to the externally oriented believer was an inward-looking and more mystical religious type.

A further aspect of the contrast between sociability and unsociability appears in Joseph Addison's figures of the Clown and the Courtier, representing enthusiasm and superstition respectively: "an Enthusiast in Religion is like an obstinate Clown, a Superstitious Man like an insipid Courtier. Enthusiasm has something in it of Madness, Superstition of Folly."[6] Addison's enthusiast and superstitious man corresponded to the abstracters and concretizers in

---

4.   Benjamin Whichcote, *Moral and Religious Aphorisms* (Norwich, 1703), 53.
5.   By implication, at least, there was also a contrast here between the spatially located and the placeless.
6.   Donald F. Bond, ed., *The Spectator*, 5 vols. (Oxford, 1965), 2:289 (No. 201, 20 October 1711).

Whichcote's statement, and Addison was pointing to the same contrast between introverted and extroverted styles of religious practice that is evident in both Whichcote and Coleridge. But more noticeable here, even remarkable, is that Addison cast these distinctions in the language of manners and civility. In that language, as I will explain below, the Clown was an insufficiently socialized figure while the Courtier was an overly socialized one. For Addison, the Clown's madness was the unhinging of the isolated mind whereas the Courtier's folly was the heteronomic vacuity of the mind incapable of independence. Addison's assertion, then, implied a spectrum from excessive autonomy to excessive sociability. Its mean, occupied by a figure who might be called the fully polite gentleman, involved some balance between autonomy and sociability, between the capacities for moral solitude and for social engagement. This was a poise eighteenth-century writers were anxious to achieve, though it often eluded them.[7]

The relation between sociability and solitude is an interesting issue in light of several strands of historical interpretation. As social practice, sociability is now understood as a defining trait of eighteenth-century intellectual culture (including the Enlightenment); and study of the forms of intellectual sociability has helped to establish both continuities and discontinuities among the diffuse centers of eighteenth-century European intellectual and cultural activity.[8] Although deriving in part from a general interest in the understandings that eighteenth-century individuals had of their own social practices,[9] this attention

7. The tensions surrounding sociability were cast and can be understood as tensions between self-absorption and theatricality; see Michael Fried's analysis in *Absorption and Theatricality: Painting and Beholder in the Age of Diderot* (Berkeley, Calif., 1980). Other treatments of these tensions are David Marshall, *The Figure of Theater* (New York, 1986); John Mullan, *Sentiment and Sociability: The Language of Feeling in the Eighteenth Century* (Oxford, 1988); and several of the essays in Peter France, *Politeness and Its Discontents* (Cambridge, 1992).

8. To mention just a few recent examples: Dena Goodman, *The Republic of Letters* (Ithaca, N.Y., 1994); Peter Borsay, *The English Urban Renaissance: Culture and Society in the Provincial Town, 1660–1770* (Oxford, 1989); Anne Goldgar, *Impolite Learning: Conduct and Community in the Republic of Letters, 1680–1750* (New Haven, Conn., and London, 1995); Richard van Dülmen, *The Society of the Enlightenment: The Rise of the Middle Class and Enlightenment Culture in Germany*, trans. Anthony Williams (New York, 1992); Margaret Jacob, *Living the Enlightenment: Freemasonry and Politics in Eighteenth-Century Europe* (New York, 1991); and several articles in "The Public and the Nation," a special issue of *Eighteenth-Century Studies*, 29 (1995), no. 1, especially Anthony La Vopa, "Herder's *Publikum*: Language, Print, and Sociability in Eighteenth-Century Germany," 5–24. Explorations of this theme have been encouraged by the translation and reception of the work of Jürgen Habermas, especially *The Structural Transformation of the Public Sphere*, originally published in 1962 and translated into English in 1989.

9. See, for example, Marvin B. Becker, *The Emergence of Civil Society in the Eighteenth Century* (Bloomington and Indianapolis, 1994); Daniel Gordon, *Citizens without Sovereignty: Equality and Sociability in French Thought, 1670–1789* (Princeton, N.J., 1994); and Lawrence E. Klein, *Shaftesbury and the Culture of Politeness* (Cambridge, 1994).

is also a specific reaction in the historiography of political discourse against a history focused on a particularly individualistic vein of liberalism.[10]

The recent interpretive emphasis on eighteenth-century sociability also provides a useful perspective on the important innovations traced in intellectual history from the time of Rousseau. It is often observed that a reaction against emphatic sociability took shape in the form of a rehabilitation of solitude or, more dramatically, the invention of authenticity as individual and of Romantic individualism.[11] Seen against the background of eighteenth-century sociability, the solitary turn expressed by writers from Rousseau to Thoreau and beyond becomes a novel, even a polemical, gesture. Such a gesture was related to a new kind of principled nonconformity, a rebellion against social oppression that was in turn built on a new reification of "society."[12] But even under the older sense of "society" (where and when sociability occurs), forms of solitude had their place. While sociability was often defined and invoked against varieties of unsociability (including solitude), the possibility of true sociability sometimes depended on solitude.

However, another innovation often associated with the late eighteenth century was the reassertion of the claims of community, of society viewed as "organic." Such a reassertion is inevitably portrayed as a reaction against an eighteenth century marked not by sociability but by an individualistic liberalism. The object of this essay is to move beyond narratives that depict a shift from either sociability to individualism or from individualism to community. In the thought and writings of the period, the themes of self and society, individual and other, solitude and sociability, are all present in a complicated configuration. Here I examine treatments of enthusiasm in order to illuminate this configuration. First I show how the attack on enthusiasm was motivated by a

10. Some representative examples of work in this vein on the themes of manners, civility, and sociability are J. G. A. Pocock, "Virtue, Rights, and Manners: A Model for Historians of Political Thought" and "The Varieties of Whiggism from Exclusion to Reform" in *Virtue, Commerce, and History* (Cambridge, 1985), especially 48–50, 230–53; John Burrow, *Whigs and Liberals: Continuity and Change in English Political Thought* (Oxford, 1988); Nicholas Phillipson, "Politics and Politeness in the Reigns of Anne and the Early Hanoverians," in J. G. A. Pocock, ed., *The Varieties of British Political Thought, 1500–1800* (Cambridge, 1993), 211–45; and Istvan Hont, "The Language of Sociability and Commerce: Samuel Pufendorf and the Theoretical Foundations of the 'Four-Stages Theory,'" in Anthony Pagden, ed., *The Languages of Political Theory in Early Modern Europe* (Cambridge, 1987), 253–76.
11. Lionel Trilling, *Sincerity and Authenticity* (Cambridge, Mass., 1971).
12. Raymond Williams, *Keywords* (London, 1976), 243–47. For the changing idea of "society" (with its consequences for the status of sociability), compare the entrance of Frances Burney's *Evelina* (1778) "into the World" with the experiences of Denis Diderot's Suzanne in *La Réligieuse* or Mary Wollstonecraft's Mary and Maria in *Mary* (1788) and *The Wrongs of Woman* (1798).

defense of sociability, examining instances, from the Restoration through the time of Joseph Addison and Richard Steele, in which enthusiasm was castigated for its unsociability. In the Restoration period, the divines who made this point were interested in doing two things: reasserting the authority of the Church, the Word, or the Clergy against the nonconformity of the enthusiast, which was traced to a kind of willful self-absorption; and asserting the morally beneficial (specifically, civilizing and socializing) impact of sound Christianity. After 1688, as I go on to show, Whig ideologists used the idea that the enthusiast was unsociable to define the sociable norms of public discourse in the new regime. However, while the "public sphere" depended on sociability and civility, it also depended on autonomy. Sociability was built on affiliation while autonomy required independence; civility was the art of pleasing while autonomy might not be very ingratiating. These tensions between sociability and autonomy surrounded the project of inventing a public sphere and they were reflected in treatments of enthusiasm. Though often identified as a condition of self-absorbed unsociability, enthusiasm could also be seen as a condition of uncontrolled gregariousness: imitative, contagious, and heteronomic. The latter view, evident in some Restoration texts, appeared conspicuously in the writings of the third earl of Shaftesbury. Indeed, in Shaftesbury, the social nature of enthusiasm helped animate a Whig moralism. Against enthusiastic heteronomy, he defended the public sphere by reasserting the necessity of autonomy.

The fact that enthusiasm could be seen as both unsociable and sociable meant that the proposed antidotes to enthusiasm were diverse. Insofar as enthusiasm represented a deficiency of sociability, its cure involved socialization. However, insofar as enthusiasm represented an excess or unregulated form of socializing, its cure required a degree of social abstinence, a kind of solitude in which the social passions could be understood and addressed.

✒ ∾

The disruptions and dislocations of the 1640s and 1650s in England led many to conclude, with Whichcote, that "some are worse for their *Religion*." Terrible things, it had been seen, could be done in the name of faith. Moreover, it was recognized that, while the perpetrators were sometimes easily identifiable opportunists ("Hypocrites!" Whichcote called them), they were often Christians whose faith, it had to be admitted, was sincere, however misdirected. One reaction was to adjust the hierarchy of virtues—de-emphasizing "faith" in favor of "charity," or morality. In the words of Whichcote, "That must not be done in the Defence of Religion, which is contrary to Religion."[13]

Thus, even before 1660 and certainly after, morality as a test of religiosity became an important theme in religious discourse. The ethical demands of Christian godliness expressed themselves in the great moral categories of charity and justice, but Restoration divines of the Anglican Church emphasized such apparently humbler qualities as good nature and sociability. Whichcote himself made "temper" and "action" the touchstones of religion. True religion, he wrote, led humans to be "well Informed in our Judgements, well Refined in our Spirits, and well Reformed in our Manners."[14] Reviewing the distempers that arose from alienation from God, Whichcote wrote: "It is Devilish to be *Spiteful* and *Revengeful:* For, Man, by Nature, is *Sociable;* and wishes well to them in whose Company he takes delight."[15] The design of Christianity, according to the latitudinarian divine and future bishop Edward Fowler, was, precisely, the reformation of life and manners, of which affability was an important aspect.[16] Fowler went out of his way to defend those who had been smeared as "latitudinarian":

> They are not onely not *scandalous,* but very *lovely* also in their behaviour, and greatly *obliging.* I never in any one *sort* of men observed so much of openheartedness and ingenuity, freedom, sociableness, and affability, as in *these* generally. They have nothing of that Crabbed authority, foolish affectation, or sullen gravity that render too many of their Censurers to *wise men* not a little contemptible.[17]

Though noted for his own polemical ferocity, Samuel Parker, the future bishop of Oxford, agreed, writing: "there is nothing more noble and generous, more cheerful and sprightly, more courteous and affable, more free and ingenuous, more sober and rational, than the Spirit and Genius of true Religion."[18] Pointing out that Jesus taught love and good nature, Parker insisted that "a peevish ill-natur'd Christian, is the greatest contradiction in the World." Indeed, he

---

13. Whichcote, *Moral and Religious Aphorisms*, 19–20. On moralism in Restoration divinity, see John Spurr, *The Restoration Church of England, 1646–1689* (New Haven, Conn., and London, 1991), 279–330.
14. Whichcote, *Moral and Religious Aphorisms*, 81.
15. Benjamin Whichcote, *Select Sermons* (London, 1698), 181.
16. Edward Fowler, *The Design of Christianity* (London, 1671), esp. chap. 5.
17. Edward Fowler, *The Principles and Practices, of Certain Moderate Divines of the Church of England* (London, 1670), 37.
18. Samuel Parker, *A Discourse of Ecclesiastical Politie*, 3d ed. (London, 1671), xxviii.

went so far as to ascribe a genteel amiability to Jesus, referring to "the unparallel'd civility and obligingness of his Deportment . . . almost as high an Evidence of the Truth and Divinity of his Doctrine, as his unparallel'd Miracles were."[19]

The counterpoint to proper Anglican sociability was sketched in terms of the "*Spiteful* and *Revengeful*," or "Crabbed authority, foolish affectation, or sullen gravity." These pointed in the direction of enthusiasm, which was certainly outside the range of Anglican sociability. Again, Whichcote's aphorisms are indicative:

> The *Good nature* of an Heathen is more God-like, than the furious Zeal of a Christian.
>
> Nothing Spoils Human Nature [which for Whichcote was both rational and sociable] more than False *Zeal*.
>
> The more *False* any one is in his *Religion*, the more Fierce and Furious in Maintaining it: the more Mistaken, the more Imposing.
>
> Fierceness in a Sect [is thought] to be Zeal for Religion, and speaking *without sense*, to be the simplicity of the Spirit.

Enthusiasm had helped to spark the intense moral concerns of Anglican divinity from the middle of the seventeenth century, and it continued to be a favorite polemical target, recognizable by its unsociability. Of course, enthusiasm had a specific and technical sense—"counterfeited inspiration," in one pithy formulation.[20] This is what Ephraim Pagitt meant by including "enthusiasm," in which misguided individuals believed "that they have the gift of Prophecy," in his taxonomy of anabaptisms.[21] Enthusiasm might be limited to those relatively few who claimed to be the vehicles of new revelation or millenial news. However, "counterfeited inspiration" was a flexible category, since Spirit and inspiration were such central notions in Christian theology. Thus, various sects, notably the Quakers, were regarded as enthusiastic. Moreover, especially

19. Samuel Parker, *A Free and Impartial Censure of the Platonick Philosophie* (Oxford, 1666), 23–24.
20. In William Lloyd's "alphabetical dictionary," printed, by Samuel Gellibrand and John Martin, as an unpaginated addendum to John Wilkins, *An Essay towards a Real Character, and a Philosophical Language* (London, 1668). For a survey of the attack on enthusiasm in this period, see Michael Heyd, *"Be Sober and Reasonable": The Critique of Enthusiasm in the Seventeenth and Early Eighteenth Centuries* (Leiden, 1995); see also Hillel Schwartz, *The French Prophets: The History of a Millenarian Group in Eighteenth-Century England* (Berkeley, Calif., 1980); and *Knaves, Fools, Madmen, and That Subtile Effluvium: A Study of the Opposition to the French Prophets in England, 1706–1710* (Gainesville, Fla., 1978).
21. Ephraim Pagitt, *Heresiography, Or A Description and History of the Hereticks and Sectaries Sprang up in These Latter Times* (London, 1662), 35.

after 1660, it became easy to use the term "enthusiast" to smear all Noncon-formists and, in time, anyone who questioned authority in Church or State. It did not take long for enthusiasms other than spiritual ones—namely, philo-sophical, linguistic, and political enthusiasms—to become the object of discus-sion.[22] Thus, though "counterfeited inspiration" may have been the technical core of "enthusiasm," the term came to cover ever-widening spheres of meaning and reference in which the technical sense was easily marginalized or lost.

Among the important associations enthusiasm picked up in time was unsociability. In what ways was the enthusiast unsociable? A number of answers can be found in an anonymous 1671 attack on Quakers, *The Charac-ter of a Quaker in His True and Proper Colours*. Though the pamphlet did not use the word "enthusiasm" (it did call the Quaker "a *Vessel of Phanaticisme*"), the attributes ascribed to Quakers were those commonly ascribed to enthusi-asts; moreover, the views of Quakers were generally regarded in the Restoration decades as the epitome of enthusiasm.

What Quaker unsociability meant, on one level, was incivility—a refusal to conform to, or a negligence about practicing the rules of, decorous behavior. The Quaker "thinks that to be *religious* one is obliged to be *uncivil*, and flings his Wits overboard to make room for *Inspiration*."[23] This unsociability had a number of aspects. To begin with, the Quakers got their name from physical expressions of spiritual possession. They were criticized in this pamphlet for refusing to discipline the body. Instead, they comported themselves with "*extravagant gestures* and *odd distortions* of body."[24] Moreover, Quakers engaged in social practices, such as using "thou" and refusing the customary removal of one's hat, through which they turned what were perceived as bad manners into marks of spiritual accomplishment. Quakers were said to interpret common civilities as signs of impiety. For example, the Quaker "cannot endure *Cere-monies* or *Complements*, especially where his Belly is concerned, and therefore falls to all meat (as *Gallants* do to a *Wench* or *Oysters*) *without saying Grace*"; or the Quaker manifests an "obstinate zeal to keep his Noddle *covered*."[25]

More generally, the Quakers refused to be affable. In *The Character of a Quaker*, the Quaker was "a *Cynick* in Religion, one that would have *Ill-nature*

---

22. The extensive bibliography on these transformations is available in Heyd, *Critique of Enthusiasm,* 289–300. See also J. G. A. Pocock, "Thomas Hobbes: Atheist or Enthusiast? His Place in a Restoration Debate," *History of Political Thought* 11 (1990): 737–49. Cf. *Heraclitus Ridens,* No. 19, 7 June 1681, which distinguished Church and State enthusiasts.
23. *The Character of a Quaker* (London, 1671), 2.
24. Ibid., 4.
25. Ibid., 10, 12–13.

translated *Grace*; as if the *Holy Spirit* (that *pure sweet gentle Dove*) did inspire men with *sullen humours* and *waspish dispositions*."[26] He had "a *sullen meagre look*" and "like a *Hedge-hog* wrapt up in his own warm down, turns out *Brisles* [*sic*] to all the World besides; you can come in no side of him but he *pricks* and *bites*, and all his Coasts are *craggy* and *inhospitable*."[27] Together, lack of physical discipline, resistance to common etiquette, and lack of affability combined to create an image of Quaker "clownishness." This term (with which Addison identified his enthusiast) appeared in this pamphlet in the summation of the Quaker's character as "a meer composition of *Contradiction* & *Clownishness*" and also in the pamphlet's subtitle, "*the Clownish Hypocrite Anatomized*."[28]

The refusal to conform to sociable expectations fit with and was indeed an expression of a deeper nonconformity—the Quaker's refusal to accept forms of authority outside the self. Of course, the enthusiast did imagine the self being moved by the highest authority, that of Divinity itself. But that was just the point of contention: the enthusiast made a claim to contact and communication with God that was wholly unmediated by the restraints on such contact that early modern states and churches had developed: "refusing the *Polestar* of Gods Word and the *Churches Compass*, he will needs *steer* by the wandring motion of a treacherous *Ignis fatuus* within, subject to be *blown any* way, and often *extinguisht* by the Hurricanes of *Passion*."[29] Thus, the Quaker claimed a dangerous autonomy from all forms of authority: "he hates both *Magistracie* and *Ministrie*, and never speaks well of *Authority* or *Obedience*."[30]

Paradoxically, this refusal to acknowledge the institutional mediations between the individual and the divine encouraged the analogy between the Protestant enthusiast and the Catholic. *The Character of a Quaker* repeated what was indeed a commonplace of the Restoration: Catholics assigned all authority to a universal Pope whereas "the Quaker sets up a Pope in *every Individual Breast*, to whom all *Scripture* and *Reason* must *truckle*."[31] In this analogy, critics of enthusiasm depicted the nightmare of Protestantism, discovered long before by Martin Luther—the metamorphosis of the priesthood of all believers into the personal papacy of each believer.

26. Ibid., 9.
27. Ibid., 1, 6.
28. Ibid., title page, 2.
29. Ibid., 5.
30. Ibid., 10.
31. Ibid., 4–5. On the analogy of Catholicism and Dissent, see Spurr, *Restoration Church of England*, 267. The idea also appears in George Hickes, *The Spirit of Enthusiasm Exorcised* (London, 1681), 38; and Robert South, *Sermons Preached upon Several Occasions*, 5 vols. (Oxford, 1842), 3:147ff.

Enthusiasm thus implied an anarchy of religious individualism. It involved a distension of selfhood about which *The Character of the Quaker* was quite explicit when it asserted that the Quaker "makes *Self* the Centre whereunto the Lines of all his Actions tend."[32] The Quaker refused not only to conform to the civilities that conduced to society but also to acknowledge the institutions that constituted the entire social regime. Enthusiasm's unsociability was related to a kind of hypertrophic egoism in which the interior life of the self stood uncorrected and undisciplined by social institutions or intercourse, and it therefore magnified and inflated its own workings into ontological realities.

Arguments against the incivility and the unsociable autonomy of sectaries, such as Quakers, were part of the battery of criticisms of enthusiasm and, like the rest of the kit, were flexible in application. As John Spurr has pointed out, though Nonconformity after 1660 ranged from millenially minded antinomians to modest presbyterians, it was still "tempting for churchmen to bracket the fanatic with the sober Nonconformist and to portray Dissent as a single enthusiastic, schismatic sect with a common cant of extravagant antinomianism."[33]

Although certain charges brought against Quakers (the principled objection to specific rules of social behavior and the lapses in bodily deportment) were not easily transferable to Nonconformists in general, deficiencies in affability and complaisance were a common charge against the broader category. The polemics of Samuel Parker against Nonconformists were a repository of this idiom. He justified his own "Zeal," saying that it was warranted "when it vents it self against the Arrogance of haughty, peevish, and sullen Religionists, that under higher pretences to Godliness supplant all Principles of Civility and good Nature, that strip Religion of its outside to make it a covering for Spight and Malice."[34] He elaborated on the Nonconformists' "sullen and unsociable Niceness" by reference to such attributes as peevishness, ill nature, moroseness, churlishness, surliness, rudeness, and barbarity.[35] Decked out with these characteristics, Nonconformity, not surprisingly, proved destructive of "Common Peace and Amity" and "Humane Society" and made for both bad subjects and bad neighbors.[36]

The sullenness and moroseness ascribed to the Nonconformist reflected the long-standing medical interpretation of enthusiasm.[37] Enthusiasm was sus-

---

32. *Character of a Quaker*, 6.
33. Spurr, *Restoration Church of England*, 321.
34. Parker, *Discourse of Ecclesiastical Politie*, iv.
35. These terms are sprinkled through the text; see pp. iv through xi.
36. Parker, *Discourse of Ecclesiastical Politie*, vi–vii.
37. This and the next paragraph summarize sections of Heyd, *Critique of Enthusiasm*, 44–71, 191–210.

ceptible to diagnosis within the Galenic humoral scheme and thus was related to melancholy. But by the second half of the seventeenth century, Galenic medicine was losing its authority and being replaced by new languages for interpreting the physical basis for distempers such as enthusiasm. However, if melancholy (in the physical sense of black bile) ceased to be an explanation of enthusiasm, the melancholic emotional tenor nonetheless remained an important component of it. Of course, as an emotional tenor, melancholy had all the traits of an unsociable frame of mind: either the withdrawn and self-absorbed condition of the classic melancholic or the temporarily agitated and aggressive state into which it was believed melancholics were liable to flare.

Melancholy also, it should be remembered, had a special relation with solitude. This relation was both causal and symptomatic. The melancholic was naturally drawn to a solitary condition because his temper directed him inward. The classic melancholic was meditative or contemplative. At the same time, solitude was an encouragement to melancholy. Insofar, then, as enthusiasm was an expression of melancholy (and not all melancholics were enthusiasts), enthusiasm was an expression of the solitary frame of mind. This was consistent not only with the sorts of incivil social behaviors by which it was said to express itself, but also with the kinds of self-centeredness and self-absorption from which it was thought to arise.

ʿ· ·ʾ

In considering enthusiasm, Joseph Addison drew on these themes, although the political and ideological map on which they had arisen as issues was now radically altered. The pre-1688 attack on enthusiasm, directed largely at Nonconformists, was easily extended to Whigs, with whom the Nonconformists were usually allied and who, in any case, were easily targeted as opponents of authority in Church and State.[38] After the 1688 Revolution, the Whigs had an entirely new relationship with authority since they served and defended the new regime. Although some historians of political discourse have dwelled on the real and enduring radicalism of Whiggism before and after 1688,[39] a theme of equal importance is how Whiggism made the transition from opposition to

38. On the association of Whiggism with religious extremism, see T. N. Corns, W. A. Speck, and J. A. Downie, "Archetypal Mystification: Polemic and Reality in English Political Literature, 1640–1750," *Eighteenth-Century Life*, n.s., 7 (1982): 7–11. Roger L'Estrange's periodical *The Observator* (1681–87) referred to this association constantly.

39. For example, Richard Ashcraft, *Revolutionary Politics and Locke's Two Treatises of Government* (Princeton, N.J., 1986); and Melinda S. Zook, *Propagators of Revolution: Conspiratorial Politics and Radical Whig Culture in Late Stuart England* (Ph.D. diss., Georgetown University, 1993).

ideological bulwark of a standing regime. The work of writers such as Addison, Steele, and the third earl of Shaftesbury provides a crucial perspective on this transition. Among other things, these writers made themselves masters of the language of sociability and, with it, the critique of enthusiasm. If, during the Restoration, sociability could be used to idealize a holy church,[40] it came to be used, after 1688, to imagine a new culture of gentlemen, with an elitist politics, an Erastian church, and a public culture of civil discourse. Part of the Whig project was the depiction of a sociable religion, a religion that could be imagined as decorous in its rituals and affable in the behavior of its adherents.

In the intervening years, from the Restoration divines to the Whig ideologists, an interesting discursive shift occurred. In elaborating a social and political vision based on sociability, the periodical writers Addison and Steele, as well as the philosopher Shaftesbury, adapted notions of politeness. Their writings, including their discussions of religion, were permeated with thoughts and figures out of the courtesy book. For instance, one of the central requirements of civility was good form, the supplemental grace required for true excellence. In the words of a popular collection of polite truisms, "Merit will not do the Work if it be not seconded by Agreeableness."[41] This idea made many appearances in both the *Tatler* and the *Spectator*. For instance, *Tatler* No. 149 stated that "a sullen wise Man is as bad as a good-natured Fool. Knowledge, softened with Complacency and good Breeding, will make a Man equally beloved and respected; but when joined with a severe, distant, and unsociable Temper, it creates rather Fear than Love."[42] For its own effectiveness, then, wisdom required the techniques of sociability. The same insight could be applied to religion. In *Spectator* No. 292, a discussion of the importance of the "becoming manner" led to the reflection that "even Religion its self, unless Decency be the Handmaid which waits upon her, is apt to make People appear guilty of Sourness and ill Humour: But this [Decency] shews Virtue in her first original Form, adds a Comeliness to Religion, and gives its Professors the justest Title to the Beauty of Holiness."[43] Thus religion, like a wide range of other practices, had to submit to the discipline of polite sociability. Indeed, according to Addison, it was a great mistake to promote too somber a religion—for instance, to object sanctimoniously to "the Pleasures of Conversation, and all those Social Entertainments, which are not only innocent but laudable." Such solemnity deterred people from a religious life "by representing it as an unsociable State."[44]

40. It could also be used in the Restoration decades to idealize a noble court.
41. Abel Boyer, *The English Theophrastus* (London, 1702), 104.
42. Donald F. Bond, ed., *The Tatler*, 3 vols. (Oxford, 1987), 2:341 (No. 149, 23 March 1710).
43. Bond, *Spectator*, 3:40 (No. 292, 4 February 1712).
44. Bond, *Spectator*, 4:253 (No. 494, 26 September 1712).

Enthusiasm was, of course, a good instance of religion in "an unsociable State." One extended discussion of enthusiasm appeared in *Spectator* No. 201, which treated the subject of religious devotion.[45] For Addison, devotion was the imaginative and passionate aspect of religious experience: "Devotion opens the Mind to great Conceptions, and fills it with more sublime Ideas than any that are to be met with in the most exalted Science; and at the same time warms and agitates the Soul more than sensual Pleasure." It was a defining trait of religion since "a State of Temperance, Sobriety and Justice without Devotion, is a cold, lifeless, insipid Condition of Virtue; and is rather to be stiled Philosophy than Religion."

Of course, devotion was susceptible to abuses, which, in this *Spectator*, took the form of that perverted pair of extremes, enthusiasm and superstition. Each was an excess of devotion—devotion without restraint: "since Devotion it self (which one would be apt to think could not be too warm) may disorder the Mind, unless its Heats are tempered with Caution and Prudence, we should be particularly careful to keep our Reason as cool as possible, and to guard our selves in all Parts of Life against the Influence of Passion, Imagination, and Constitution."

Enthusiasm could be differentiated from superstition according to the varying ways in which excessive devotion manifested itself—in particular, the different objects that it fixed on and tended to magnify. Enthusiasm involved a turn inward:

> When the Mind finds her self very much inflamed with her Devotions, she is too much inclined to think they are not of her own kindling, but blown up by something Divine within her. If she indulges this Thought too far, and humours the growing Passion, she at last flings her self into imaginary Raptures and Extasies; and when once she fancies her self under the Influence of a Divine Impulse, it is no wonder if she slights Human Ordinances, and refuses to comply with any established Form of Religion, as thinking her self directed by a much superior Guide.

Like the enthusiasts depicted during the Restoration, Addison's enthusiast was a victim of self-absorption who tended to get lost in a maze of imaginings. In enthusiasm, the mind's own products were exaggerated and overestimated so that the line between the divine and the mortal began to be effaced.[46] In consequence, the enthusiast disregarded the established forms.

45. Bond, *Spectator*, 2:287–90 (No. 201, 20 October 1711).
46. This is a theme in J. G. A. Pocock's essay in this volume.

By contrast, superstition involved a fixation on and magnification of things external to the mind. It dwelled on external objects and forms, organizing and overdramatizing external appearances—an excess of formalism. While enthusiasm could be found in "most of the Sects that fall short of the Church of *England*," superstition was best illustrated in the agglutinative history of Roman Catholicism:

> . . . a Habit or Ceremony, tho' never so ridiculous, which has taken Sanctuary in the Church sticks in it for ever. A *Gothic* Bishop, perhaps, thought it proper to repeat such a Form in such particular Shoes or Slippers. Another fancied it would be very decent if such a Part of publick Devotions were performed with a Mitre on his Head, and a Crosier in his Hand. To this a Brother *Vandal*, as wise as the others, adds an antick Dress, which he conceived would allude very aptly to such and such Mysteries, till by Degrees the whole Office has degenerated into an empty Show. Their Successors see the Vanity and Inconvenience of these Ceremonies, but instead of reforming, perhaps add others, which they think more significant, and which take Possession in the same manner, and are never to be driven out after they have been once admitted. I have seen the Pope officiate at Saint *Peters*, where, for two Hours together, he was busied in putting on or off his different Accoutrements, according to the different Parts he was to act in them.

The theatricality of this sort of worship was the direct opposite of the self-absorption ascribed to enthusiasm. If, as Addison said, the enthusiast rebelled against form, so the superstitious person submitted uncritically.[47]

Having laid out the parameters of introversion and extroversion and of formlessness and formalism, Addison continued: "An Enthusiast in Religion is like an obstinate Clown, a Superstitious Man like an insipid Courtier." The Clown and Courtier were figures out of the discourse of good manners and civility. They represented extreme points on a spectrum of sociability that

---

47. In the Restoration period, this attentiveness to religious form, most commonly diagnosed among Catholics, was frequently called "foppery"; see *Reasons for the Repeal of That Part of the Statutes of Colleges in the Universities of Cambridge and Oxford, which Required the Taking of Orders* (n.d.); *The Second Advice to the Painter* (London, 1679); and *A Letter to the Earl of Shaftesbury* (London, 1680), 1. Many of the main points made by Addison in *Spectator* No. 201 are echoed in Hume's essay "Of Superstition and Enthusiasm"; see David Hume, *Essays Moral, Political, and Literary*, ed. Eugene F. Miller (Indianapolis, 1985), 73–79.

ranged from those untutored in worldly matters to those schooled in nothing but such worldliness. The Clown, a victim of class or provinciality, was remote from or untouched by the sophisticating influences suggested by the Court. By contrast, the Courtier was overqualified in sophistication. While isolation from the Court produced a comportment lacking in refinement, grace, decorum, or measure, overexposure to the Court produced a comportment that was over-refined and unmeasured in its very preoccupation with form. As Shaftesbury himself described the balance point in his private papers, "the Perfection of Carriage & Manners, is between the Ruggedness of one who cares not how he gives offense, and the Suppleness of one who only studdyes how to please."[48] The enthusiast was a Clown because of his negligence about form, which was itself rooted in his self-absorption, the magnified and yet uncorrected character of his inner life. The superstitious man approximated the Courtier because of his over-solicitousness about form.

By taking up the themes of the Restoration discourse of enthusiasm and supplementing them by casting them in the language of manners, Addison brought religion into the horizon of polite sociability. For the Restoration divines, true religion made the believer sociable. For Addison, a true gentleman knew how to behave in religious matters as in other departments of life. Enthusiasm remained an enemy of true religion but, according to Addison, it became an enemy of gentility as well.

✒   ✒

The third earl of Shaftesbury, Addison's contemporary, certainly agreed with Addison that enthusiasm endangered polite sociability. Echoing the language of Bishops Parker and Fowler, he painted a picture of "the fierce unsociable way of modern zealots, those starched, gruff gentlemen, who guard religion as bullies do a mistress, and give us the while a very indifferent opinion of their lady's merit and their own wit, by adoring what they neither allow to be inspected by others nor care themselves to examine in a fair light."[49] The "bully" enthusiast lacked social grace and affability; moreover, he demanded an exaggerated privacy suggesting not spirituality but, perhaps, the jealousy and possessiveness characteristic of more earthly transactions.

48. Shaftesbury Papers, Public Record Office, London, 30/24/27/10, 67.
49. Anthony Ashley Cooper, third earl of Shaftesbury, *Characteristics*, ed. John Robertson, 2 vols. (London, 1900; reprint, Indianapolis, 1964), 2:24–25 ("The Moralists," I.iii).

However, Shaftesbury made some distinctive—although not totally original—moves in his account of enthusiasm. First, he offered a different diagnosis of the underlying pathology: although, as the lines just quoted indicate, he recognized the unsociability of the enthusiast, he saw enthusism as a problem of misdirected or excessive rather than deficient sociability. Second, he transvaluated the term "enthusiasm," embracing it as a foundation for morality and sociability in the best sense.[50] Shaftesbury's account of the "savage air of the vulgar enthusiastic kind" was offered as a contrast to the "serene, soft, and harmonious" aspect of a different kind of enthusiast—specifically, Theocles, the philosophical hero of Shaftesbury's dialogue *The Moralists*.

Although, as stressed above, critics of enthusiasm in the later seventeenth and eighteenth centuries pointed out the unsociability of the enthusiast, they also assigned the enthusiast a certain social character. Typically, enthusiasts were members of sects, so they were simultaneously separatist and social. Having cast the Quakers as antisocial in numerous ways, the author of *The Character of a Quaker* admitted that they "doe yet generally throughout *England* keep themselves up *in one entire Body*, glewed together with a strict Unity, as to *Affection*, and *Correspondence*."[51] Quakers were unsociable in relation to society at large but, among themselves, they were a friendly and mutually supportive swarm.

In addition, the very egoism of the enthusiast subtly enmeshed him in social relations. Because the pretension to inspiration was often described as a kind of spiritual pride, the Quaker was "very curious to be in all things *contrary to the common Mode*, that he may be taken notice of, for a *singular man*."[52] Animated by *"Pride and singularity blended,"* the Quaker's "looks and habit cry; *Pray observe me*, and his whole deportment is *starched* and *affected*, you may take his *Face*, for a new fashioned *Sun-Dyal*."[53] Thus, the negligence of the Quaker with respect to the social code was guided by a careful attentiveness to the opinions of others. More generally, any claim to "special gifts" from God was a temptation to pride since they "make us glorious in the eyes of men. Whereupon Gifted persons [even in apostolic times] were often tempted by popular applause to pride themselves in their gifts."[54] The spiritual pride of the enthusiast, which apparently set him apart, in fact tied him into the theater of

50. See Heyd, *Critique of Enthusiasm,* 211–40; and Klein, *Shaftesbury and the Culture of Politeness,* 165–69.
51. *Character of a Quaker*, 16. On the herding of religious enthusiasts, *Heraclitus Ridens*, No. 19, 7 June 1681.
52. *Character of a Quaker,* 8.
53. *Plus Ultra or the Second Part of the Character of a Quaker* (London, 1672), 2.
54. Hickes, *Spirit of Enthusiasm Exorcised,* 7.

social interaction. Thus, long before Shaftesbury, critics of enthusiasm acknowledged the social aspects of even the unsociable attributes of the enthusiastic personality.

Similarly, Shaftesbury was not the first writer to transvaluate the term enthusiasm. Even writers who insisted that enthusiasm was always and in its entirety a bad thing often recognized that enthusiasm was an excessive version or an illegitimate form of some core quality, aptitude, process, or phenomenon that they valued: a critique of enthusiasm had to protect what was valued while aspersing enthusiasm. Thus, Roger L'Estrange, inveterate enemy of Nonconformists, had to protest that he was not attacking "conscience" per se.[55] Similarly, Henry Wharton had to make clear that an attack on enthusiasm did not extend to "the power of judging for himself in matters of Religion" that belonged legitimately to "every private Person."[56] The Cambridge Platonists, while attacking wrong-headed zeal and enthusiasm, were keen to preserve, in one way or another, forms of imaginative and/or passionate engagement with the spiritual domain. Thus, Henry More's allegory of the soul, *Psychozoia*, insisted on distinctions between a desirable Platonic and mystical piety, on the one hand, and, on the other, mistaken uses of "Holy Spirit" and downright enthusiasm[57]; and Whichcote's attacks on zeal did not preclude an endorsement of the presence of "the *Spirit of God* in *us*" as "a Living Law, Informing the Soul."[58]

In Addison's *Spectator*, as quoted above, a passionate and imaginative animation of religious experience was preserved under the category "devotion" while its distortions were labeled "enthusiasm" and "superstition." However, in another number, Addison neglected those careful distinctions and noted how passages in Milton's *Paradise Lost* "fill the Mind with glorious Ideas of God's Works, and awaken that Divine Enthusiasm, which is so natural to Devotion."[59] This categorial slippage points up that the distance is not that great between, on the one hand, making one word ("enthusiasm") an aspersion while preserving some of its defining traits in another term ("devotion") and, on the other, making one word ("enthusiasm") both an aspersion and a compliment, a repository of both the good and bad configuration of the traits that define it.

55. Roger L'Estrange, *A Memento: Directed to All that Truly Reverence the Memory of King Charles the Martyr* (London, 1662), 86.
56. Henry Wharton, *The Enthusiasm of the Church of Rome Demonstrated* (London, 1688), sigs. A3v–A4r.
57. See Nigel Smith, *Literature and Revolution in England, 1640–1660* (New Haven, Conn., and London, 1994), 218–21.
58. Whichcote, *Moral and Religious Aphorisms*, 90, 136.
59. Bond, *Spectator*, 3:200 (No. 327, 15 March 1712).

Prior to Shaftesbury, John Dennis had sought to redeem enthusiasm from aspersion. Dennis was a critic and playwright who never successfully fended off the derision of many of his contemporaries, but his writings continue to be of much interest.[60] Like Shaftesbury, Dennis was a Whig who sought to deploy the resources of culture on behalf of moral improvement. Such moral improvement was itself part of the legitimation of the post-1688 regime. In his early uses of the word, "enthusiasm" was artistic susceptibility. Dedicating his *Miscellanies in Verse and Prose* to the earl of Dorset, Dennis described the genius and largeness of soul required to perceive literary beauty: Dorset was an ideal patron and connoisseur of others' work because, a poet himself, he knew "those happy Enthusiasms, those violent Emotions, those supernatural transports which exalt a mortal above mortality." Dennis went on to specify:

> tho mear Enthusiasm is but Madness, nothing can be more noble than that which is rightly regulated; and nothing can come nearer that which I fancy to be a true description of Wit; which is a just mixture of Reason and Extravagance, that is such a mixture as reason may always be sure to predominate, and make its mortal Enemy subservient to its grand design of discovering and illustrating sacred Truth.[61]

So enthusiasm here was something not to be excluded but to be regulated, since it was a crucial source of value and of insight into experience. Although this early usage was primarily aesthetic, Dennis later sought to relate enthusiasm to its religious sources. He argued that, to perform its moral functions ("to reform the Manners"), poetry had to move the passions, and that religion was "a perpetual source of extraordinary Passion, which is commonly call'd Enthusiasm."[62] He thus proposed an alliance between poetry and religion that would support morality, religion, and liberty. Enthusiasm thus expressed what was best and most important in religion.

Shaftesbury went further than Dennis. As enthusiasm functioned for Dennis—indeed, as devotion functioned for Addison—so enthusiasm functioned for Shaftesbury: it provided the passionate and imaginative energy to animate the human soul. However, where Dennis's "enthusiasm" and Addison's "devotion" were categories of religious experience, Shaftesbury's "enthusiasm" was a much broader category, "wonderfully powerful and extensive":

---

60. On Dennis, see Harry G. Paul, *John Dennis: His Life and Criticism* (New York, 1911); and *The Critical Works of John Dennis,* ed. Edward Niles Hooker (Baltimore, 1939).
61. John Dennis, *Miscellanies in Verse and Prose* (London, 1693), dedication and preface.
62. John Dennis, *The Advancement and Reformation of Modern Poetry* (London, 1701), dedication; and *The Grounds of Criticism in Poetry* (London, 1704), preface, chaps. 3 and 4.

Something there will be of extravagance and fury, when the ideas or images received are too big for the narrow human vessel to contain. So that inspiration may be justly called divine enthusiasm; for the word itself signifies divine presence, and was made use of by the philosopher whom the earliest Christian Fathers called divine, to express whatever was sublime in human passions. This was the spirit he allotted to heroes, statesmen, poets, orators, musicians, and even philosophers themselves. Nor can we, of our own accord, forbear ascribing to a noble enthusiasm whatever is performed by any of these. So that almost all of us know something of this principle.[63]

In this extension, enthusiasm assumed new roles and responsibilities—or perhaps resumed them—as a progenitor of art, intellect, culture, and even civilization; indeed, of a modern heroics.[64]

Motivating this reappraisal of enthusiasm was Shaftesbury's polemic against philosophical egoism and ethical nominalism.[65] He was resisting the disenchantment of the world (and its arch-disenchanters Descartes, Hobbes, and Locke), even as he shifted enchantment's grounds:

Whether, in fact, there be any real enchantment, any influence of stars, any power of demons or of foreign natures over our own minds, is thought questionable by many. Some there are who assert the negative, and endeavour to solve the appearances of this kind by the natural operation of our passions and the common course of outward things. For my own part, I cannot but at this present apprehend a kind of enchantment or magic in that which we call enthusiasm.[66]

Shaftesburian heroics remained social, however, since enthusiasm was ultimately constitutive of society, a foundational instrument of moral order. In his view, even virtue was "no other than a noble enthusiasm justly directed and regulated by that high standard . . . in the nature of things."[67] It was enthusiasm that offered people access to an ontologically secured realm of both ethical and aesthetic value. The lover, the friend, the patriot, and the saint were

63. Shaftesbury, *Characteristics*, 1:38–39 ("Letter Concerning Enthusiasm," vii).
64. See Peter Fenves's essay in this volume.
65. Klein, *Shaftesbury and the Culture of Politeness*, 60–68.
66. Shaftesbury, *Characteristics*, 2:173 ("Miscellaneous Reflections," II.i).
67. Ibid., 2:176 ("Miscellaneous Reflections," II.i).

all "actuated by this passion, and prove themselves in effect so many different enthusiasts." Thus, an enthusiasm for the good pushed people toward "the manners and conduct of a truly social life."[68]

Enlisting enthusiasm in this way—on the side of virtue, society, civility, and sociability—involved a significant repositioning of it. Usually associated with self-absorption, hypertrophic selfhood, and even egoism, enthusiasm in Shaftesbury's reconfiguration allowed individuals to transcend the limits of the self or, at least, to see and situate themselves in the moral frameworks of society and cosmos.

This is not to deny that enthusiasm had its drawbacks for Shaftesbury. His *Letter Concerning Enthusiasm* was simultaneously a critique of wrong-headed enthusiasm and a rehabilitation of the concept. Its central point was the universality and inevitability of enthusiasm, since it was a condition of the passions: the choice was not between enthusiasm and an alternative but between kinds of enthusiasm. Thus Shaftesbury transvaluated enthusiasm without denying its many negative associations. Good enthusiasm was philosophical, informed by wide principles of sympathy and intelligence; bad enthusiasm was narrow and crabbed and, as noted above, radiated "that savage air of the vulgar enthusiastic kind."

However, even in this perverted form, and even if enthusiasm's manner was unsociable, Shaftesbury insisted on its fundamentally social nature. As an effect of human passion, enthusiasm was susceptible to amplification by "contact or sympathy." It was a kind of contagious panic in which looks conveyed infection:

> The fury flies from face to face; and the disease is no sooner seen than caught. They who in a better situation of mind have beheld a multitude under the power of this passion, have owned that they saw in the countenances of men something more ghastly and terrible than at other times is expressed on the most passionate occasion. Such force has society in ill as well as in good passions: and so much stronger any affection is for being social and communicative.[69]

Thus, enthusiasm is a social form of unsociability, and could account for the swarming of the sect or mob that sets itself against social order and authority—the sorts of enthusiasts against whom Restoration divines had directed so much criticism.

68. Ibid., 2:176–77 ("Miscellaneous Reflections," II.i).
69. Ibid., 1:13 ("Letter Concerning Enthusiasm," ii).

The solution for enthusiasm depended on the nature of the problem that it was taken to be.

Insofar as the enthusiast refused to accept the authority of mediations erected by society between the individual and the divine, enthusiasm's critics often simply reasserted the authority of those mediations. They reminded readers of "the *Polestar* of Gods Word and the *Churches Compass*."[70] They reiterated not only "the Use and Authority of the Scriptures," but also "the Tradition of the Universal Church, the Orders of the Ministry, and the Study of Divinity."[71]

Insofar as the enthusiast engaged in extravagancies of passion or imagination, enthusiasm's critics often asserted the moderate principles of reason and prudence. Addison, as quoted above, invoked "Caution and Prudence" and "Reason as cool as possible" to prevent the overheating of "Passion, Imagination and Constitution" in enthusiastic displays.[72] Addison drew extensively on the themes of the "natural religion" of the later seventeenth and early eighteenth centuries, of which an important attraction was the authority it assigned to reason. In natural religion, Divinity was largely, if not entirely, accessible by means of ordinary reason. Thus, natural religion was a contraceptive to those extraordinary penetrations of Divinity into everyday life that were claimed by enthusiasts. To the spiritual claims of enthusiasm (that "Confounder of Reason, and Religion"), Whichcote retorted, "I oppose not *Rational* to *Spiritual*: for Spiritual is most Rational."[73] The Restoration bishop John Wilkins offered natural religion as the antidote to "pernicious Doctrines of the *Antinomians*, and of all other *Libertine-Enthusiasts* whatsoever: Nothing being more incredible, than that *Divine Revelation* should contradict the clear & unquestionable Dictates of *Natural Light*; nor any thing more vain, than to fancy that the *Grace of God* does release men from the *Laws of Nature*."[74]

Reason offered a collateral benefit in remedying enthusiasm. Insofar as the enthusiast was a victim of solitude and privacy, reason was a public, social, and even sociable process. In this period, rationality was conceived as a principle structuring the universe, but it was coming to be conceived also, less grandly, as an activity of the human mind, one that was often pursued interactively

---

70. *Character of a Quaker*, 5.
71. Hickes, *Spirit of Enthusiasm Exorcised*, 1.
72. Bond, *Spectator*, 2:289 (No. 201, 20 October 1711).
73. Whichcote, *Moral and Religious Aphorisms*, 107, 136.
74. John Wilkins, *Of the Principles and Duties of Natural Religion* (London, 1675), sig. A4v.

with other people. For Wilkins, for instance, God's existence was an idea accessible to natural reason. It was also

> promoted by the experience and instruction of others; Because mankind is naturally designed for a Sociable life, and to be helpful to one another by mutual conversation. And without this advantage of discourse and conversation, whereby they communicate their thoughts and opinions to one another, it could not otherwise be, but that men must needs be strangely ignorant, and have many wild and gross apprehensions of such things as are in themselves very plain and obvious, and do appear so to others.[75]

Solitude bred phantasms of the mind, of which enthusiastic delusions were but one sort. Enthusiasm was associated with unsociability and solitude in ways, explored above, that made Wilkins's observation relevant to it. The "natural light" that Wilkins proposed for dispelling antinomianism and enthusiasm was not simply natural reason: it was, more specifically, what "men of a mature age, in the ordinary use of their faculties, with the common help of mutual Society, may know and be sufficiently assured of, without the help of any special Revelation."[76]

The resources of publicity and sociability, which were already being mined in the Restoration decades by writers such as Wilkins, came into their own after 1688 as part of the public ideology of Whiggism. Steele noted in the *Tatler* that "it is natural for the Imaginations of Men, who lead their Lives in too solitary a Manner, to prey upon themselves, and form from their own Conceptions Beings and Things which have no Place in Nature."[77] The remedies for the corruptions of mind brought on by solitude in general or enthusiasm in particular were, according to Shaftesbury, public ones. Certainly, one of the most controversial points in the *Letter Concerning Enthusiasm* when it first appeared was the toleration with which Shaftesbury thought enthusiasm should be handled. Shaftesbury's toleration supposed a public sphere in which enthusiastic claims could be evaluated. Indeed, enthusiasm elicited many of the lines that make the *Letter* a founding document of eighteenth-century publicity:

> There can be no impartial and free censure of manners where any peculiar custom or national opinion is set apart. . . . 'Tis only in a free nation, such as ours, that imposture has no privilege. . . . 'Tis

---

75. Ibid., 59.
76. Ibid., 60–61.
77. Bond, *Tatler*, 3:81 (No. 203, 27 July 1710).

true, this liberty may seem to run too far. We may perhaps be said to make ill use of it. So every one will say, when he himself is touched, and his opinion freely examined. But who shall be judge of what may be freely examined and what may not? . . . Justness of thought and style, refinement in manners, good breeding, and politeness of every kind can come only from the trial and experience of what is best. . . . Whatever humour has got the start, if it be unnatural, it cannot hold; and the ridicule, if ill-placed at first, will certainly fall at last where it deserves.[78]

However, the *Letter Concerning Enthusiasm* offered another remedy for enthusiasm, different but perhaps symmetrical. Insofar as enthusiasm was disobedient, irrational, and private, authority, reason, and public debate were the appropriate antidotes. However, insofar as enthusiasm itself was an effect of human sociability, a communication or sympathy of perverse sentiments and ideas, it required something else:

it would be well for us if, before we ascended into the higher regions of divinity, we would vouchsafe to descend a little into ourselves, and bestow some poor thoughts upon plain honest morals. When we had once looked into ourselves, and distinguished well the nature of our own affections, we should probably be fitter judges of the divineness of a character, and discern better what affections were suitable or unsuitable to a perfect being.[79]

Here, the inwardness that characterized so many manifestations of enthusiasm returned as a remedy to cure the same phenomenon. In other cases, inwardness was presented as self-indulgence, a granting of license to one's own imaginations, passions, and ideas. In its ultimate form, that kind of introversion sacralized the interior; enthusiasm led to self-apotheosis; and the self, in all sincerity, masqueraded as prophet or even avatar. For Shaftesbury, inwardness was the search for self-knowledge or, more precisely, the practice of self-inquiry, a reiterated cross-examination of "the temper of our own mind and passions."[80] It helped to unmask the self's own masquerades, which Shaftesbury conceived as effects of the insufficiently autonomous self, of the self insufficiently disengaged from the theatrics of sociability.[81]

---

78. Shaftesbury, *Characteristics*, 1:9–10 ("Letter Concerning Enthusiasm," ii).
79. Ibid., 1:29–30 ("Letter Concerning Enthusiasm," v).
80. Ibid., 1:24 ("Letter Concerning Enthusiasm," iv).
81. Much of his thinking was dedicated to combatting this sort of psychic heteronomy; see Klein, *Shaftesbury and the Culture of Politeness*, 72–80.

For Shaftesbury, religion was a breeding ground for imposture: "in all religions except the true I look upon the greatest zeal to be accompanied with the strongest inclinations to deceive." The deceptions practiced in public were, in Shaftesbury's view, coordinated with self-deceptions: "there is more of innocent delusion than voluntary imposture in the world, and . . . they who have most imposed on mankind have been happy in a certain faculty of imposing first upon themselves, by which they have a kind of salve for their consciences, and are so much the more successful, as they can act their part more naturally and to the life."[82] Shaftesbury was pointing to the way that an exterior role colonized and even created the self. The pretensions of a public persona were reflected inward so that the self had no independence from its social being.

In turn, the effectiveness of such pretensions depended on a lack of self-inquiry:

> the chief interest of ambition, avarice, corruption, and every sly insinuating vice is to prevent this interview and familiarity of discourse which is consequent upon close retirement and inward recess. 'Tis the grand artifice of villainy and lewdness, as well as of *superstition and bigotry*, to put us upon terms of greater distance and formality with ourselves.[83]

Of "the imaginary saint, or mystic," in particular, Shaftesbury wrote:

> Instead of looking narrowly into his own nature and mind, that he may be no longer a mystery to himself, he is taken up with the contemplation of other mysterious natures, which he can never explain or comprehend. He has the spectres of his zeal before his eyes, and is as familiar with his modes, essences, personages, and exhibitions of deity, as the conjuror with his different forms, species, and orders of genii or daemons. So that we make no doubt to assert that not so much as a recluse religionist, a votary, or hermit, was ever truly by himself.[84]

Once again, the enthusiast had a mind filled with figments. But here, this was an effect not of true inwardness or solitude but of an imaginary kind of *extroversion*. The inwardness that had always been ascribed to enthusiasts turned out in Shaftesbury to be something else: the colonization of the interior by figments of social life. Shaftesbury measured this state against a true solitude, the necessary condition for a bracing self-inquiry.

---

82. Shaftesbury, *Characteristics*, 2:86 ("The Moralists," II.v).
83. Ibid., 1:115 ("Soliloquy," I.ii); italics added.
84. Ibid., 1:116 ("Soliloquy," I.ii).

ᴗ ᴗ

English writers in the later seventeenth and early eighteenth centuries had many reasons to invoke sociability. One important reason was the desire to confront and restrain the disorder and disruption of the many different phenomena that could be called "enthusiasm." On this basis, sociability entered into the self-understanding of both the Restoration and the post-1688 regimes, albeit in quite different ways. At the same time, sociability had its discontents. The social and sociable character of human personality might in some circumstances appear a good brake on the anarchic energy of an enthusiasm conceived as unsociable, solitary, and private. However, human sociability itself was liable to manifest itself in reckless and rootless imitation and theatricality. Enthusiasm might be construed as an effect not of an excess of self but rather of its deficiency. Against the social self whose lability could issue in enthusiasms, self-absorption could seem something of a remedy.

University of Nevada, Las Vegas

Anxieties of Enthusiasm:
Coleridge, Prophecy, and Popular
Politics in the 1790s

JON MEE

W riting in 1763, Martin Madan offered a confident definition of
the term enthusiasm:

> To equal the *imaginations* of men to the *holy scripture of God*, and
> think them as much the *inspiration of God*, as what was dictated
> as such, to the *holy prophets* and *apostles*, is strictly and properly
> *Enthusiasm*.[1]

Throughout Europe in the eighteenth century, as the essays in this volume
demonstrate in their different ways, "enthusiasm" was a term used to draw
cultural boundaries. Indeed, it was a term against which ideas about the
Enlightenment and its "public sphere" were defined, although such definitions were always complicated by issues of inclusion and exclusion.[2] In
Britain, particularly after the publication of Thomas Paine's *Rights of Man*
(1791–92), previously excluded voices, perhaps constituting counter-publics
of their own, were clamoring more and more to be heard. The popular radical movement that sprang up in the 1790s, under the influence of Paine's
book, is sometimes represented as seeking to remove the barriers of class and
education that continued to obstruct the path to "Reason." The radicals of
the 1790s urged the extension of Enlightenment principles with this end in

---

1. M[artin] M[adan], *A Full and Compleat Answer to the Capital Errors, Contained in the writings of the late Rev.
   William Law* (1763), vi.
2. For a discussion of some of these issues in relation to Jürgen Habermas's notion of the "public sphere," see
   Anthony J. La Vopa, "Conceiving a Public: Ideas and Society in Eighteenth-Century Europe," *Journal of Mod-
   ern History* 64 (1992): 79–116; and Geoff Eley's discussion of Günther Lottes's work in "Nations, Publics, and
   Political Cultures," in Craig Calhoun, ed., *Habermas and the Public Sphere* (Cambridge, Mass., 1992), 327–31.

view, but not everyone involved in the radical ferment of that decade concurred in their definition of what the public sphere should look like. Rational Dissenters such as Joseph Priestley and Samuel Taylor Coleridge wanted to align themselves with a narrative of the progress of reason in the eighteenth century, but they also claimed to see God's hand at work in that progress. Their attempts to create a respectable public space for a reform-minded politics that still found a place for revealed religion were complicated by the existence of a culture of unapologetic enthusiasm at the popular level. Within this culture, the continuing reality of prophetic illumination was proclaimed, and it was sometimes presented as the proper basis for a radical politics. This was a perspective from which the Enlightenment cult of reason could be viewed, quite self-consciously, as simply another means by which the power and knowledge of an educated elite were perpetuated. Here was a different notion of the public sphere, and even of Enlightenment.

The first part of my essay is concerned with the problems caused for the reform movement in the 1790s by this chiastic relationship between Enlightenment and enthusiasm. The second part is concerned with the relationship between radical enthusiasm and Romanticism, both of which have often been regarded as reactions against the radicalism associated with the French Revolution, in particular, and Enlightenment rationality, more generally. The Romanticism developed in the poetry and theory of Wordsworth and Coleridge frequently figured the poet in terms of the prophet and poetic inspiration in terms of a private revelation, or apocalypse, which might tempt us to think of such inspiration as a species of enthusiasm. Indeed, specifically in relation to literary inspiration, the word enthusiasm was sometimes given a positive inflection, albeit a qualified one. But as I shall argue, the relationship between poetry and prophecy was a very fraught one in this period. Enthusiasm was associated with a kind of revelation that might shatter the notion of the autonomous individual reader that was fundamental to both Enlightenment and Romantic ways of thinking about the public sphere. Thus, for someone such as Coleridge, who provides the focus for the issues discussed here, the journey from politically committed Rational Dissent to Romanticism did not lead from Enlightenment to enthusiasm. Starting out on his public career in the 1790s, Coleridge was well aware of the spectacular outpourings of politicized prophecy of the time, but in subsequent decades he continued to grapple with the spectre of enthusiasm as a scandalous mirror-image against which to define himself.

I begin with the difficulties caused by prophetic enthusiasm for the kinds of reformist opinion supposedly committed to the expansion of the public sphere in the late eighteenth century. Dipesh Chakrabarty has recently argued that "we do not have the analytical categories in academic discourse that do justice to the real, everyday and multiple connections we have to what we, in becoming modern, have come to see as 'non-rational.'"[3] In this regard, as we might expect, modern historiography is merely acting as the child of the Enlightenment, which saw the birth of the discipline of modern history-writing. Chakrabarty's specific concern is with India, but his judgment could well be applied to historians of radicalism in the 1790s. Notwithstanding the influence of E. P. Thompson's interest in the politics of popular religious dissent, the modern historian usually finds it easiest to identify the main current of the radical movement in the 1790s with figures such as John Thelwall, who were confident that enthusiasm was steadily retreating in the face of the same progress of truth and reason that would ultimately bring with it political reform.[4] Of course, it is far from true that only radicals were confident of the demise of enthusiasm; many commentators at the time regarded outbursts of popular religious fervor as out of step with the direction of history. The periodical press was particularly harsh on manifestations of popular enthusiasm—not surprisingly, given the status of the press as a key site for the rational exchange of opinion constitutive of the enlightened public sphere. A typical example of this attitude can be found in the *Analytical Review*, a leading journal of dissenting opinion by and large committed to an agenda of political and social reform:

> Facts sometimes occur, which, though not miraculous, almost as much astonish the philosopher, as if he saw a miracle. Such a fact is the recent attention, which at the close of the 18th century, and in the metropolis of one of the most enlightened nations of Europe, has been paid by people of all ranks to a mad prophet.[5]

The mad prophet in question was Richard Brothers, who was at the center of an efflorescence of enthusiasm that fascinated public opinion in 1795—to the extent that even the *Analytical Review*, much to its own chagrin, was forced for a few months in the middle of that year to devote a special section to reviewing prophecies.

Brothers was a former naval lieutenant who had been discharged on half pay at the end of the American War. In 1790 he had refused on religious

3. Dipesh Chakrabarty, "Radical Histories and [the] Question of Enlightenment Rationalism: Some Recent Critiques of Subaltern Studies," *Economic and Political Weekly*, 8 April 1995, 751–59 at 753.
4. Thompson himself notes a revival of interest in John Thelwall in "Hunting the Radical Fox," *Past and Present* 142 (1994): 94–140, n. 2.
5. See the *Analytical Review* 21 (1795): 318.

grounds to swear the oath of loyalty to the king, required for him to draw his pay. The result was a period in a workhouse, followed by a brief stay in Newgate. When he was released in 1792, Brothers began writing prophetic letters to the government claiming that God had revealed to him that the French Revolution was the fulfillment of biblical prophecy and should not be challenged by force of British arms. His prophecies became the center of a very public controversy when he published, in several different editions, *A Revealed Knowledge of the Prophecies and Times* (1794–95). Although this kind of prophecy, as Clarke Garrett has pointed out, was a staple of popular literature in the eighteenth century, the Brothers controversy witnessed an outpouring of enthusiasm not seen for decades.[6] Anthologies filled with visionary material, such as George Riebau's *God's Awful Warning* (1795) and Garnet Terry's *Prophetical Extracts* (1794–95), soon appeared, bewildering the press with their zealous predictions of the imminent fulfillment of biblical prophecy.

Enthusiasm was commonly figured as a kind of disease in the eighteenth century, a disease to which it was feared the unenlightened masses were particularly vulnerable.[7] The prophecies of Brothers looked like a virus peculiarly well suited to exploit vulgar susceptibilities and potentially to destabilize the social order. The Foxite author of *A Word of Admonition to the Rt. Honourable William Pitt* (1795), typically making use of the metaphor of infection, mocked the government's failure to take action against "the poison prophetic that is infused and making rapid progress through the great body of society." Though not sharing the pamphlet's oppositionist politics, the *Gentleman's Magazine* echoed this point of view when it argued that the enthusiasm of Brothers's books, together with their cheapness, made them particularly attractive to "the bulk of the people, whose minds in these days do not need disquiet." The government finally acknowledged the danger and had Brothers arrested on suspicion of treasonable practices. He was subsequently interrogated by the Privy Council and then confined to a madhouse until Pitt's death in 1806.[8]

Not that everyone who saw in contemporary events the fulfillment of biblical prophecy was to be identified with enthusiasm so easily. A more respectable scholarly tradition of millenarianism played its part in the radical

---

6. See Clarke Garrett, *Respectable Folly: Millenarians and the French Revolution in France and England* (Baltimore and London, 1975), 169.

7. See Susie Tucker, *Enthusiasm: A Study in Semantic Change* (Cambridge, 1972), 145–48.

8. See *A Word of Admonition to the Rt. Honourable William Pitt* (1795), 14; and *The Gentleman's Magazine*, 65 (1795): 208. Robert Southey, looking back on the phenomenon of Brothers's popularity, wrote: "When a madman calls himself inspired from that moment the disorder becomes infectious"; see *Letters from England*, ed. Jack Simmons (1807; reprint, London, 1951), 428.

response to the French Revolution. The scientist and dissenting minister Joseph Priestley, for instance, could be counted among this number (as could Coleridge, who came under the sway of the Rational Dissenter William Frend while at Cambridge in the early 1790s).[9] Much as his politics were vilified in the conservative press, Priestley retained a reputation as a key player of the Enlightenment in England, at least in those journals such as the *Analytical Review* that remained sympathetic to Rational Dissent, even during the reactionary backlash of the 1790s. Brothers, on the other hand, was universally regarded in the periodical press as a crazy product of popular enthusiasm and was represented as a throwback to an age of superstition. Priestley looked to the fulfillment of the events in history as proof of the Bible's veracity. Brothers, as the *Analytical Review* put it, was a "prophet commentator" who claimed to interpret and *add to* the biblical canon through his own visions.[10] Priestley was a commentator and interpreter for whom reason—as he told Edmund Burke—was "the umpire in all disputes," and he even claimed to use it in his biblical divinations; while Brothers belonged with those who, in the words of the *Evangelical Magazine*, "not content with so sober and commendable enquiry, have been bold enough to boast of a prophetic spirit."[11] The claim to be able to supplement and even supersede the biblical canon with one's own "prophetic spirit" was key to eighteenth-century definitions of enthusiasm. Applying the terms of Martin Madan's understanding of the word would identify Brothers as guilty of enthusiasm but not Priestley, although, as we shall see, conservative opponents of Rational Dissent were not given to observing such a distinction. Even deists and atheists, as J. G. A. Pocock's article in this volume suggests, could be smeared with "enthusiasm" for mistaking their own imaginary utopias for the truth, a point that helps explain, as we shall see later, why Rational Dissenters and deists alike were often quick to dissociate themselves from popular prophets such as Brothers.

The government itself seemed unsure of the significance of Brothers. Although the initial charge was treason, the government suggested it might proceed on the basis of an Elizabethan statute against false prophecy, before finally confining him to a lunatic asylum. Similarly, for the periodical press, as participants in the enlightened public sphere, prophetic practice had no easily identifiable place. Reviewers of material published during the Brothers controversy

9. For the fullest recent treatment of Coleridge and Cambridge Dissent, see Nicholas Roe, *Wordsworth and Coleridge: The Radical Years* (Oxford, 1988), chap. 3.
10. *Analytical Review* 21 (1795): 213.
11. *Letters to the Right Honourable Edmund Burke* (Birmingham, 1791), 141; *Evangelical Magazine* 4 (1796): 303.

often expressed uncertainty as to whether it was serious or not.[12] John Barrell has judiciously pointed out some of the complications involved in understanding the politics surrounding the controversy. Perhaps himself whiggishly unable to take enthusiasm seriously, Barrell has suggested that the intention of some of the pamphlets condemning Brothers as a democrat was to lure the government into arresting the prophet so as to expose him to public ridicule. Barrell's view is that most of the pamphlets that came from the radical press "treat [Brothers] as a lunatic or impostor." According to Barrell, these "are atheist or agnostic attacks not only on the prophet but on the doctrines of Christianity as well, and are part of the explicit move toward atheism of many London radicals following the publication of *The Age of Reason*."[13] But to suggest that the radical movement in general was necessarily hostile to prophetic politics is to underplay the complicated nature of radical ideology in the period.

It is true that important radicals were hostile to popular enthusiasm, regarding it as contrary to the spirit of enlightenment that they believed was being fulfilled in the French Revolution. Thelwall, in particular, sought to distance the Jacobinism of the 1790s from what he saw as the fanaticism of the 1640s.[14] At the same time, he claimed an inheritance from a republican tradition that included such seventeenth-century forebears as Milton and Harrington. This Commonwealth tradition was also claimed as their inheritance by Rational Dissenters such as Priestley, but their genealogy of the Enlightenment, unlike Thelwall's, kept open a space for a Christian millenarianism able

12. See the different reviews in the *Analytical* for March 1795, where some hesitation is expressed about which pamphlets are satirical and which are not (no. 21, pp. 318–23). This difficulty can also trip up modern historians, including myself. As John Barrell correctly points out (see reference in n. 13 below), in my discussion of Brothers in *Dangerous Enthusiasm: William Blake and the Culture of Radicalism in the 1790s* (Oxford, 1992), I read the anonymous pamphlet *The Age of Prophecy!* as if it were a radical text written in support of Brothers (p. 29), whereas it is almost certainly satirizing both Brothers and the popular radical movement. The *Analytical* calls the pamphlet "in part a feeble attempt at ironical drollery and in part a serious refutation of Mr Brothers and Mr Halhed's method of interpreting scripture" (no. 21, p. 490). As an organ of Rational Dissent, the *Analytical* thought contemporary "prophets" particularly deserving of ridicule, identifying "all pretensions to prophecy, or other supernatural powers, as effects of enthusiasm or imposture" (p. 321). That journal was much more comfortable with the position of the Reverend Frank James, whose *Memoirs of Pretended Prophets* (London, 1795) claimed that "since the sacred canon was completed, no person has given satisfactory evidence of his being a prophet" (p. 20). For the *Analytical*'s positive response, see no. 22 (1795).
13. John Barrell, "Imagining the King's Death: The Arrest of Richard Brothers," *History Workshop Journal* 37 (1994): 1–32 at 13–14.
14. For an excellent discussion of Thelwall's attitudes to the republican tradition of the seventeenth century, see Peter Kitson, "'Sages and patriots that being dead do yet speak to us': Readings of the English Revolution in the Late Eighteenth Century," in James Holstun, ed., *Pamphlet Wars: Prose in the English Revolution* (London and Portland, 1992), 205–30 at 218.

to read in the French Revolution the fulfillment of biblical prophecy. For both Thelwall and Priestley, the universal application of reason was to be the passport for entry into an expanded public sphere, but the Christian millenarianism of the latter made the spectre of popular enthusiasm a particularly uncomfortable double. The anxiety that reformers would be associated with the religious enthusiasm of the Commonwealth was particularly acute for Dissenters, especially after the publication in 1790 of Edmund Burke's *Reflections on the Revolution in France*. Although Burke represented reformers in general and Rational Dissenters in particular as rationalist system-builders, cut off from feeling and experience by the coldness of their faith in reason, he also succeeded in crystallizing an image of Dissenters as the heirs of the Fifth Monarchy men and other sectarian enthusiasts of the seventeenth century. Such was Burke's success that radicalism of any kind was frequently figured in terms of enthusiasm. In relation to politics, the term enthusiasm almost left behind its religious application, except that conservative representations of radicalism were keen to exploit a "memory" of the chaos caused by religious fanaticism in the previous century. Thus at Thomas Hardy's trial for treason in 1794, the prosecution suggested that "the idea that by the establishment of the Rights of Man, universal peace would be established throughout the world" was "an enthusiasm dangerous in the highest degree . . . as dangerous as the enthusiasm of the millenarians, or the Fifth Monarchy-men, who in the last century occasioned some disturbance."[15]

The immediate object of Burke's polemic in his *Reflections* was Richard Price, Priestley's fellow Rational Dissenter, who had welcomed the advent of the French Revolution in the famous sermon given at the Old Jewry in 1789. However, Iain McCalman has recently suggested a previously overlooked target in the figure of Lord George Gordon. Gordon had played an important role in keeping the flame of popular radicalism alive during the 1780s and 1790s. Partly because the government feared his ability to appeal to popular religious enthusiasm, he had been incarcerated in 1787 on charges of libeling the queen of France and for publishing a libelous attack on the British constitution. When he died of jail fever in 1793, he became something of a popular martyr to the radical movement.[16] It is conceivable that Brothers fulfilled the need within the culture of enthusiasm for a focal point after the death of Gordon. And Brothers,

---

15. T. B. Howell, *A Complete Collection of State Trials*, 24:1214–15.
16. See Iain McCalman, "Mad Lord George and Madame La Motte: Riot and Sexuality in the Genesis of Burke's *Reflections on the Revolution in France*," *Journal of British Studies* 35 (1996): 343–67. For further details of Gordon's relationship with the popular radical movement, see also McCalman's "New Jerusalems: Prophecy, Dissent, and Radical Culture in England, 1786–1830," in K. Haakonssen, ed., *Enlightenment and*

although perhaps the most notorious successor to Gordon, was only one among such figures, part of the vibrant metropolitan culture of enthusiasm, of field preachers and prophets. Hardy, to take one example, was a deeply religious man and an intimate of Gordon's whose millenarianism reinforced his political opinions.[17] The reference at Hardy's treason trial to seventeenth-century enthusiasm was perhaps not so unfair as it may at first seem.[18]

These and other examples suggest that Paineite natural-rights thinking did not simply eradicate an older tradition of religiously oriented radicalism in the popular culture. Despite Barrell's stress on the dominance of deistical beliefs in the popular radical movement, even he acknowledges that "beyond question, . . . millenarian beliefs of one kind or another were held by many in that movement."[19] It is all too easy to slip into assumptions about the demise of enthusiasm on the basis of a teleology derived in part from those radicals who, like Thelwall, wanted to present the popular movement as above all a product of Enlightenment rationality. Brothers may or may not have been a democrat himself, but there is no doubt that his fame rested in part on the continuing existence of a public confident that the inner light could provide a guide for political action. Nor should it be assumed that religious radicalism was aligned with the more moderate, constitutionalist thinking. Quite the contrary, in fact, since there is evidence that the most incendiary radical republicanism, which went underground after the middle of the decade, was often fiercely religious. This led to various tensions and fissures within the radical movement, as well as strange accommodations, a situation that can be illustrated by looking briefly at the career of Richard "Citizen" Lee.

Apart from Thompson's passing comment that he was "one of the few English Jacobins who referred to the guillotine in terms of warm approval,"

Religion: Rational Dissent in Eighteenth-Century Religion (Cambridge, 1996), 312–35; and Douglas Hay, "The Laws of God and the Laws of Man," in John Rule and Robert Malcolmson, eds., *Protest and Survival: Essays for E. P. Thompson* (London, 1993), 60–111. Brothers and Gordon may have met in Newgate, but Barrell points out that when interviewed by the Privy Council, Brothers denied he had ever known Gordon ("The Arrest of Richard Brothers," 15). His subsequent claim in the interview that he "was a Man of Peace, and the other was not" suggests that he at least knew of Gordon and had an idea of what he stood for. Obviously, Brothers would have wanted to distance himself from Gordon before the Privy Council, whatever the truth of the matter, since Gordon's millenarian politics had brought him what amounted to a life sentence.

17. Mary Thale, ed., *Selections from the Papers of the London Corresponding Society, 1792–99* (Cambridge, 1983), 306n; and Thomas Hardy, *Memoir of Thomas Hardy* (1832), reprinted in David Vincent, ed., *Testaments of Radicalism: Memoirs of Working-Class Politicians, 1790–1885* (London, 1977), 31–102 at 39.

18. George Riebau, Brothers's publisher, was also a member of the London Corresponding Society, the leading radical organization in the metropolis. Riebau, like "Citizen" Lee, discussed below, produced a great many cheap, incendiary handbills attacking the government in 1795. See Garrett, *Millenarians and the French Revolution,* 205–6.

19. Barrell, "The Arrest of Richard Brothers," 12.

Richard Lee has received little attention from historians.[20] Yet in 1795 Lee was discussed in Parliament during the debates on the so-called Gagging Acts. In order to justify its repressive legislation, the government wanted to present Lee, who had been publishing pamphlets for the previous year under such incendiary titles as *King Killing* and *The Happy Reign of George the Last*, as the London Corresponding Society's official printer. While he had been involved with the society at various times, it appears that by late 1795 Lee had finally seceded from it.[21] At least one of Lee's secessions was founded on religious matters. W. H. Reid claimed that Lee and John Bone were *"proscribed* for refusing to sell Volney's *Ruins* and Paine's *Age of Reason.*"[22] Lee's shop, "The Tree of Liberty," was, in fact, a bastion of the metropolitan culture of enthusiasm that remained committed to the radical movement while at the same time resisting the attempts of sections of the leadership, including Thelwall, to spread the deism of Paine's *Age of Reason*.

As far as I have been able to discover, the first writings to which Lee ever signed his own name were the poems collected together as *Flowers from Sharon* (1794). Among the booksellers listed on the book's title page were J. S. Jordan and Garnet Terry, both of whom, and especially the former, appear as shadowy but persistent figures in the world of millenarian radicalism in the 1790s. Jordan, who took over the publication of the first edition of Paine's *Rights of Man* from Joseph Johnson, also worked with Terry in republishing an Old Ranter text from the seventeenth century, Samuel How's *The Sufficiency of the Spirit's Teaching*, in 1792. W. H. Reid later claimed that it was by reading How that Paine came to his conclusion that God existed only in the human mind—itself a demonstration of the ways in which deism and enthusiasm could come together as well as diverge within radical culture.[23] Although Lee's *Flowers from Sharon* gives no hint of the republican pamphleteering that was to come from his shop in 1795, its stress on free grace asserts the authority of the inner light of the believer over the claims of education or reason:

> It is not from a vain Supposition of their Poetical Merit, that the
> ensuing Sheets are offered to the Public; but from a Conviction
> of the Divine Truths they contain: Truths, which I own, fallen

---

20. See Thompson, *The Making of the English Working Class*, revised ed. (Harmondsworth, England, 1968), 155. An exception to the general neglect is Jane Douglas's brief account of Lee's career in "Citizen Lee and the Tree of Liberty," *Factotum* 7 (1979): 8–12.
21. For mention of Lee in Parliament, see the anonymous *The History of Two Acts* (London, 1796), 273–35, 279–80, 368–69.
22. See W. H. Reid, *The Rise and Dissolution of the Infidel Societies in this Metropolis* (London, 1800), 6.
23. Ibid., 69.

and depraved Reason will always stumble at; and which the unregenerate Heart will never cordially receive; they are too humbling for proud Nature to be in love with;—too dazzling for carnal Eyes to behold.

A review of *Flowers from Sharon* in the *Evangelical Magazine* described Lee as a "laborious mechanic" and mentions "defects in grammar, accent, rhyme, and meter" that "might have been removed by the previous correction of some judicious friend."[24] Acknowledging these lapses, Lee nevertheless rejected the claims of learning in favor of a different kind of subaltern knowledge. For Lee, inspiration was a universally available free grace that transcended the barriers of education erected by what William Blake called the "Classical Learned."[25] The Enlightenment appeal to critical reasoning as constitutive of the public sphere, while potentially democratic, was always defined in terms of certain minimum requirements that guaranteed the exclusion of the unlearned and unlettered.[26] "Enthusiasm" had a role as a term of abuse within Enlightenment discourse as one of the barriers used to exclude this constituency from the public sphere, but there also existed enthusiasts who countered by offering a vision of an expanded public sphere on the basis of a universally available free grace. Whereas Samuel Johnson (quoted by Blake in his annotations) claimed that the Bible could not "be understood at all by the unlearned," Blake believed that "Ignorant and Simple Minds Understand it Best" (Erdman, 667). Garnet Terry, Lee's former publisher, held a similar opinion of the Bible:

> The scriptures are plain and easy—as is Christ's example clear and obvious to view: he is no hard master, nor are the scriptures a sealed book to you, but a plain clear guide, and easy to be understood, written to suit the meanest capacities, independent of the glosses of mercenaries who would make us believe to the contrary.[27]

For all the megalomania of proclaiming himself Prince of the Hebrews, Richard Brothers, too, identified his visions as countering a restricted notion of participation in the public sphere: "the vulgar are precluded from being

---

24. See Lee, "Advertisement" to *Flowers from Sharon* (London, 1794); and the anonymous review of the volume in *Evangelical Magazine* (1794): 82–83.
25. *The Complete Poetry and Prose of William Blake,* newly rev. ed., ed. David V. Erdman (Berkeley and Los Angeles, 1982), 667; page references to this edition are given henceforward in the text.
26. See La Vopa, "Conceiving a Public," 95.
27. Onesimus [Garnett Terry], *Letters on Godly and Religious Subjects,* 2d ed., 2 vols. (London, 1808), 1:iii.

judges of this or any other," he wrote in his confinement, "because they are not learned—a very silly reason indeed."[28] Taken together, comments such as these could be understood as the assertion of a counter-public of enthusiasm, one for which the inner light of prophecy had at least as much claim to be the legitimate basis of public opinion as rational judgment. Not long after the publication of *Flowers from Sharon,* something happened to Richard "Citizen" Lee that transformed his anti-hegemonic assertion of the public legitimacy of enthusiasm into an explicitly radical politics.

Whatever was at the root of Lee's transformation, it needs to be stressed that his republicanism did not entail the abandonment of his religious enthusiasm. Indeed, it may have enabled the millenarian fervor for the guillotine noticed by Thompson, since millenarian enthusiasm remains a powerful part of the explicitly political material Lee published in 1795, from broadsides such as the notorious *King Killing* to his second collection of verse, *Songs from the Rock.* In poems such as "Rights of God," the wrath of God is called down on the head of monarchy in the register of an Old Testament prophet:

> SOLE KING of NATIONS, rise! assert thy Sway,
> THOU JEALOUS GOD! thy potent Arm display;
> Tumble the Blood-Built Thrones of *Despots* down
> Let Dust and Darkness be the *Tyrant's* Crown![29]

Showing the disdain that he shared with Terry for "framed studied speech," Lee's language—its violence, its taste for the imperative case, and even its typographical penchant for capitalization—breathes what the eighteenth century recognized as the spirit of enthusiasm. There is little restraint in Lee's adoption of the prophetic stance. Indeed, where the poetry adopts an anti-Catholic rhetoric, as it often does, it seems reminiscent of the Protestant extremism of the Gordon rioters of 1780, a language far from being rendered obsolete in 1795.[30]

The circulation of Lee's poetry helps illustrate the currency of the language of enthusiasm in radical circles. Two of his poems, *Death of Mrs Hardy* and "Civic Gratitude," are very personal responses to the position of Hardy as a

28. Richard Brothers, *A Description of Jerusalem* (London, 1801), 79.
29. The poem was evidently a favorite of Lee's, at least, reproduced in both *Songs from the Rock* (n.d. [1795?], pp. 17–18) and a separate pamphlet of poetry, *The Death of Despotism and the Doom of Tyrants,* which seems to have come out in the same year. Thomas Spence also chose the poem for his *Pig's Meat* (see n. 32 below).
30. For a brief discussion of the "style" of enthusiasm in relation to Blake, but which would also apply to much of Lee's poetry, see Mee, *Dangerous Enthusiasm,* 35–36. A typical example of Lee's anti-Catholic rhetoric is to be found in "The Second Advent, or The Complete overthrow of Papal Tyranny Anticipated," also published in *Songs from the Rock.*

radical hero and prophet. The former is reproduced in Hardy's autobiography, where Lee is warmly praised as a "patriot bard," and it may be that the two men were personal friends.[31] Lee also seems to have been in touch with Thomas Spence, through whose influence the culture of radical millenarianism survived well into the next century.[32] Although Spence was involved in radical politics from the 1770s, his ideas took on a more millenarian emphasis around the same time that Lee published *Flowers from Sharon*. Malcolm Chase has suggested that the experience of moving to London, with its seething subcultures of field preachers and prophets, may have sparked off a millenarianism that had remained latent since Spence's intensely religious upbringing on Tyneside.[33] Spence has been regarded by some historians as a secular radical who merely exploited the popular appeal of prophetic language, but such instrumentalist readings underestimate the vitality of the culture of enthusiasm Spence encountered in the metropolis. McCalman has observed that "Spence did not distinguish between secular and religious strands of his thought. The 'age of reason' heralded by Enlightenment philosophers paralleled God's promise of the 'Millennium', and Spence was happy to lace them together."[34]

Despite the tensions in the London Corresponding Society that I have been outlining, the boundaries between enthusiasm and Enlightenment were often porous in the popular culture. In their habitually hostile attitudes to clerical institutions, for instance, enthusiasm and Enlightenment could seem much the same thing. Superstition, in the sense of priestcraft, was a key negative term in both lexicons. Thus "Cobbler" How's confidence that every man's mind was his own church could excite both Blake's enthusiastic belief that inspiration was open to all and Paine's faith in rational judgment. Blake, while distrusting Paine's deism, could still praise him as a "worker of miracles" (Erdman, 617). Similarly, in *Pig's Meat* Spence could publish excerpts from the infidel text that caused Lee to quit the London Corresponding Society, Volney's *Ruins of Empire*, along with Lee's own religious poetry. It was this kind of intellectual exchange that had been anticipated by Burke's image of the popular politician as both rational system-builder and enthusiastic prophet.

At one stage, Spence shared a publisher, Arthur Seale, with Richard Brothers; and the government certainly seems to have viewed Spence as someone

31. *Memoir of Thomas Hardy*, 61.
32. Several of Lee's poems appeared in Spence's weekly, *Pig's Meat*, 3d ed., 2 vols. (London, [1795]): "The Triumph of Liberty" (2:176–77); "The Rights of God" (2:204); and "Sonnet to Freedom" (2:284). Spence also appears on the title page of *Songs from the Rock* as one of the booksellers who stocked the volume.
33. Malcolm Chase, *The People's Farm: English Radical Agrarianism, 1775–1840* (Oxford, 1988), 48.
34. See Iain McCalman, *Radical Underworld: Prophets, Revolutionaries, and Pornographers in London, 1795–1840* (Cambridge, 1988), 66.

with dangerous appeal to the popular culture of enthusiasm. His prosecution in 1801 came in the wake of the parliamentary Committee of Secrecy's recommendation that the activities of prophets like Brothers be checked. After hearing Spence's defense in 1801, *The Morning Chronicle* commented that he should be locked up with Brothers in Bedlam. Robert Southey believed that Spence would have been more dangerous had he been a religious rather than a political enthusiast. In fact, Spence did represent himself as something of an inspired prophet. Frequently framing his ideas in terms of his own visions and dreams, he drew around himself a group of believers who continued to propagate his message after his death in 1814. The language of prophecy remained a vital part of radical culture in Spencean works such as Thomas Evans's *Christian Policy* (1816) and Robert Wedderburn's *Axe Laid to the Root* (1817). To infidels such as Thelwall or Francis Place, seeking to argue the case for popular participation in a rational public sphere, Evans was a fanatical throwback to an unrespectable culture of metropolitan enthusiasm. Place claimed that "like many other half-crazy people, . . . [Evans] . . . found the principle of his system in the Bible, . . . as other fanatics before him . . . attempted to found a society which was to renovate the world and produce a millennium." Even so, Place, at least, was conscious enough of the importance of the Spenceans to prepare a thorough manuscript biography of their prophet, which still survives in the British Library.[35]

Thus the enthusiasm of people like Lee and Spence remained a live and contentious issue within radical circles well into the nineteenth century, never entirely to be displaced by Place's vision of rational self-improvement or Thelwall's faith in "Reason and the pure spirit of philosophy."[36] The existence of this vibrant metropolitan culture also continued to cause anxieties in other circles trying to negotiate a response to the revolutionary politics of the 1790s. For the government, religious enthusiasm always retained a social threat, which helps explain the legislation Lord Sidmouth introduced to Parliament to check field preaching in 1811. "To be a Methodist," wrote one of his correspondents, "is to be a Jacobin in the extreme."[37] Although their political perspectives could hardly have been more different, men like Place and Sidmouth were more or less agreed on the dangerous social effects of enthusiasm. Much more difficult was the position of those Christian Dissenters who, while seeking to avoid the stigma of enthusiasm, wished to retain the notion that the Bible and its

---

35. See Place, "Collection for a Memoir of Thomas Spence," BL, Add. MS. 27808, fols. 138ff. The comments on Evans can be found in Add. MS. 27809, fols. 33, 99–100. For the details of Spence's trial in 1801, see McCalman, *Radical Underworld*, 66–67.

36. See John Thelwall, *Political Lectures,* vol. 1 (London, 1795), 12.

37. Quoted in McCalman, *Radical Underworld*, 51

prophetic tradition had a relevance to contemporary politics. Coleridge fell into this category, in the 1790s at least, and I want to devote the rest of this discussion to the ways in which his need to distinguish himself from the un-respectable tradition of enthusiasm played a role in the development of his thought and of what we now call Romanticism.

❦ ❧

High Romanticism as it developed in England in the writing of Coleridge and Wordsworth is often represented as a retreat from a radical political commit-ment to the French Revolution. An influential restatement of this narrative by M. H. Abrams, published in the 1970s, represented the process in terms of the transformation of one kind of prophetic enthusiasm into another, "faith in an apocalypse by revolution . . . gave way to faith in apocalypse by imagination or cognition."[38] The system-building of Enlightenment rationalism is displaced by the idea of an aesthetic revelation involving what Abrams called an "imag-inative transformation of the self."[39] Increasingly, the poet was figured as a prophet of the imagination. For New Historicist critics, such as Alan Liu, for whom Abrams is culpable in his willingness to perpetuate the self-image pro-moted by the poets, this process involves an evasion of history, the displace-ment of public events by narratives of private revelation. In Liu's formulation, prophecy operates to displace politics.[40] What this overlooks, and what Abrams's original formulation did recognize, is that political enthusiasm had itself been frequently figured as a prophetic operation in the 1790s. The Rev-olution had been widely greeted as a form of apocalypse. As I have tried to show above, prophecy did not necessarily operate in opposition to history and politics in the 1790s; but where prophecy did lay claim to a public role, it was readily identified with enthusiasm. Elsewhere I have argued that Wordsworth's retreat from his political commitments involved him in a difficult process of defining his visionary poetics in such a way that it could not be charged with enthusiasm.[41] Here I shall discuss Coleridge's subtly different and perhaps

38. M. H. Abrams, *Natural Supernaturalism: Tradition and Revolution in Romantic Literature* (Oxford, 1971), 334.
39. Abrams, "Constructing and Deconstructing," in Morris Eaves and Michael Fischer, eds., *Romanticism and Contemporary Criticism* (Ithaca, N.Y., 1986), 167.
40. For an earlier discussion of Liu's approach to Wordsworth's apocalypticism, see Jon Mee, "Apocalypse and Ambivalence: The Politics of Millenarianism in the 1790s," *South Atlantic Quarterly* 95 (1996): 671–97, esp. 687–93.
41. Ibid.

more difficult evolution of a similar response. Unlike Wordsworth, whom he described to Thelwall in May 1796 as "at least a *Semi*-atheist," Coleridge was coming out of a dialogue with the dissenting tradition that, as I have shown, had the dual objective of sustaining the public authority of biblical prophecy even as it disavowed enthusiasm.[42] Maintaining such a position without making oneself vulnerable to the charge of enthusiasm was no easy matter. It continued to be a problem for Coleridge even after he had disavowed his radical past. Here I propose to supplement (and complicate) the often told story of Coleridge's Romantic rewriting of that past by looking at the attempts he made to dissociate himself from the spectre of enthusiasm.

I begin with a poem Coleridge wrote while still very much under the influence of Cambridge Dissent, "Religious Musings," first published in its entirety in his *Poems on Various Subjects* in April 1796.[43] Coleridge's poem is standard millenarian fare, in that it interprets contemporary political events, along with advances in science and learning, as signs of the fulfillment of biblical prophecies of the last days. In the sixth of the *Lectures on Revealed Religion* given in Bristol, probably in June 1795, Coleridge emphasized that prophecies "must be obscure in proportion to the distance, and become clear as they approach the Time of their Completion." Their fulfillment in the present was a sign of the truth of the Bible: "Prophecies are necessary to Revealed Religion as perpetual Testimonies," and were thus a means of defending revealed religion against what he perceived to be the errors of infidels such as William Godwin and, as we shall see later, Thelwall.[44] In a letter to Southey of 11 September 1794, Coleridge made his earliest recorded reference to Godwin:

> Godwin *thinks* himself *inclined* to *Atheism—acknowledges* there
> are many arguments *for* deity, he cannot answer—but not so
> many, as *against* his Existence—He is writing a book about it. I
> set him at defiance.[45]

The editors of the excellent edition of the 1795 lectures comment that Coleridge's response to infidels such as Godwin "affected his attitude to the

---

42. See Coleridge to Thelwall, 13 May 1796, *Collected Letters of Samuel Taylor Coleridge*, ed. E. L. Griggs, 6 vols. (Oxford, 1956), 1:126.

43. See Coleridge, *Poems on Various Subjects* (Bristol, 1796), 135–75. Excerpts from "Religious Musings" were printed in Coleridge's short-lived periodical, *The Watchman*, in March of that year under the title "The Present State of Society." See *The Watchman*, no. 2, 9 March 1796, in *The Collected Works of Samuel Taylor Coleridge,* vol. 2, ed. Lewis Patton (Princeton, N.J., 1970), 64–67.

44. *Lectures 1795 on Politics and Religion*, in *Collected Works*, vol. 1, ed. Lewis Patton and Peter Mann (Princeton, N.J., 1971), 151–52.

45. *Collected Letters*, 1:102.

whole radical movement," and see it as "the key to much of his social and political thinking in 1795."[46]

While "Religious Musings" was no doubt intended as a defiant statement
toward infidel radicals, proclaiming Coleridge's faith in the ability of the Bible
and Christianity to provide the basis of his politics, it is also articulated in ways
that would deflect the charge of enthusiasm. Coleridge's poem situates itself as
part of a gradual process of enlightenment that comprised scientific and political changes within the public culture, or what Priestley called "the general
Enlargement of Liberty."[47] "Religious Musings" represents the fulfillment of
prophecy as the product of a spirit of Necessity working through the agency of
an elect that comprises the heroes of the English Enlightenment generally and
Rational Dissent in particular: Milton, Newton, Franklin, Hartley, and Priestley himself. For if Coleridge set Godwin "at defiance," he did not want to
undermine the credibility of either his faith or his politics by aligning them
with the spirit of enthusiasm. In contrast to the unrestrained violence of Lee's
language, Coleridge's apocalypticism is ringed with caution. The French Revolution is not to be understood as the final fulfillment of biblical prophecy in
itself; it is the opening only of the fifth of the seven seals. The poem itself is
concerned with the ultimate descent of divine justice at the end of time:

> And lo! the Throne of the redeeming God
> Forth flashing unimaginable day
> Wraps in one blaze earth, heaven, and deepest hell
> (Lines 426–28)

The question remains open as to when that ultimate fulfillment will be. The
relatively polite constituency of Rational Dissent, as demonstrated by the
response of the *Analytical Review* to the Brothers affair, had always been wary
of popular enthusiasm and, in part because of a fear of the irrationality of the
mob, cautious about the notion of a genuinely mass participation in the
enlightened public sphere.[48] Especially after Burke succeeded in fixing the
image of Richard Price as a throwback to seventeenth-century millenarianism,
Rational Dissenters were likely to be especially cautious about claiming direct
knowledge of the imminence of the Last Days.

This reflex of caution and hesitation seems present in the ambivalence of
Coleridge's "Religious Musings." Coleridge reassures the "Children of
wretchedness" (line 321) that "Yet is the day of Retribution nigh" (line 323),

---

46. *Lectures 1795*, lxvii.
47. *Letters to the Right Honourable Edmund Burke*, 141.
48. For a discussion of this reflex in enlightenment thinking, see La Vopa, "Conceiving a Public," 12.

but he also takes care to counsel them that "More groans must rise / More blood must stream, or ere your wrongs be full" (line 321). Where in his "Rights of God" Lee calls directly on God for an immediate display of his apocalyptic power, in Coleridge's poetry images of apocalyptic violence are produced only to be controlled and contained; he twice cautions those impatient for apocalyptic change to "Rest awhile" (lines 320 and 327). Discussing a similarly cautious invocation of the Millennium in Coleridge's *Moral and Political Lecture* of the previous year, Nicholas Roe comments that "the emphasis is less on immediate fulfillment than aspiration."[49] It might be more accurate to say that the aspiration itself is being disciplined and defined against the exorbitance of enthusiasm.

Coleridge's care in these texts can be contrasted with the unashamed enthusiasm of Lee's claim to have direct access to "divine Truths . . . which . . . depraved Reason will always stumble at" or, indeed, Blake's unequivocal identification of his own poetry as prophecy. My own view is that, further, Coleridge's writing in this period is concerned to respect a distinction between poetry and prophecy disavowed by both Blake and Lee, although such an argument might sound strange given that literary criticism has for a long time now operated with the idea that a defining feature of Romanticism was its use of prophetic rhetoric. Robert Lowth's discovery that the prophets of the Old Testament were also the poets of Hebrew society was a commonplace by the 1790s; in the *Age of Reason* Paine even used the notion of the equivalence of poetry and prophecy to discredit the notion that the Bible was divine revelation. Nevertheless, what I want to argue is that poetry and prophecy were carefully distinguished as two different orders of inspiration.[50] Partly because of the way the relationship between the poet and the reader was imagined—that is, as a conversation between autonomous individuals, an idea that Coleridge played his own part in developing—poetic inspiration needed to be properly disciplined and distinct from exorbitant public claims to the immediate experience of divine illumination.

At least one commentator on the Brothers controversy remarked explicitly on the relationship between poetry and prophecy. The *Analytical*'s anonymous reviewer, still puzzled an the eruption of vulgar enthusiasm in a sophisticated modern metropolis like London, commented:

> Prophecy and poetry are so nearly allied, that in most nations
> they have been more or less confounded. In some languages, the

---

49. Roe, *The Radical Years,* 215
50. See Mee, *Dangerous Enthusiasm,* 39–46.

same term denotes both a prophet and a poet. . . . Both use a
bold metaphorical style; both utter their oracles in verse, or in a
sort of prose resembling verse; both claim the gift of inspiration;
and both are, or at least were once, believed to be inspired.[51]

The word "confounded," though, sounds a note of warning here. To continue
to believe that the poet and the prophet are identical is to be guilty of a
misguided primitivism. The regression would be social as well as historical,
leading back to the enthusiasm of Brothers and his ilk. The *Analytical Review*
suggests that two quite different kinds of inspiration are at stake, even while
pointing out the formal similarities between them. To claim quite literally to
be a prophet—to claim that one's own visions had the status of divine revelation, as Brothers, Blake, and others did in the 1790s—was to ignore the difference between poet and prophet, and effectively to abrogate the conventions
of the enlightened public sphere.

Toward the close of "Religious Musings," Coleridge swerves away from
laying claim to the power of prophecy. His province is poetry, dealing with
prophetic matter, inspired and sublime to be sure, but not itself claiming to be
prophecy. As the poem approaches what would be a climactic vision of the last
days, Coleridge draws back. His "Fancy Falls" (line 409). The apocalyptic
moment invites representation, but remains unimaginable. The veil must ultimately remain unlifted and the poem concludes, accepting that divine inspiration is not enjoyed by mere mortals:

> I haply journeying my immortal course
> Shall sometime join your mystic choir! Till then
> I discipline my young noviciate thought
> In ministries of heart-stirring song.
>
> (Lines 436–39)

A recognition of Coleridge's attempt to discipline his inspiration helps
explain the generally positive reviews the poem received at a time when
prophecy, in the wake of the Brothers affair, was a particularly sensitive subject.[52] One reviewer in particular, John Aikin, who wrote for the *Monthly*

---

51. *Analytical Review* 21 (1795): 213.
52. Coleridge wrote with delight about the reviews to his friend J. P. Estrlin on 4 July 1796 (*Collected Let-
    ters*, 1:135): "The Reviews have been wonderful—The Monthly has *cataracted* panegyric on my poems;
    the Critical has cascaded it; and the Analytical has *dribbled* it with very tolerable civility. The Monthly
    has at least done justice to my Religious Musings—They place it 'on the very top of the scale of Sub-
    limity[']—!" It is worth contrasting these remarks with his comments on "Religious Musings" in *The
    Biographia Literaria*, discussed below.

Review, showed that he was well aware of the dangers with which Coleridge was flirting, but decided that the poet stopped short of enthusiasm:

> Often obscure, uncouth, and verging to extravagance, but generally striking and impressive to a supreme degree, it exhibits that ungoverned career of fancy and feeling which equally belongs to the poet and the enthusiast. The book of Revelations may be a dangerous fount of prophecy, but it is no mean Helicon of poetic inspiration. Who will deny genius to such conceptions as the following.[53]

A Dissenter himself, educated at the Warrington Academy, where Priestley taught, Aikin could well sympathize with Coleridge's attempt to articulate a variety of Christian politics distinct from the enthusiasm of Brothers and Lee.

A rather less sympathetic response to Coleridge's poem came from John Thelwall who, unlike Aikin, was inclined to conflate any kind of millenarianism with enthusiasm. As I have noted, Thelwall's radicalism laid claim to an Enlightenment pedigree. In lectures given in 1795, Thelwall carefully distinguished the "spirit" of the French Revolution from the English Revolution of the 1640s. Of the latter he wrote that "the intolerance of religious sects, and the visions of Fanaticism had poisoned the judgment and embittered the spirit of the Republicans of the day." In contrast he argued "the peaceable diffusion of knowledge" was "our object": "this is not the rant of inconsiderate enthusiasm."[54] Thelwall's Enlightenment disdain for popular superstition aside, no doubt his response was conditioned in part by his own urgent need to escape the Burkian identification of radicalism of all kinds with the enthusiasm of the seventeenth century, and he was not always successful, as a matter of style if not of substance. Thomas Amyot, reporting on Thelwall's populist style of lecturing, claimed "he raves like a mad Methodist parson: the most ranting Actor in the most ranting Character never made so much noise as Citizen Thelwall." Enthusiasm can be equated with theatricality because both represent the dissolution of the autonomous subject from an "enlightened" perspective. Thelwall loses himself in the character of the demagogue and his subjectivity is scattered to the mob who form the audience for his performance. The same identification operates in the depictions of Thelwall as "Citizen Rant" in both Isaac Disraeli's *Vaurien* (1797) and George Walker's *The Vagabond* (1799).[55] Ranting enthusiasm was the last thing with which the Jacobin orator, proclaiming his

53. *Monthly Review,* 2d ser., 20 (1796): 197–98.
54. Thelwall, *Political Lectures,* 40, 13, 26.
55. See Thompson, "Hunting the Jacobin Fox," 96, 124.

vision of an enlightened public sphere open to the scrutiny of individual reason, wanted to be connected.

Ranting enthusiasm was precisely what Thelwall saw in "Religious Musings," and he was quick to condemn it. Coleridge wrote Thelwall late in April 1796:

> I build all my poetic pretensions on the Religious Musings—
> which you will read with a POET'S EYE, with the same unpreju-
> diceness, I wish, I could add, the same pleasure, with which the
> atheistic Poem of Lucretius.[56]

By mentioning the atheism of Lucretius, Coleridge is provocatively raising for Thelwall the context of their ongoing disagreement about "Modern patriotism." In a spoof published in *The Watchman* in March 1796, Coleridge made clear his view that patriotism without Christian principles amounted to libertinism.[57] Thelwall's reply to Coleridge's letter reaffirmed his own position that any politics based on an appeal to revealed religion rather than reason was no better than enthusiasm. Thelwall's opinion of "Religious Musings" was correspondingly negative.[58] What praise he could muster

> belongs almost exclusively to those parts which are not at all reli-
> gious. As for the generality of those passages which are most so,
> they are certainly anything in the world rather than poetry. . . .
> they are the very acme of abstruse, metaphysical, mistical rant, &
> all ranting abstractions, metaphysic & mysticism are wider from
> true poetry than the equator from the poles.

Thelwall's distinction between "rant" and "poetry" is consistent with Aikin's distinction between prophecy and literature, but Thelwall draws his line in a different place. Ironically, Thelwall the radical accepts something from Burke's terms, seeing in the Rational Dissenter of the 1790s the spectre of the regicides of the seventeenth century: "the licencious (I mean pious) nonsense of the conventicle." Later on in the letter he directly accuses Coleridge of "enthusiasm."[59]

Unsurprisingly, Coleridge rejected Thelwall's analysis and, more particularly, he rejected the reading of his version of millenarianism as unenlightened enthusiasm. For Coleridge believed himself to be as in touch with the true spirit of the Enlightenment as any classical republican: "how are these opinions

56. To Thelwall, [late April 1796], *Collected Letters*, 1:122.
57. *The Watchman*, no. 3, 17 March 1796, 98–100.
58. For the text of Thelwall's reply of 10 May, 1796, see Warren E. Gibbs, "An Unpublished Letter from John Thelwall to S. T. Coleridge," *Modern Language Review* 25 (1930): 85–90.
59. Ibid., 87–89.

connected with the *Conventicle* more than with the Stoa, the Lyceum, or the grove of Academus?" he asks Thelwall in his reply.[60] Nevertheless, the anxiety evident in the poem about going too far toward enthusiasm in its prophetic politics was only likely to have been confirmed by the tussle with Thelwall. Indeed, for all his defiance of Thelwall's infidelism, he wrote in February 1797 to assure him:

> The Religious Musings, I have altered monstrously, since I read them to you, and received your criticisms.[61]

Roe has shown that around 1795–96 Coleridge shared with Thelwall a fear that popular tumults and social disorder would induce a government crackdown on the radical movement more generally.[62] Enthusiasm, as I have shown, was feared across the political spectrum as the spark that could light the fuse of popular unrest and thus result in social dislocation.

Others moving in Coleridge's orbit at this time were alive to the dangers of enthusiasm in this respect. Southey visited William Bryan, a follower of Brothers who lived in Bristol, in October 1794. On Bryan's millennial ravings, Southey later commented that "few subjects appear to me more worthy of attention than the aberration of the human intellect upon the most momentous subject which can ever employ it." A chapter is devoted to Brothers in Southey's *Letters from England*, the purpose of which, he later revealed, was to control through ridicule what he regarded as the socially disruptive power of enthusiasm:

> Bedlam is the place for such half lunatics, half impostors, because they infect others. I have seen the instances of the mischief Brothers did in making tradesmen leave their business and their families, all that relates to him, and Bryan is written from personal knowledge, I knew Bryan and heard the whole system from his own mouth, and he it was who went with the knife to stab Brothers, and told me the fact himself.[63]

---

60. To Thelwall, 13 May 1796, *Collected Letters*, 1:127.
61. Ibid., 1:309.
62. Roe, *The Radical Years,* 174.
63. To James Graham, 4 January 1808, *New Letters of Robert Southey,* ed. Kenneth Curry, 2 vols. (New York and London, 1965), 1:467–68, 468–69. In addition to the chapter on Brothers in *Letters from England* (pp. 427–33), there are chapters on his follower William Bryan (pp. 415–27) and the prophetess Joanna Southcott (pp. 433–46). Not only was enthusiasm associated with the dissolution of proper domesticity, but it was also frequently figured in terms of the dissolution of gender boundaries, a matter that I intend to take up at length elsewhere in relation to Southcott, who played an important role in keeping enthusiasm before the public eye after 1800.

Coleridge shared with both Southey and Thelwall a fear of the social consequences of popular enthusiasm and consequently was careful to distance his
opinions from the enthusiasm of the crowd. The sixth of his *Lectures on
Revealed Religion* makes it quite clear that his millenarian politics has more to
do with the exertions of the kind of elect mentioned in "Religious Musings"
than with any more general rising up of the spirit of enthusiasm:

> Universal Equality is the object of the Mess[iah's] mission not to
> be procured by the tumultuous uprising of an indignant multi-
> tude but this final result of an unresisting yet deeply principled
> Minority, which gradually absorbing kindred minds shall at last
> become the whole.

Earlier in 1795, in his *Moral and Political Lectures*, Coleridge had contrasted the
wildness of some reformers with "that small but glorious band, whom we may
truly distinguish by the name of thinking and disinterested Patriots." Men like
Bryan and Brothers, Coleridge would have feared, were speaking to the wild
element, while he aligned himself with the disinterested band of the elect.[64]

Indeed, the few explicit references to Brothers in Coleridge's lectures and
other writings of this period suggest that he sought to define his own enlightened
millenarianism against the enthusiasm of the popular prophet. Coleridge used
the contrast to assure his political opponents, both in the government and
among radical infidels, that he shared their notion of what properly constituted
public discourse—even if he is arguing that revealed religion has a proper role to
play in politics.[65] An often noted, and in my view related, feature of Coleridge's
poetry after "Religious Musings" is a withdrawal from the public into a more
domestic world. Morton D. Paley suggests that this setting "is not necessarily the
antithesis of the millennial for it is at least potentially a millennium in microcosm."[66] A "millennium in microcosm" it may be, but it is also an attempt to do
disciplinary work on the idea of poetic revelation so that it might be distinguished from enthusiasm. Indeed, given Southey's stress on the way enthusiasm
could break families apart, Coleridge's poetic reinscription of the millennial
moment within the domestic sphere in poems such as "Frost at Midnight" could
be seen as a quite deliberate strategy for indicating what was different about his

---

64. *Lectures 1795*, 218, 12.
65. See Morton D. Paley's two excellent essays on the millenarianism of Coleridge's poetry in the 1790s:
"'These promised Years': Coleridge's 'Religious Musings' and the Millenarianism of the 1790s," in Keith
Hanley and Raman Selden, eds., *Revolution and English Romanticism* (1990), 49–60; and "Apocalypse
and Millennium in the Poetry of Coleridge," *Wordsworth Circle* 23 (1992): 24–34. On the contrast
with Brothers, see especially "These promised Years," 59.
66. "Apocalypse and Millennium," 26.

own form of inspiration. Whereas enthusiasm threatens to splinter disciplined subjectivity through a violent eruption of revelation into the public world, Coleridge's poetic revelation increasingly affirms the Enlightenment notion of "the modern public as a communion of autonomous readers."[67] Private judgment is the basis of public opinion in the bourgeois public sphere. Where the prophetic figure who threatens to speak directly to a public does appear in Coleridge's poetry of this period, it is as a figure of potential danger:

> Beware! beware!
> His flashing eyes, his floating hair!
> Weave a circle round him thrice,
> And close your eyes with holy dread,
> For he on honey-dew hath fed,
> And drunk the milk of Paradise
> ("Kubla Khan," lines 49–54)[68]

This image may glamorize the figure of the poet-prophet, but it also isolates him, separating him from any public discourse of prophetic utterance, a point reinforced by the unfinished, fragmentary nature of the poem. This characterization effaces the existence of the subculture of enthusiasm, policing the boundary between poetry and prophecy, and cutting the prophetic stance off from its public as effectively as the government cut Brothers off from his. This reflex in Coleridge's writing continued beyond the 1790s, and I would like to conclude by sketching the way in which he continued to distinguish himself from the tradition of prophetic enthusiasm as he retreated from Rational Dissent and political radicalism toward trinitarianism in religion, conservatism in politics, and Romanticism in literature.

Part of Coleridge's strategy was an attempt to fix the meaning of the word enthusiast by its etymology (contrary to more general usage in the period). As early as *The Friend*, he was trying to contrast "the demons of fanaticism," which had to be driven out "from the people," with "true Christian enthusiasm."[69] The latter was identified with a quiet certainty in the nearness of God, the former with crowds and public performance (an idea present in the representation of Thelwall as "Citizen Rant"). Distinguishing "fanaticism" from "enthusiasm" was an attempt to quarantine the latter from its association with

---

67. See La Vopa's essay in this volume for a discussion of this model in relation to idea of enthusiasm.
68. "Kubla Khan: or, A Vision in a Dream," *The Complete Poetical Works of Samuel Taylor Coleridge,* ed. E. H. Coleridge, 2 vols. (Oxford, 1912), 1:295–98.
69. For a brief account of Coleridge's attempts to distinguish fanaticism from enthusiasm, see Tucker, *Enthusiasm,* 19, 47–48.

a popular culture in which prophecy and the illumination of the spirit were
proclaimed as the true basis of public discourse—a task that Wordsworth was
undertaking in *The Prelude* at about the same time. This kind of quarantining
meant that Coleridge had to return to the matter of his own past, and to the
fear that his own millenarian politics in the 1790s were tainted by the spirit of
fanaticism. Significantly for this process, the *Biographia Literaria* (1817) begins
with a discussion of "Religious Musings" and an attempt to define Coleridge's
Romantic aesthetics against the errors he made in framing that poem: "I for-
got to enquire, whether the thoughts themselves did not demand a degree of
attention unsuitable to the nature and objects of poetry." Implicit here is the
distinction between poetry and prophecy. Coleridge implies that he now sees
a clear distinction between the former and the latter. He claims to have "used
my best efforts to tame the swell and glitter both of thought and diction" in
later editions of the poem,[70] but this taming is not simply a matter of choosing more appropriate poetic diction. Thelwall had seen in the swell and glitter
of Coleridge's poem the rant of enthusiasm; the attempt to tame that rant was
a reflex of Coleridge's writing from the very beginning.[71] Thus Romanticism,
in Coleridge's case at least, involved not only a counter to Enlightenment
thinking but also a distancing from the spectre of enthusiasm, the disavowal of
a popular tradition of public prophecy. In fact, paradoxically, the two were
ineluctably bound together for Coleridge. In *The Lay Sermons*, the first volume
of which was published in 1817, as in the much earlier lectures on revealed
religion, Coleridge was defending the integrity of the Bible against both the
slurs of infidels and "the false prophets" of the radical movement, but in a passing footnote he comments that the Bible "has been strangely abused and
perverted from the Millenarians of the primitive Church to the religious Politicians of our own time."[72] Buried in the notes here is the acknowledgment of a
quite different religious politics from his own in 1817, one against which he
had been in an uneasy process of defining himself from the early 1790s.

    To pursue this argument further would involve investigating the possibility
that Coleridge's Kantianism, which is adduced in order to prove the theory of
the Imagination in the *Biographia Literaria*, should be understood in terms of

---

70. *Biographia Literaria*, ed. James Engell and W. Jackson Bate, in *Collected Works*, vol. 7 (Princeton, N.J.,
1983), 1:7.
71. Cf. B. R. Pollin (assisted by Redmond Burke), "John Thelwall's Marginalia in a Copy of Coleridge's
Biographia Literaria," *Bulletin of the New York Public Library* 74 (1970): 73–94. Thelwall still believed
the *Biographia* to contain "the rant & cant of the conventicle" (p. 94), a phrase that echoes his letter of
1796 on "Religious Musings." Evidently he saw what he calls Coleridge's "Metaphysics" merely as a bid
to make his enthusiasm seem philosophically respectable.
72. *Lay Sermons*, in *Collected Works*, ed. R. J. White, vol. 6, 145, 147n.

a lifelong attempt to discover a framing discipline for his ideas about the Imagination, which would mark it off conclusively from dangerous enthusiasm. It is the discipline of philosophy itself that is increasingly invoked by Coleridge as the secure ground of his theories—just as it is emerging as a discipline in the strict sense. Ironically, as Anthony La Vopa has shown, Kant's philosophy was itself was being attacked in Germany at this time as a secular mutation of *Schwärmerei*.[73] La Vopa's discussion of German responses to Kant places them in the context of more general fears about the expansion of the reading public—that is, the idea that reading itself might be a species of secular enthusiasm capable of overwhelming the rational judgment on which the self-image of the enlightened public sphere was predicated. His account of the nexus between enthusiasm and reading is suggestive in relation to Coleridge's own attitude to "the luxuriant misgrowth of our activity, a Reading Public," but that story is not one that I can pursue here.[74] I'd rather close on a recuperative turn by reiterating that enthusiasm is a term that operates across the boundaries of those histories that seek to negotiate the narrative from Enlightenment to Romanticism. In Coleridge's case, at least, High Romanticism may have been defining itself against a Jacobin materialism that we are apt to identify with the Enlightenment, but it was also involved on a different front, throwing up earthworks to defend itself from the charge of enthusiasm. In the process, Coleridge was distancing himself from a very different culture, one for which prophecy, rather than transcending history and politics, could open up a space within them.

University College, Oxford

73. See the discussion on reading as a form of *Schwärmerei* in La Vopa's essay in this volume.
74. For a useful discussion of Coleridge's attitude to the expansion of the reading public, see Jon Klancher, *The Making of English Reading Audiences, 1789–1832* (Madison, Wis., 1987), 150–70.

Contributors

Lawrence E. Klein, who teaches history at the University of Nevada, Las Vegas, is the author of *Shaftesbury and the Culture of Politeness: Moral Discourse and Cultural Politics in Early-Eighteenth-Century England* (1994). He is working on a new edition of the third earl of Shaftesbury's *Characteristics* for Cambridge University Press.

Anthony J. La Vopa, who teaches history at North Carolina State University, Raleigh, is currently a fellow at the National Humanities Center. He is the author of a number of articles on eighteenth-century German social and intellectual history, and of *Grace, Talent, and Merit: Poor Students, Clerical Careers, and Professional Ideology in Eighteenth-Century Germany* (1988). He is working on a biography of Johann Gottlieb Fichte.

☙ ❧

Peter Fenves is a professor of German and Comparative Literature at Northwestern University. His book *Raising the Tone of Philosophy: Late Essays by Kant, Transformative Critique by Derrida* will be published in a new edition in autumn 1998. He has recently published articles on Moses Mendelssohn, Adalbert Stifter, Walter Benjamin, Jacques Derrida, Luce Irigaray, and Jean-Luc Nancy, as well as on Kant and Hölderlin.

Jan Goldstein is a professor of history at the University of Chicago, where she is also a member of the Committee on the Conceptual Foundations of Science and an editor of the *Journal of Modern History*. Her books include *Console and Classify: The French Psychiatric Profession in the Nineteenth Century* (1990) and *Foucault and the Writing of History* (1994). Her current work includes a translation of a manuscript on a case of hysteria in a Savoyard peasant girl and a study of competing psychologies in nineteenth-century France.

Jon Mee is Margaret Candfield Fellow in English at University College and lecturer in the Faculty of English, Oxford University. His recent publications have been devoted to William Blake, popular print culture in the 1790s, and contemporary Indian writing in English. He is one of the editors of the forthcoming *Oxford Companion to British Culture of the Romantic Period*.

continued overleaf

J. G. A. Pocock, the author of many works on British political thought, is Professor Emeritus of History at the Johns Hopkins University. His essay in this volume is part of a projected series of studies on Edward Gibbon and his age, "Barbarism and Religion," to be published by Cambridge University Press.

Mary D. Sheriff, a professor of art at the University of North Carolina, Chapel Hill, is the author of *J. H. Fragonard: Art and Eroticism* (1990) and *The Exceptional Woman: Elisabeth Vigée-Lebrun and the Cultural Politics of Art* (1996). She is working on a study of art and enthusiasm in the French Enlightenment.

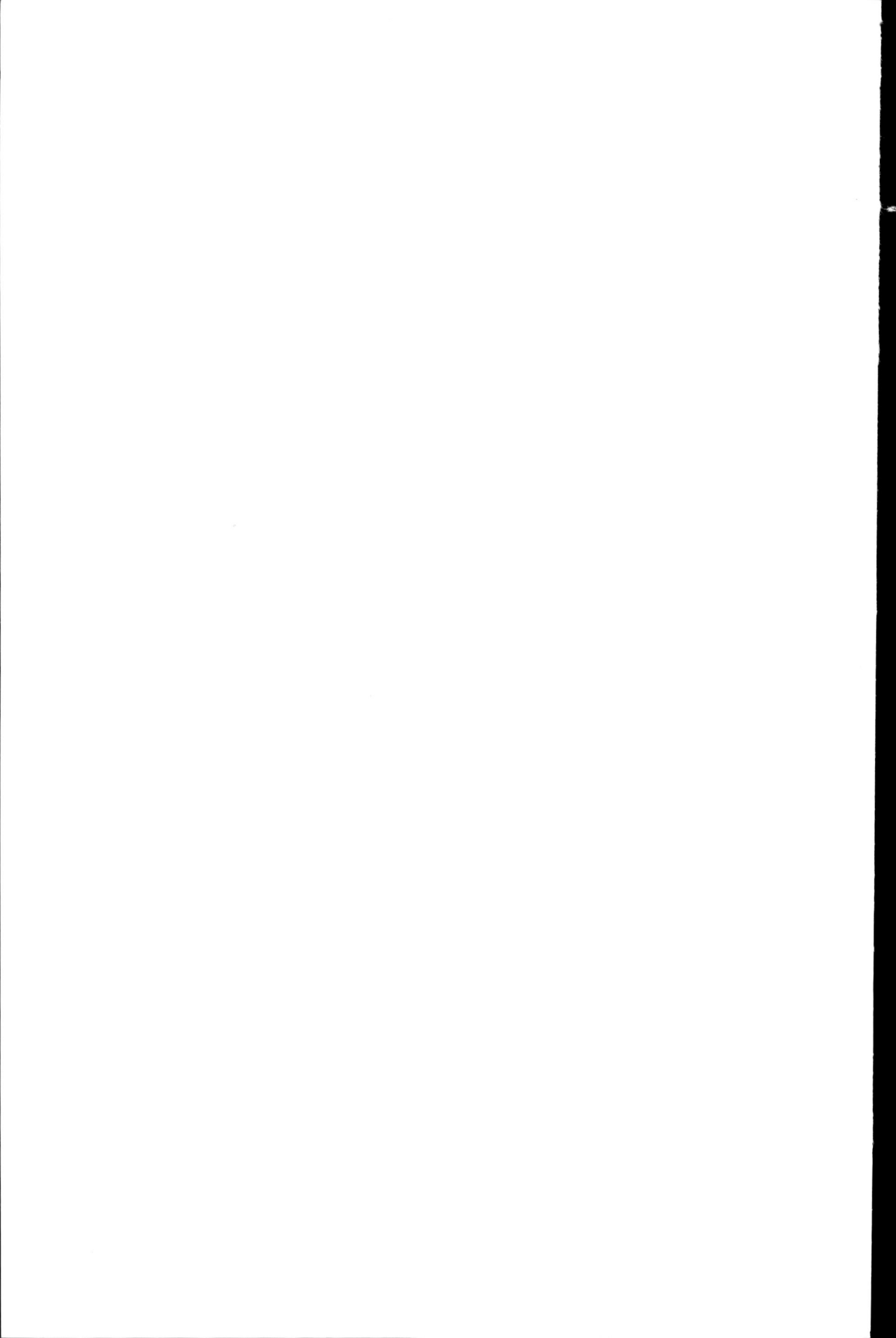